Sneaky Uses
for Everyday
Things

Gadgets, Gizmos
& Gimmicks

Cy Tymony

**Andrews McMeel
Publishing, LLC**

Kansas City • Sydney • London

Disclaimer

This book is for the entertainment and edification of its readers. While reasonable care has been exercised with respect to its accuracy, the publisher and the author assume no responsibility for errors or omissions in its content. Nor do we assume liability for any damages resulting from use of the information presented here.

This book contains references to electrical safety that *must* be observed. *Do not use AC power for any projects listed.* Do not place or store magnets near such magnetically sensitive media as videotapes, audiotapes, or computer disks.

Disparities in materials and design methods and the application of components may cause your results to vary from those shown here. The publisher and the author disclaim any liability for injury that may result from the use, proper or improper, of the information contained in this book. We do not guarantee that the information contained herein is complete, safe, or acurate, nor should it be considered a substitute for your good judgment and common sense.

Nothing in this book should be construed or interpreted to infringe on the rights of other persons or to violate criminal statutes. We urge you to obey all laws and respect all rights, including property rights, of others.

Sneaky Uses for Everyday Things: Gadgets, Gizmos & Gimmicks
copyright © 2009 by Cy Tymony.

This 2009 edition is a compilation of three previously published books by Cy Tymony: *Sneaky Uses for Everyday Things* © 2003; *Sneakier Uses for Everyday Things* © 2005; and *Sneakiest Uses for Everyday Things* © 2007; published exclusively for Barnes & Noble, Inc. by Andrews McMeel Publishing, LLC.

Barnes & Noble, Inc.
122 Fifth Avenue
New York, NY 10011

ISBN: 978-0-7407-8424-8

Printed in China

10 11 12 13 TEN 10 9 8 7 6 5 4 3 2

SNEAKY USES FOR EVERYDAY THINGS:
Gadgets, Gizmos & Gimmicks

Sneaky Uses for Everyday Things

How to Turn a Penny into a Radio,
Make a Flood Alarm with an Aspirin,
Change Milk into Plastic, Extract
Water and Electricity from Thin Air,
Turn On a TV with Your Ring,
and Other Amazing Feats

Contents

Part I

Sneaky Tricks and Gimmicks

Part II

Sneaky Gadgets and Gizmos

Part III

Security Gadgets and Gizmos

Part IV

Sneaky Survival Techniques

Foreword

I was one of those kids who loved to tear things apart and put them back together. Old black-and-white TVs, washing machine motors, and solenoids littered my basement. Countless hours would be spent dissecting and building electronic gadgets in the coolness of that dark refuge.

I was what we would call today a "geek." I even wore a pocket protector (and when I studied engineering in college, I collected four slide rules).

Those postwar days, in the late 1950s and '60s, were ripe for we subterranean gadgeteers. Lower Manhattan was filled with surplus electronic parts and WWII junk just waiting for vultures like myself to descend and buy them by the pound or part. Decades before the World Trade Center was ever built, the streets that define that neighborhood were cluttered with cardboard boxes and tables overflowing with resistors, vacuum tubes, circuit boards, and knobs of every kind. Radios and TVs spilled into the streets, and lucky was the kid who could afford to bring home the innards of a real, live radarscope. Who knows what ship it had served, what foreign planes had blipped across its screen? These were our fields of dreams, where hobbyists could find all the ingredients they needed for home-brew creations.

It was a paradise. And then I grew up. I left home, abandoning my Heathkits and Popular Electronics projects (I made a four-transistor radio!). My science fair punch-card reader collected dust, my oscilloscope never to be turned on again.
Those days of wonderful creativity slowly faded away, becoming cherished memories of youth. Modern computer chips made once-simple soldering techniques more risky and unnecessary. Heathkit went out of business. Radio Shack cut way back on its

hobbyist section. The Internet captured most of my attention. My tinkering juices were never to be stirred up again, I thought.

Then I discovered Cy Tymony. His books drew me like a moth to a flame. There, amid the pages of hand-drawn illustrations, were the kinds of projects I hadn't seen in years. Decades. Half a lifetime. With a few twists of a screwdriver, you could turn an ordinary radio into a magical box where airline pilots talk to one other. You could make all kinds of "stuff" out all parts just lying around the house. I could tinker again!

Thank you, Cy, for reinvigorating those creative juices. We all owe you debt of gratitude for reinventing the old days for we veterans of the vacuum tube era. And for opening up the world of tinkering and creativity to a whole new generation of hobbyists looking to get their hands dirty with new and exciting projects.

Ira Flatow
Science Friday

Acknowledgments

Special thanks go to my agent, Sheree Bykofsky, for her enthusi-astic encouragement and for believing in this book from the start. I am also appreciative of the assistance provided by Janet Rosen and Megan Buckley at her agency.

I wish to thank Jennifer Fox, my editor at Andrews McMeel, and copy editor, Janet Baker, for their invaluable work.

A warm thank-you goes to Bill Melzer for insights and opinions that helped shape this book.

I am also grateful for the project evaluation assistance pro-vided by Jerry Anderson, Isaac English, Carlos Daza, Sybil Smith, and Serrenity Smith.

And I hope the following is adequate to show my invaluable appreciation and love for Cloise Shaw. Thanks, Mom. I love you.

Introduction

"Life . . . is what we make it."
—William James

You don't have to be 007 to adapt unique gadgets, secure a room from intruders, or get the upper hand over aggressors. Anyone can learn how to become a real-life MacGyver in minutes, using nothing but a few hodgepodge items fate has put at our disposal. Sometimes you have to be sneaky.

Sure, it never hurts to have the smarts of Einstein or the strength of Superman, but they're not necessary with *Sneaky Uses for Everyday Things*. When life puts us in a bind, the best solution is frequently not the obvious one. It'll be the sneaky one.

Solutions to a dilemma can come from the most unlikely sources:

- A motorist stranded with a bad heater-valve gasket made a new one by cutting and shaping the tongue from an old track shoe. It worked well enough to get him home safely.

- U.S. prisoners of war devised a stealthy makeshift radio receiver using nothing more than a razor blade, a pencil, and the wire fence of the prison camp as an antenna.

- Convicts at Wisconsin's Green Bay Correctional Institution scaled the prison walls using rope they braided from thousands of yards of dental floss.

- On September 11, 2001, a window washer trapped in a Twin Towers elevator with five other passengers used his squeegee to pry open the doors and chisel through the wall to escape the inferno.

People rarely think about the common items and devices they use in everyday life. They think even less about adapting them to perform other functions. For lovers of self-reliance and gadgetry, *Sneaky Uses for Everyday Things* is an amazing assortment of more than forty fabulous build-it-yourself projects, security procedures, self-defense and survival strategies, unique gift ideas, and more.

Did you know that the coins in your pocket can generate electricity or receive radio signals? Want to know what household item can identify counterfeit paper currency? How to turn milk into plastic or glue? How to locate directions using the sun or the stars? How to make a compass without a magnet, extract water from thin air, use water to start a fire, or make a ring that can turn on your TV? It's all here. Even wire hangers and coffee-cream-container tops get their moment in the sun.

Sneaky Uses for Everyday Things does not include conventional projects found in most crafts and household hints books. Nor are instructions supplied for first aid, fishing, making a shelter, or spotting edible plants. The Resources section at the back includes lists of books and Web sites for obtaining science tricks, frugal facts, and camping information.

Sneaky Uses for Everyday Things avoids projects or procedures that require expensive or unusual materials not found in the average home. No special knowledge or tools are needed. Whether you like to conserve resources or like the idea of getting something for nothing, you can use the book as a practical tool, a fantasy escape, or a trivia guide; it's up to you. "Things" will never appear the same again.

Let's start now. You can do more than you think!

Part I

Sneaky Tricks and Gimmicks

You too can do more with less! Many household items you use every day can perform other functions. Using nothing but a few supplies like paper clips, rubber bands, and refrigerator magnets, you can quickly make unique gadgets and gifts.

Want to know how to tell real paper currency from fake? How to make plastic and glue out of milk? Generate electricity from fruits?

If you have an insatiable curiosity for sneaky secrets of everyday things, look no further. The projects that follow can be made in no time. Start your entry into clever resourcefulness here.

The Fear of Small Sums:
Detect Counterfeit Bills

Whether it's a hundred-dollar bill or a one, getting stuck with counterfeit money is a fear many of us have. In the United States in 2002, $43 million in fake currency was circulated. When counterfeit currency is seized, neither consumers nor companies are compensated for the loss. So what can we do about it? This project describes two methods to tell good currency from bad.

The first method is a careful visual inspection of the bill. Compare a suspect note with a genuine note of the same denomination and series. Look for the following telltale signs:

1. The paper on a genuine bill has tiny red and blue fibers embedded in it. Counterfeit bills may have a few red and blue lines on them but they are printed on the surface and are not really embedded in the paper.
2. The portrait and the sawtooth points on Federal Reserve and Treasury seals are distinct and clear on the real thing.
3. The edge lines of the border on a genuine bill are sharp and unbroken.
4. The serial number on a good bill is evenly spaced and printed with the same color as the Treasury seal.

The second way to verify paper currency is to test the ink. How can we do this in a sneaky way, at home or in the office? Easy: by using one important feature of the ink used on U.S. currency. A legitimate bill has iron particles in the ink that are attracted to a strong magnet. To verify a bill, obtain a very strong magnet or a rare-earth magnet. Rare-earth magnets are extremely strong for their small size. They can be obtained from electronic parts stores and scientific supply outlets. See the Resources section at the back of this book.

You can also use small refrigerator magnets, connecting them end to end to create collectively a much stronger single magnet. See Figure 1.

What's Needed
- Dollar bill
- Strong magnet

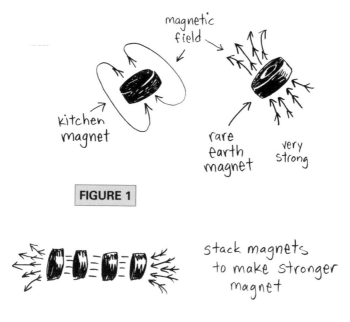

magnetic field

kitchen magnet

rare earth magnet

very strong

FIGURE 1

stack magnets to make stronger magnet

What to Do

Fold the bill in half crosswise and lay it on a table, as shown in Figure 2. Point the strong magnet near the portrait of the president on the bill, but do not touch it. A legitimate bill will move toward the magnet, as shown in Figure 3.

Whenever you doubt the authenticity of paper currency, simply pull out your magnet and perform the magnetic attraction test. If you create the Power Ring shown in Part II of this book, it can be used for currency tests too.

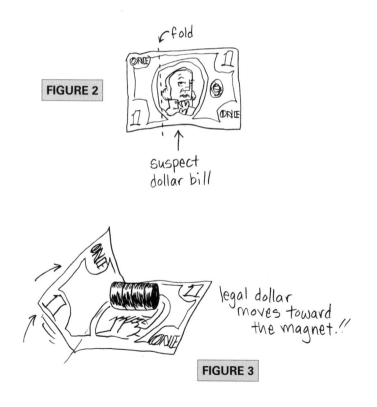

fold

FIGURE 2

suspect
dollar bill

legal dollar
moves toward
the magnet.''

FIGURE 3

Slushy Fun:
Cheap Gel Packs for Swollen Muscles

People in physically demanding jobs and weekend warriors get muscle aches often. When they do, an icy gel pack can relieve the pain and swelling.

Gel packs work to reduce swelling because they can be fitted around joints to cool them thoroughly. You can save money by making your own version—a slushy pack—from everyday things found in the home.

What's Needed
- Water
- Rubbing alcohol
- Watertight freezer bag—typically 6½" x 5⅞"

1½ cups water

rubbing alcohol

½ cup rubbing alcohol

the kind that seals ↘

waterproof sandwich bag

FIGURE 1

What to Do

Add 1½ cups water and ½ cup alcohol to the plastic bag and seal it. Ensure that the bag is not overfilled. Place bag in the freezer for 3 hours (see Figure 1).

The fluid inside will not freeze solid. Instead, the alcohol keeps the water flexible and slushy for a better fit (see Figure 2).

When needed, remove the bag from the freezer and apply it to the swollen area as shown in Figure 3. To prevent frostbite or cold burns, place a towel or cloth between the plastic and the skin.

Once you're done, place the slushy pack back in the freezer for future use.

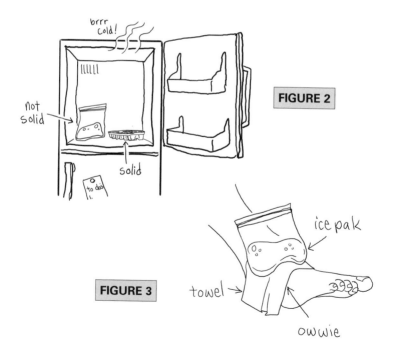

FIGURE 2

FIGURE 3

Got Plastic?
Turn Milk into Sneaky Plastic

Have you ever needed plastic molding material for a repair or a craft project? Perhaps you broke off a plastic piece from a toy or an appliance and need to fill in the unsightly gap. Well, you can transform commonplace items in your kitchen into a flexible compound that will do such repairs and even allow you to paint to match.

Believe it or not, you can make a malleable plastic material from plain household milk and only one other ingredient—vinegar. It's easy.

What's Needed
- Milk
- Small pot
- Spoon
- Vinegar
- Strainer
- Jar
- Paper towels

milk

vinegar

8 oz

← don't boil!

FIGURE 1

What to Do

Pour an 8-ounce cup of milk in a pot and heat it on a stove. Let it warm but not boil. Add a tablespoon of vinegar and stir the mixture. Soon, clumps of a solid material will form on the surface. Continue stirring (see Figure 1).

Place the strainer on top of the jar and pour the mixture through the strainer. Use the spoon to press the clumps and squeeze out the liquid, which is discarded. Remove the material from the strainer and place it on a paper towel. Dab paper towels on top of the material to absorb excess moisture (see Figure 2).

The solid material that has formed is called casein. It separates from milk when an acid, like vinegar, is added. Casein is used in industry to make glue, paint, and some plastics. You can now form the "sneaky plastic" into shape with a mold or use your hands. Allow the shaped material to dry for 1 to 2 days.

Sneaky plastic has many uses. First, it allows you to recycle spoiled milk that would be discarded anyway. You can make impressions of coins and other small objects. You can shape the plastic into parts to replace items such as broken Walkman belt clips. Or you can make a personalized key ring ornament (see Figure 3).

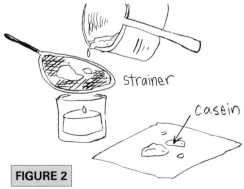

strainer

casein

FIGURE 2

Here are some more ideas for putting this plastic compound to use:

Child-proofing items with sharp edges or points
Toy assembly aid (to hold wood and plastic pieces together)
Caulk for small holes in a boat
Pendant holder
Wheels for carts and toys
Tool handle
Material for a spacer or washer
Guitar pick
Bottle cap
Temporary plumbing repairs
Waterproof container
Fishing lure and float
Replacement button

Sneaky plastic can also be used to create a Power Ring (see Part II under "Superman and Green Lantern Ain't Got Nothin' on Me"). Whether you use the compound for critical repairs or just for fun craft projects, you'll discover it provides plenty of versatility with only a small investment of time.

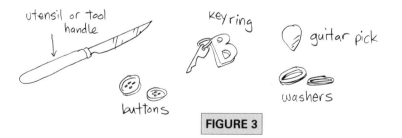

FIGURE 3

Need Glue?
Create Sneaky Glue from Milk

If you have an emergency need to secure items together and you're out of glue, don't have a cow. Milk one.

By adding two common ingredients to milk, you can make sneaky glue! When vinegar is added to milk, a sticky substance called casein is formed. By adding baking soda, you can create a gluelike substance.

What's Needed

- Milk
- Small pot
- Spoon
- Vinegar
- Strainer
- Jar
- Paper towels
- Baking soda

FIGURE 1

What to Do

Pour an 8-ounce cup of milk in a pot and heat it on a stove to 250 degrees. Let it warm but not boil. Add a tablespoon of vinegar and stir the mixture. Soon, clumps of a solid material will form on the surface. Continue stirring (see Figure 1).

Place the strainer on top of the jar and pour the mixture through the strainer. Use the spoon to press the clumps and squeeze out the liquid, as shown in Figure 2.

Remove the material from the strainer and place it back in the pot, on the stove. Add ¼ cup of water and a tablespoon of baking soda (see Figure 3). The casein material will begin to bubble. When it stops, use the leftover material as glue.

Note: Wait several hours before using any item secured with sneaky glue.

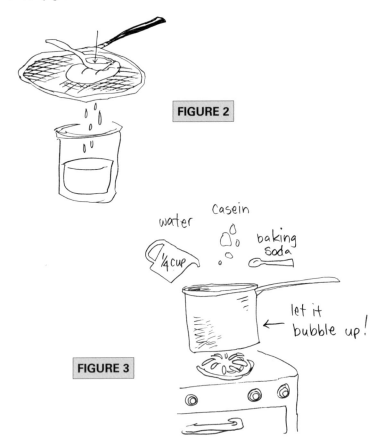

FIGURE 2

water   Casein   baking
¼ cup   soda

let it
← bubble up!

FIGURE 3

Spin Thrift:
Make a
Videotape Rewinder

Do you want to exercise and lose weight from the comfort of your easy chair? Would you like to do it while you watch television and prevent needless wear and tear of your VCR at the same time? Well, now you can!

If this sounds like a TV-infomercial pitch for a new exercise system, guess again. You'll be able to do all of the above and not spend a dime. If you own a VCR, you know what an inconvenience it is to rewind your videotapes. You must sit and wait for up to five minutes while your VCR is generating lots of heat and wearing out its motor. If you have a rental tape, it must be rewound before it is returned. Some video rental stores will charge a fine if their tapes are not returned fully rewound.

You could purchase an electric videotape rewinder, but they are costly, use electricity, and eventually break down. Some of the cheaper models have even been know to break tapes because they do not properly sense where they end. If you own a camcorder, you know how valuable your limited battery life is. Unnecessarily fast-forwarding and rewinding tapes will quickly drain a camcorder's battery. By using a free portable manual tape rewinder, you will save your battery power for recording additional scenes in the field.

You can easily make a manual tape rewinder yourself within ten minutes from ordinary household items: a wire garment hanger and a paper clip. Then you can rewind your videotapes while you watch television so it won't seem tedious. I do it all the time.

What's Needed

- Wire hanger
- Paper clip
- Tape (any type)
- Pliers

What to Do

First, let's find out why you can't just rewind a videotape with a pen or your fingers. Figure 1 illustrates the bottom view of a typical VHS cassette. There is a supply reel, which has the tape wrapped around it, and a take-up reel, which holds the tape after it plays to the end. If you try to turn either reel, they will not move. There is a catch mechanism in the tape shell that prevents tape reel rotation unless a small thin object is pushed through the small reel-release hole.

VCR manufacturers designed their machines this way to prevent damage to a tape in the event of a malfunction. When a tape is loaded in a VCR, a small thin part of the chassis protrudes through the tape shell's reel-release hole, allowing the reels to rotate. In case of a problem, the machine immediately stops the tape and shuts down or ejects the tape to prevent breakage. You can design your rewinding device for a VHS, Betamax, or 8-millimeter cassette tape.

Using pliers, untwist a standard wire garment hanger into a long straight line and cut it in half with the pliers. If you cannot cut the wire, bend it back and forth rapidly, and the heat generated by the motion will eventually cause it to break in two. Then bend a paper clip into the shape shown in Figure 2.

Next, bend the hanger with the pliers into the shape shown in Figure 2. The only size that is crucial is the width of the **C**-shaped end. If you want to rewind a VHS tape, the **C**-shaped end should be approximately ⅗ inch wide.

For a Beta tape, the **C** shape width should be approximately ⁷⁄₁₀ inch. An 8-millimeter tape rewinder requires a ⅖ inch **C** shape at the end of the hanger. These dimensions are approximate because you'll need to bend the **C**-shaped end outward slightly to attain a snug fit when it's positioned in the cassette's tape reel sprocket.

Note: If you wrap the **C** area of the hanger with tape—masking tape, duct tape, or electrical tape will do nicely—it will reduce the chances that the videotape rewinder will slip out of the sprocket reel.

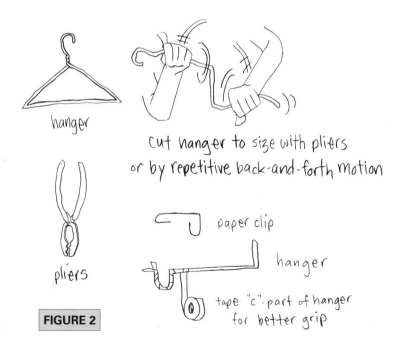

hanger

Cut hanger to size with pliers
or by repetitive back-and-forth motion

pliers

paper clip

hanger

tape "c"-part of hanger
for better grip

FIGURE 2

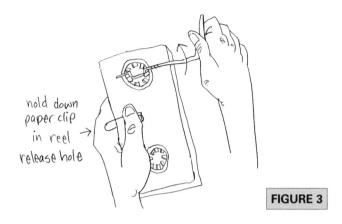

hold down
paper clip
in reel →
release hole

FIGURE 3

Now push the paper clip into the release hole of the cassette. See Figure 3 for the location of the release hole on Beta and VHS tapes (8-millimeter tapes have no reel-release mechanism).

Press the **C**-shaped end of the rewinder into the take-up reel sprocket of the cassette. Hold the paper clip in the release hole in one hand and turn the rewinder's crank arm with the other (see Figure 4). If the rewinder slips out of the reel sprocket, bend the **C** shape outward to achieve a tighter fit.

There you have it: a no-cost manual videotape rewinder!

BONUS APPLICATION:
MINI SPIN ME, AN
AUDIOCASSETTE REWINDER

You've seen how easy it is to make a videotape rewinder. Why not make one for your audiocassettes too? If you use a portable cassette recorder or a Walkman tape player, you can extend their battery life tremendously by rewinding the tapes yourself.

What's Needed

• One large paper clip

What to Do

Bend the paper clip into the shape shown in Figure 1. The **C**-shaped end should be approximately ⅜ inch wide. The **C**-shaped end should fit tightly enough to produce a *click* sound when inserted into the cassette's reel sprocket.

Press the **C** end into the tape reel sprocket and turn the rewinder's crank handle (see Figure 2).

Look through the cassette's tape window to see when the tape reaches the end (or desired position). It only takes about three minutes to rewind a 60-minute cassette from one end to the other.

Once you've finished, you can feel confident that you've saved a little battery power and burned calories to boot.

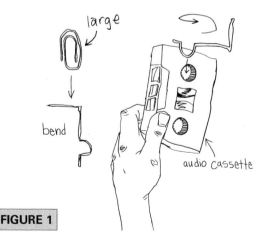

large

bend

audio cassette

FIGURE 1

Getting Wired:
Sneaky Wire Sources Are Everywhere

It will soon become obvious that many projects in this book use electrical wire. In an emergency, you can obtain wire—or items that can be used as wire—from some very unlikely sources.

To test an item's conductivity (its ability to let electricity flow through it), use a flashlight bulb or an LED. (LED is short for light-emitting diode; LEDs are used in most electronic devices and toys as function indicators because they draw very little electrical current, operate with very little heat, and have no filament to burn out.

Lay a small 3-volt watch battery on the item to be tested, as shown in Figure 1. If the bulb LED lights, the item can be used as wire for battery-powered projects.

Ready-to-use wire can be obtained from telephone cord, TV/ VCR cable, headphone wire, earphone wire, and speaker wire, and also from inside toys, radios, and other electrical devices. (*Note:* Some of these sources have from one to six separate wires inside.)

Wire for projects can also be made from take-out food container handles, twist-ties, paper clips, envelope clasps, ballpoint pen springs, fast-food wrappers, and potato-chip bag liners.

You can also use aluminum from the following items:

Margarine wrapper
Ketchup or condiment package
Breath-mint-container label

FIGURE 1

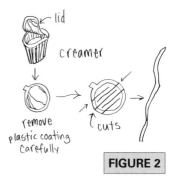

FIGURE 2

Chewing-gum wrapper
Trading-card packaging
Coffee-creamer-container lid

You can cut strips of aluminum material from food wrappers easily enough. With smaller items—such as aluminum obtained from a coffee-creamer-container lid—use the sneaky cutting

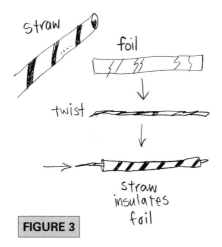

FIGURE 3

pattern shown in Figure 2. Special care must be taken handling the fragile aluminum materials listed. In some instances, aluminum material will be covered by a wax or plastic coating that you may be able to remove.

Note: Wire from aluminum sources is only to be used for low-voltage battery-powered projects.

Figure 3 illustrates how items as small as a cut-up coffee-creamer-container lid can be insulated from other items using a straw, hollow stirrer, or paper.

The resourceful use of items to make sneaky wire is not only intriguing, it's fun, too.

good wire Candidates

twist ties

paper clips

ball point pen

envelope clasps

spring

take out container handle

ketchup

gum

fast food

foil wrappers

CHiPs

potato chips

phone cord

head phones cord

speaker wire

BONUS APPLICATION:
HOW TO CONNECT THINGS

So far, this project has illustrated how to obtain wires from everyday things. Now you'll learn how to connect the wires to provide consistent performance. A tight connection is crucial in electrical projects; otherwise, faulty and erratic operation may result.

Figure 1 shows a piece of insulated wire. Strip the insulation material away to make a connection to other electrical parts. Remove one to two inches of insulation from the end of the wire; see Figure 2.

To connect the wire to a similarly stripped wire, wrap the stripped ends around each other, as shown in Figure 3's three steps.

When connecting the wire to the end of a stiff lead (like the end of an LED), wrap the wire around the lead and bend the lead back over the wire; see Figure 4.

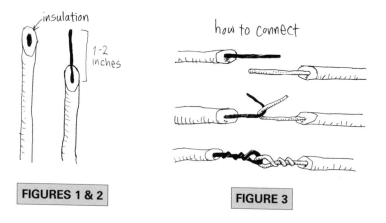

FIGURES 1 & 2

FIGURE 3

To connect wire to the end of a small battery, bend the wire into a circular shape, place it on the battery terminal, and wrap the connection tightly with tape, as shown in Figure 5.

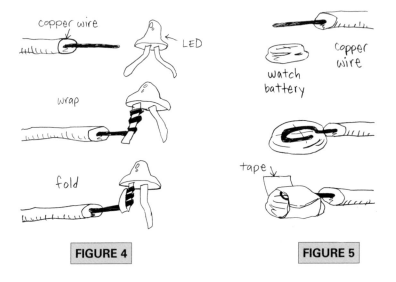

FIGURE 4

FIGURE 5

More Power to You:
Make Batteries from Everyday Things

No one can dispute the usefulness of electricity. But what do you do if you're in a remote area without AC power or batteries? Make sneaky batteries, of course!

In this project, you'll learn how to use fruits, vegetable juices, paper clips, and coins to generate electricity.

What's Needed
- Lemon or other fruit
- Nail
- Heavy copper wire
- Paper clip or twist-tie
- Water
- Salt
- Paper towel
- Pennies and nickels
- Plate

What to Do
THE FRUIT BATTERY

Insert a nail or paper clip into a lemon. Then stick a piece of heavy copper wire into the lemon. Make sure that the wire is close to, but does not touch, the nail (See Figure 1). The nail has become the battery's negative electrode and the copper wire is the positive electrode. The lemon juice, which is acidic, acts as

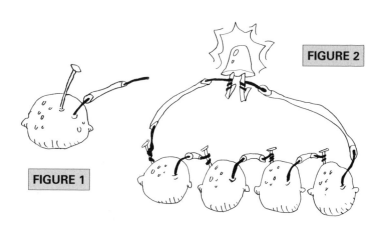

FIGURE 2

FIGURE 1

the electrolyte. You can use other item pairs besides a paper clip and copper wire, as long as they are made of different metals.

The lemon battery will supply about one-fourth to one-third of a volt of electricity. To use a sneaky battery as the battery to power a small electrical device, like an LED light, you must connect a few of them in series, as shown in Figure 2.

THE COIN BATTERY

With the fruit battery, you stuck the metal into the fruit. You can also make a battery by placing a chemical solution between two coins.

Dissolve 2 tablespoons of salt in a glass of water. This is the electrolyte you will place between two dissimilar metal coins.

Now moisten a piece of paper towel or tissue in the salt water. Put a nickel on a plate and put a small piece of the wet absorbent paper on the nickel. Then place a penny on top of the paper (see Figure 3).

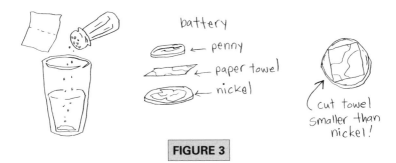

battery
← penny
← paper towel
← nickel

(cut towel
smaller than
nickel!

FIGURE 3

In order for the homemade battery to do useful work, you must make a series of them stacked up as seen in Figure 4. Be sure the paper separators do not touch one another.

The more pairs of coins you add, the higher the voltage output will be. One coin pair should produce about one-third of a volt. With six pairs stacked up, you should be able to power a small flashlight bulb, LED, or other device when the regular batteries have failed. See Figure 5. *Power will last up to two hours.*

Once you know how to make sneaky batteries, you'll never again be totally out of power sources.

Six pairs of
coin batteries
stacked

FIGURE 4

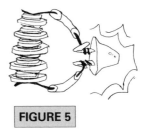

FIGURE 5

You Light Up My Life:
Construct Electronic Greeting Cards

To make an impression on someone, give a gift. For a unique and lasting impression, give a handmade sneaky personalized gift. This project will show you how to use parts from discarded toys and gadgets to make electronic greeting cards, posters, and more.

LEDs are found in most electronic devices and in toys and appliances. They are little lights that indicate whether a device or a function is on. Unlike ordinary lightbulbs, these miniature marvels do not have a filament, produce virtually no heat, consume very little power, and (when properly powered) never burn out!

You can obtain LEDs from old discarded toys and other devices. You will need to cut their leads away from the small circuit board, using pliers or wire cutters. You can also purchase LEDs at electronic parts stores locally or from sites shown in the Resources section at the back of the book. You can also obtain blinking LEDs that flash on and off without requiring other components.

What's Needed
- LED
- 3-volt watch battery
- Business card
- Tape
- Wire

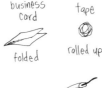

business card
folded

tape
rolled up

insulated wire
(with stripped ends)

Insulated wire
(with stripped ends)
curled

L.E.D.

battery

L.E.D.

FIGURE 1

What to Do

Since LEDs require 2 to 5 volts to operate, the best compact power supply for them is a 3-volt lithium watch battery. Since AA, C, and D cell batteries provide just 1½ volts each, you would need two cells to provide 3 volts (although larger cells will last longer).

To see how an LED works, press its leads on both sides of a 3-volt battery, as shown in

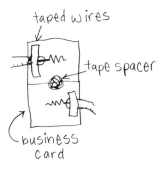

taped wires

tape spacer

business card

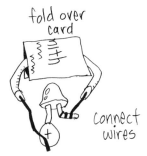

fold over card

connect wires

FIGURE 2

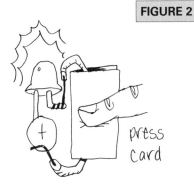

press card

press

You light up my life

Figure 1. If the LED doesn't light, reverse the battery position or reverse the LED leads.

Figure 2 shows how to make a sneaky "touch switch" with a folded business card, stiff wire, and tape. Tape the wires to the card and roll up a piece of tape to act as a spacer. When properly positioned, a slight press of the folded card will connect the wires and light the LED. See the "Invite the Power" section of Part II for methods of controlling LEDs and other devices with a ring.

LEDs can be mounted on greeting cards and bookmarks, belts and bracelets, behind posters, on trophies—and even on clothing! They can add value to items you might otherwise throw away.

Part II

Sneaky Gadgets and Gizmos

All too often people discard older or broken but still functional high-tech gadgets without realizing what other functions they can serve.

Despite the complexity of radios, tape recorders, and other gizmos, this section will illustrate simple, sneaky projects to take advantage of their little-known capabilities.

Want to see how to turn on a TV with your ring, open a room door with a toy car, or adapt a tape recorder into a hearing aid or megaphone? It's here.

Do you know the sneaky method to make a radio out of a penny or how to turn a screw in an FM radio to magically receive aircraft broadcasts? That's here, too, along with bonus applications.

If you're intrigued with high-tech resourcefulness, the following easy-to-build projects will fascinate and delight.

"Superman and Green Lantern Ain't Got Nothin' on Me": **Make a Power Ring**

What can you do with a commonly worn trinket? More than you might think. Here's a novel project you can make with everyday things that will allow you to activate LEDs, toys—even appliances—with your *ring*!

What's Needed
- Toy ring (with a flat surface)
- Small magnet
- Glue

flat surface

ring

small magnet

What to Do
The power ring works with a magnet attached to its front surface. It is aimed at a magnetically sensitive switch you will make in the next project.

Glue a small magnet to the surface of a toy ring. You can use a refrigerator magnet or, preferably, a small rare-earth magnet. A rare-earth magnet will allow the power ring to activate devices from a longer distance. Rare-earth magnets can be obtained from electronic part stores and scientific supply outlets (see Figure 1).

You can also create a custom-made ring using the sneaky plastic made from the *Got Plastic?* project in Part I.

magnet on ring

FIGURE 1

Power Ring Uses

As a Secret Signaling Device. Attach a small toy compass to a door or window with tape. A friend with a power ring can aim the ring from a secret location and the compass needle will spin, signaling that it's your friend.

To Verify Currency. Fold a bill in half and lay it on a table. Point the power ring close to the portrait of the president on the bill. A legitimate bill has iron particles in the ink and will move toward the magnet.

For an Emergency Compass. Need to make a compass? Use your power ring. Obtain a small thin piece of metal (but not aluminum) and stroke the power ring repeatedly in one direction at least fifty times. You can use a straightened paper clip, a needle, a twist-tie, or a staple from a magazine. Place the metal on a piece of paper or leaf and let it float on the surface of a

FIGURE 2

container of water. The metal will be magnetized enough to be attracted to the Earth's north and south magnetic poles and act as a "Sneaky" compass.

To Activate Toys and Devices. The next project—"Invite the Power"—illustrates how to make a magnetically-activated switch using aluminum foil and a paper clip. With it, only you will be able to activate small lights and buzzers placed inside greeting cards, toys, and gifts as shown in Figure 2.

To Control Appliances. "Invite the Power!" also illustrates how the power ring can be used safely to control household lights and appliances with a device called the X-10® Universal Interface, available from home supply, hardware, and electronic parts stores.

BONUS APPLICATIONS

If you prefer not to activate devices with a ring, a magnet can be mounted in other ways.

Glue a magnet to the end of a plunger dowel (or decorative stick), and you've got a magic wand. Or place a thin rare-earth magnet between two business cards and tape them together. Now you can activate selected devices in the style of a magnetic-strip security card; see Figure 3.

dowel from plunger

magnet

business cards

rare-earth magnet

magic wand

magnet glued to end of dowel

cards glued together with magnet inside

FIGURE 3

"Invite the Power!":
Make Power-Ring-Activated Gadgets

What's the good of having a unique power ring without something for it to control? Not much. After you've made a power ring, as just described, you can use it to activate a variety of devices. This project will show how to make a magnetically sensitive switch. With it, the power ring can turn on a variety of devices, including AC-operated appliances.

What's Needed

- Power ring
- Paper clip or twist-tie
- Aluminum foil
- Business card or cardboard
- LED or flashlight bulb
- Wire
- Tape
- Optional X-10® Universal Powerflash Interface and Appliance Module

power ring.

LED

paper twist-clip or tie

business card

aluminum foil

insulated wire
(with stripped ends)

tape

screw terminals

X-10® Universal Interface

button

X-10® Appliance Module

What to Do

To create a magnetically activated switch, tape the aluminum foil to the business card. Then tape a piece of wire to the aluminum foil. Roll up a small piece of tape and place it adjacent to the foil, as shown in Figure 1.

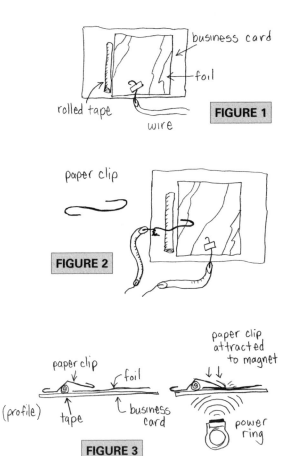

business card

foil

rolled tape

wire

FIGURE 1

paper clip

FIGURE 2

paper clip

foil

(profile)

tape

business card

paper clip attracted to magnet

power ring

FIGURE 3

greeting card

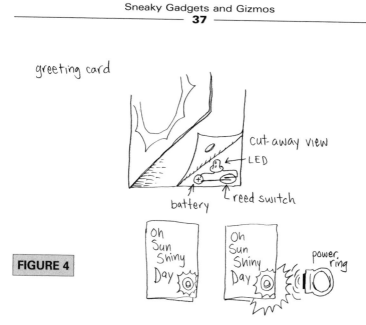

cut-away view

LED

battery

reed switch

Oh Sun Shiny Day

Oh Sun Shiny Day

power ring

FIGURE 4

Next, bend the paper clip into an **S** shape and wrap another piece of wire around it. Tape the paper clip near the foil and over the tape so that one end of it rests slightly above, but not touching, the foil; see Figure 2.

Test the switch by aiming the power ring close to the switch. The paper clip should move forward and make contact with the aluminum when the power ring is close; see Figure 3.

Now the ends of the two wires can be attached to a battery and an LED, and when the power ring is aimed at the paper clip the LED will light. Cover the parts with a piece of cardboard and tape the covers closed for protection.

The power-ring–activated switch can be used in a variety of applications, such as activation of LEDs in greeting cards, posters, and jewelry; see Figure 4.

CONTROLLING APPLIANCES WITH A POWER RING

In many homes, people use X-10® controllers and appliance modules to activate TVs, stereos, and lights by remote control. Typically, appliances are plugged into X-10® modules. The controller can turn the appliances on or off from another room, as shown in Figure 5.

There is a special X-10® controller model called the Universal Powerflash Interface that includes two connections for wires to be attached to it. Figure 6 shows how to attach the power-ring–activated switch wires to the Universal Interface contact screws. If you plug in an appliance to an X-10® appliance module, you can turn it on when you aim the ring at the switch; see Figure 7.

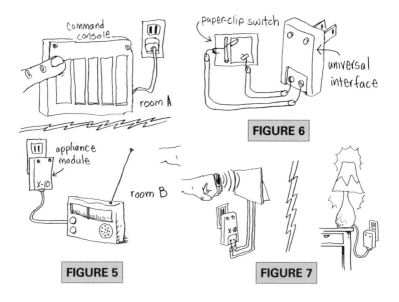

command console

paper-clip switch

universal interface

room A

FIGURE 6

appliance module

X-10

room B

X-10

FIGURE 5

FIGURE 7

A sneaky switch can be hidden behind or inside of items. Only you will know where to point the power ring and turn on the appliance of your choice.

For more information about X-10® modules and controllers, see www.X10.com.

Gifts of a Feather
You Make Together:
Build Togetherness Gifts

Here's a novel project, which illustrates that some gifts, like people, need each other. The gift set will illuminate an LED only when they are facing each other.

Togetherness gifts work with the same parts and design used in the power ring project, but each gift has a magnet inside that will activate the other gift's magnetically sensitive sneaky switch.

What's Needed

- Two small strong magnets
- Paper clips
- Aluminum foil
- Cardboard
- Two gift boxes
- Two LEDs
- Wire

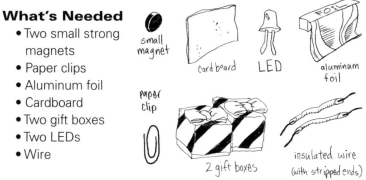

small magnet

Cardboard

LED

aluminum foil

paper clip

2 gift boxes

insulated wire (with stripped ends)

What to Do

First, using the instructions given in the "Invite the Power!" section, build two sets of sneaky switches and connect a battery and LED to each as shown in Figure 1.

Mount the sneaky-switch circuits with batteries and LEDs in the two gift boxes. Cut a small hole through which the LEDs can be seen. Then, with the gift boxes facing each other, tape the two magnets so they are positioned opposite the sneaky switches; see Figure 2.

Test the togetherness gift set by placing them close to each other and see if the LEDs will light. If they do not, adjust the positioning of the two magnets until they do.

Last, secure the covers on the gift boxes with tape and write a passage on the outside (or tape a card to each box) with an appropriate message: For instance, *We both need each other.*

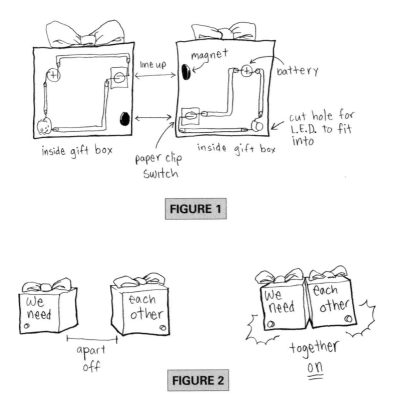

FIGURE 1

FIGURE 2

Listen Impossible:
Make Recordings Only You Can Hear

Many people are reluctant to preserve their personal thoughts on tape out of fear of someone's finding and listening to it later. If that sounds like you, this project will illustrate a sneaky technique you can use to make private messages that stay private.

How is a tape recorded? As seen in Figure 1, a cassette tape is positioned in a recorder's case so that the tape moves past the RECORD/PLAY tape head at a 90-degree angle. This is called the tape head's "azimuth angle." The tape-head position can be adjusted by turning a small screw. If this is done, the quality of a prerecorded tape will suffer.

However, if a blank tape is recorded on a machine with a repositioned tape head, the quality will be fine—but only on that tape recorder. If the tape is played on another recorder, the sound will be garbled.

You can take advantage of azimuth loss by recording personal messages on your tape recorder with the tape head's position changed and then readjust the head so you can use the recorder in a normal fashion. If someone plays the tape, the signal will be virtually inaudible. When needed, you can play back the tape after adjusting the tape head to hear the sounds clearly.

Phillips head

tape recorder

small jeweler's screwdriver

What's Needed
- Tape recorder
- Small jeweler's screwdriver

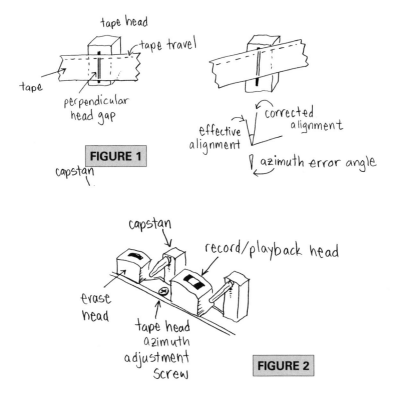

FIGURE 1

FIGURE 2

What to Do

Since the screw slot that allows adjustment of the tape-head position is cross-shaped and very small, you will need a tiny Phillips screwdriver. This tool is commonly found in eyeglass repair kits available from drugstores.

Place a tape in a portable tape recorder and press the PLAY button. Look carefully at the tiny hole or slot on the case near the tape head. As shown in Figure 2, there will be a small screw that allows you to adjust the head position. By turning the screw

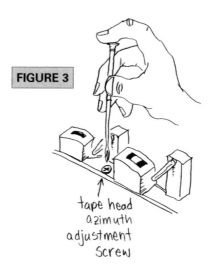

FIGURE 3

tape head
azimuth
adjustment
screw

in either direction, you can alter the azimuth angle of the tape head (see Figure 3).

Note the original position of the screw. Then, with a small screwdriver, adjust the tape head while playing a prerecorded tape. You'll hear the sound quality decrease as you turn the screw in either direction from its starting point. Leave the screw in the position that produces the lowest audio and quality level.

Next, place a blank tape in the recorder and, with some music playing in the background (to make it more difficult for an eavesdropper to understand what is being said), press the RECORD button and speak into the microphone. When you play back the tape, you'll hear your voice clearly. But if you play the tape in another tape player, your voice will be incomprehensible. When you want to hear a specially recorded tape, simply adjust the tape head to where it was originally. Now you can make personal tapes wherever you wish, and only you can successfully play them back.

For Your Ears Only:
Use a Tape Recorder as a Sound Amplifier

In the movies, spies always seem to have a sound-snooping device so they can hear across a room or through walls. But you don't have to request special ordnance from Q to have this sneaky accessory. With a common tape recorder, an earphone, and a small microphone, you'll be able to make a sneaky hearing aid, stethoscope, and more.

Sneaky Fact: A tape recorder sends sound signals to its earphone jack while it is in the RECORD mode. You can prove this by listening with an earphone while you record a tape.

What's Needed

- Portable tape recorder
- Earphone
- Small microphone
- Suction cup (optional)
- Hanger
- Cardboard
- Aluminum foil

tape recorder

earphone

small microphone

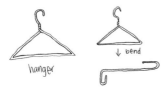
hanger
↓ bend

cardboard

suction cup

aluminum foil

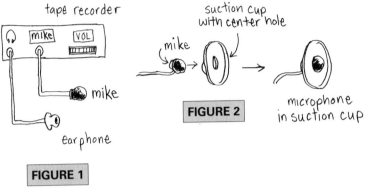

tape recorder

mike

earphone

FIGURE 1

suction cup
with center hole

mike

FIGURE 2

microphone
in suction cup

What to Do

When placed in the RECORD mode, a tape recorder will amplify sounds from the microphone and send signals to the tape head. It also sends audio signals to the earphone jack. In essence, it is an audio amplifier.

To use this function, place a cassette tape in the recorder. Then plug the microphone and earphone into their appropriate jacks. Attach the wires to the plug as shown in Figure 1. Press the RECORD button; then press the PAUSE button. This will stop the motor from turning and will save battery power.

Turn up the volume control. You'll be able to monitor distant sounds with the microphone, and they will be heard from the earphone. Congratulations! You've just made a portable sneaky sound-snooper system.

If you puncture a small hole in a suction cup and place the microphone in it, you can place the microphone on a door or wall and hear sounds through it. Place the microphone on your chest and you'll have an electronic stethoscope (see Figure 2).

BONUS APPLICATION

For sneaky long-distance listening, cut a large sheet of aluminum foil and a piece of cardboard (11 by 17 inches or larger) into a half-moon shape as shown in Figure 3. Tape the foil to the cardboard and bend it into a cone shape. Bend a hanger into the shape shown in Figure 4 and secure the microphone and cone to the hook of the hanger. Position the microphone inside the cone so it faces the point. Tape the cone closed.

Turn up the volume control, and you'll be able to detect distant sounds with the microphone that can be heard through the earphone.

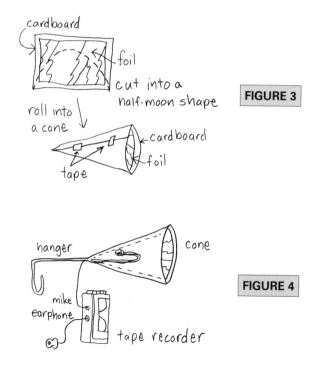

FIGURE 3

FIGURE 4

Give a Shout-out:
Make a Sneaky
Megaphone or PA

Are you tired of yelling in your house like a drill sergeant? With this project, you'll learn how to prevent the need to sound off to family members.

Most people believe a cassette tape recorder can only be used to record and play back voices and music. If the motor fails or if it eats tapes, they will usually throw it away. This project will show how it can be used for other sneaky purposes.

You've been in stores where an announcement over a public address system is being played. You can perform the same function with a common tape recorder and a small speaker.

Sneaky fact: A tape recorder sends sound signals to its earphone jack while it is in the RECORD mode. You can prove this by listening with an earphone while you record a tape. If, instead of an earphone, a small speaker is connected to the earphone jack, a PA effect will be heard while recording.

What's Needed
- Tape recorder
- Wire
- Small speaker
- Earphone plug
- Separate microphone (optional)

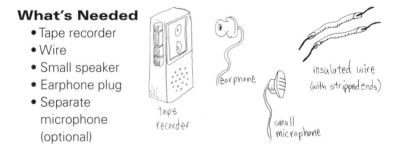

tape recorder

earphone

small microphone

insulated wire (with stripped ends)

What to Do

When placed in the RECORD mode, a tape recorder will amplify sounds from the microphone and send signals to the tape head. It also sends audio signals to the earphone jack. To use this function, place a cassette in the recorder, as shown in Figure 1. Then use the plug from an old earphone cable and attach its wires to a small speaker. Any small speaker will work; one from a car sound system or an old TV, a Walkman speaker, or one from a nonworking radio or tape player. Attach the wires to the earphone plug.

After connecting the speaker to the earphone jack, place the cassette in the recorder and press the RECORD button. Then press the PAUSE button. This will stop the motor from turning and will save battery power.

Now speak into the microphone, and your voice will be amplified and sent out through the speaker. Be sure to keep the speaker pointed away from the recorder to prevent feedback; see Figure 2. Congratulations! You've just made a portable public-address system.

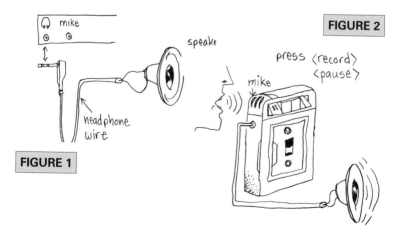

If you add a longer pair of wires, you can speak from one room and be heard in another, much like a one-way intercom (see Figure 3). You can make announcements, play prerecorded tapes, or provide long-distance music and news broadcasts.

FIGURE 3

Secret Agent:
Mr. Wireless
Has Countless Uses

Tired of missing phone calls or a doorbell ring when you leave a room? Fortunately, a sneaky remedy is available.

One of the most versatile toys available is the Mr. Microphone wireless broadcaster. Most people purchase it for their kids so they can sing on an FM radio, but this project has many other applications.

Mr. Wireless, as we'll call it, is essentially a wireless FM radio station with a broadcast range of up to 150 feet. A nearby FM radio can receive sound or music from the microphone. A small screw on the unit allows you to select the broadcast frequency. Here are just a few of its sneaky uses (see Figure 1).

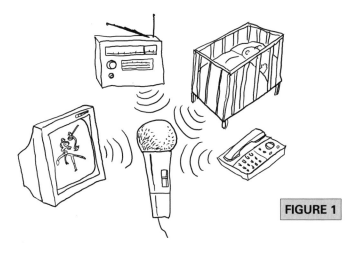

FIGURE 1

- Place a Mr. Wireless in a room near your baby and you can monitor the child with an FM radio.
- Monitor the doorbell or telephone by placing a Mr. Wireless in the vicinity.
- You can also use a Mr. Wireless to monitor a television, shortwave radio, or police scanner.

The Mr. Wireless device can be easily modified to accept a direct audio signal from an earphone jack. This will allow you to use it to play the output of a portable scanner, MP3 player, cassette player, or CD player in an automobile or boat. The car stereo will receive the Mr. Wireless broadcast and send the amplified sounds to the car speakers.

What's Needed
- Mr. Microphone toy
- Earphone plug
- Tape

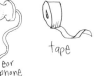

Mr. Microphone toy

ear phone

tape

What to Do
Figure 2 shows a typical Mr. Wireless toy. Remove its sponge cover and remove the case screw(s); some covers will require that you slide and twist the case until it separates into two parts.

Then remove the small microphone from the case.

Cut the wires and strip the ends of insulation (see Figure 3). You can use the plug end from an old earphone, attach it to the microphone wires, and tape them together. Push the plug jack through the top hole, replace the case cover, and screw it together.

Place fresh batteries in the Mr. Wireless, turn it on, and connect the earphone plug to the earphone of the device you

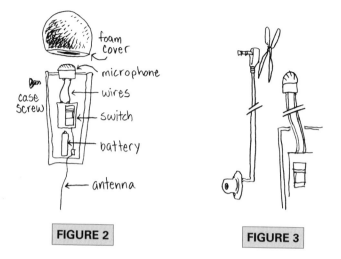

FIGURE 2

FIGURE 3

want to play. Tune the car stereo to the broadcast frequency of the Mr. Wireless and turn on the portable audio player (MP3 player or cassette or CD player). Keep the volume low on the device so it does not produce audio distortion.

Miniaturizing Mr. Wireless:
Use Him in Remote Places

They say that size matters, but that depends on what your goal is and what you have to work with. If you use the Mr. Wireless device frequently, you'll probably want to miniaturize it for more portable concealed uses. The original package is relatively large, to fit the batteries inside, but it can be made smaller.

With a smaller version, Mr. Wireless can be left at various locations for remote monitoring. Imagine the fun and sneaky applications!

What's Needed

- Mr. Microphone toy
- Lithium or other high-capacity watch battery
- Small plastic candy box or mint container
- Tape

Mr. Microphone toy

tape

MINTy Mint

plastic candy box

lithium battery

What to Do

Wireless microphone-type toys vary in design, so the following directions are general in nature.

Remove the screw(s) holding the Mr. Microphone case together. In some instances this will require sliding the two case pieces apart; see Figure 1. Then remove the circuit board, ON/OFF

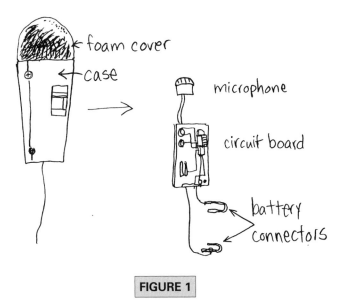

foam cover

case

microphone

circuit board

battery connectors

FIGURE 1

switch, microphone, and battery connectors from the case. Note which connectors are attached to the positive (+) and negative (–) battery terminals.

Assemble your Mr. Wireless parts inside a mint container or other small box, as shown in Figure 2. Tape the lithium watch battery to the connectors and test it with an FM radio to ensure the proper polarity. If it doesn't work, reverse the connectors on the battery. Now your Mr. Wireless is ready for undercover operation.

Keep in mind that miniaturizing the Mr. Wireless device has one disadvantage: The smaller battery used for the modification will have a shorter life.

Remember: The mini Mr. Wireless can be used just about anywhere. But don't forget to bring an FM radio along to monitor its broadcasts.

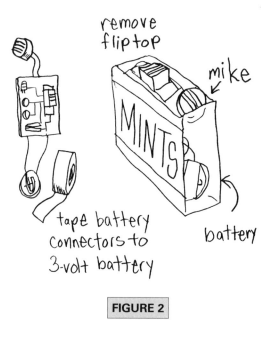

remove fliptop

mike

tape battery connectors to 3-volt battery

battery

FIGURE 2

Got a Toy Car?
Make a Power
Room Door Opener

Who among us hasn't dreamed of having a power door opener as seen in sci-fi and spy movies? This project will show you how to use a small toy car to do the trick. A small wire-controlled car has enough power to push and pull a typical room door back and forth if you know the super-sneaky way to install it.

What's Needed
- Wire-controlled toy car
- Velcro tape, adhesive-backed
- Screwdriver
- Pliers

Velcro tape

pliers

wire-controlled toy car

F R

screwdriver

What to Do
This project requires a small wire-controlled toy car, *not* a radio-controlled version. This is to prevent the batteries from running down. (With a radio-controlled car, the remote control and the car's internal receiver have to be in the ON mode, and this drains batteries.)

First, remove the body shell from the toy car with a screwdriver. Then remove the front wheel and axle, as shown in Figure 1.

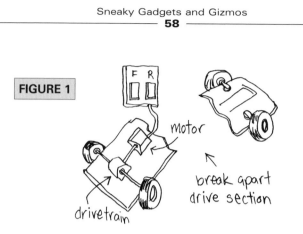

FIGURE 1

motor

break apart
drive section

drivetrain

Now, using the Velcro tape, attach the car near the bottom end
of the door (see Figure 2).

Using the remote control, see if it can push the door open
or closed. If not, reposition the car for more traction. When the
proper position is found, you will be able either to move the door
with your hand or let the car do it.

Optionally, you can break off the entire front part of the

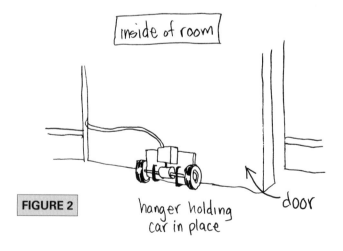

inside of room

FIGURE 2

hanger holding
car in place

door

chassis so that it takes up less space and cover it with materials for a more appealing look. Mount the remote control outside the door as desired (see Figure 3).

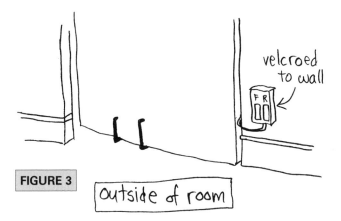

velcroed to wall

F R

FIGURE 3

outside of room

BONUS APPLICATION IDEA

Substitute a magnetically sensitive sneaky switch for the remote control's switch, and your door can be opened with a power ring. (See the "Invite the Power!" section, earlier in Part II, for details.) Now that's futuristic!

Irrational Public Radio:
Put It Together from Scratch

Ever wonder how a radio works? Would you believe that you can make a sneaky radio with nonelectronic items found in every home? It's true!

Making crystal radios was a popular activity a few generations ago. Even now, many parents show their kids how to make a radio at home that doesn't require AC power or batteries. And there is no danger of getting an electric shock. Although only a few stations will be received, there's nothing like the feeling of tuning in a station for the first time on a radio you put together from scratch.

Normally, building a crystal radio requires electronic components, such as a crystal or germanium diode to act as a detector. This involves going out to purchase a crystal radio kit or hunting for the separate electronic components.

The Irrational Public Radio is made completely out of everyday things. You should be able to receive a strong radio signal in most places in the country. You can use wire from an old telephone cord for the coil, antenna, and ground wires. Instead of a crystal or a diode you will use a penny and a twist-tie!

Radio Fun-damentals

Radio stations mix the audio (sound) signal with a carrier signal. The carrier is a high-frequency radio wave that allows for long-range transmission.

Radio receivers have four basic sections: a receiving section, using an antenna and ground wires to capture radio signals; a tuning section, using a coil of wire, to focus on a specific signal; a detector section, using a diode, to separate the audio signal from the carrier wave; and an audio output section, using a speaker or earphone to convert the audio signal into sound.

Crystal and diode detectors are electronic devices that conduct electricity in one direction better than the other. Crystals were once used in the detector sections of radio receivers, but diodes are used now. Since crystals and diodes are not considered everyday things, our sneaky radio will use a substitute detector made from a penny and a twist-tie.

What's Needed
- Toilet paper tube or small bottle
- Telephone cord, 25 feet or longer
  (or other thin wire)
- Crystal earphone (not a Walkman or
  cell phone headset or in-the-ear earphone)
- Penny
- Paper clips
- Twist-tie
- Cardboard (from a shoe box or food container)
- Pliers with insulated handles
- Screwdriver

toilet paper   paper clip or twist-tie   cardboard   pliers   screwdriver

What to Do

Remove the outer insulation from the telephone wire and separate the wires (Figure 1). One of the wires will be used for the antenna. Mount it as high as you can in your room. Lay the other end of the wire on the cardboard with a paper clip, as shown in Figure 2. Strip the insulation from the end of the wire and attach it to the paper clip.

Connect another wire, with its end stripped, to a metal water pipe under a sink in your kitchen. This will be the ground wire. Its other end connects to paper clip 2 as shown in Figure 2.

To build the radio tuning coil, remove two inches of insulation from the end of a third wire and put this stripped end through the paper tube. Wind about eighty turns around the paper tube. Secure the wire with tape if necessary. Insert the end of

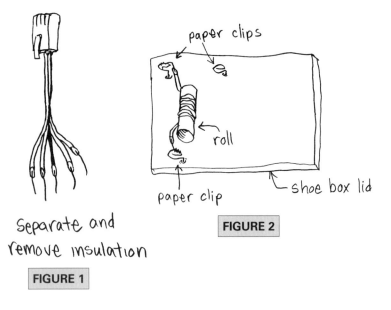

Separate and
remove insulation

FIGURE 1

paper clips

roll

paper clip

shoe box lid

FIGURE 2

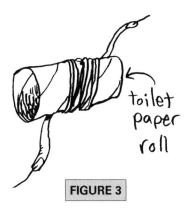

toilet paper roll

FIGURE 3

the wire into the other hole on the tube, as shown in Figure 3. Connect both wire ends to paper clips 1 and 2.

Strip an inch of insulation from both wire leads of the earphone. Connect one of the earphone wires to paper clip 1.

Scratch the surface of the penny with the screwdriver and, using pliers, hold it over a flame for three minutes until a black spot appears. After it cools, slip the penny securely under paper clip 2 (see Figure 4).

Strip off the insulation from the twist-tie and cut one end into a sharp point. Bend the twist-tie into a **V** shape and mount the dull end to paper clip 3. The pointed end should press firmly against the burnt surface of the penny, as shown in Figure 4.

Connect the remaining earphone wire to paper clip 3. Your Irrational Public Radio is completed.

Put on the earphone and slowly move the tip of the twist-tie across the surface of the penny until you hear a radio station. Be sure the tip of the twist-tie has enough pressure on the coin to maintain contact. If necessary, bend it into position again (see Figure 5).

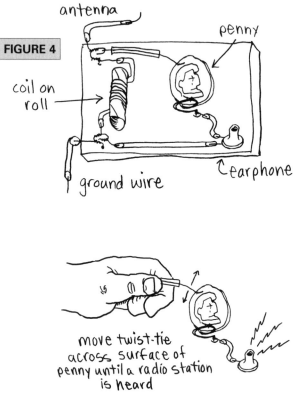

FIGURE 4

antenna

penny

coil on roll

ground wire

earphone

move twist-tie across surface of penny until a radio station is heard

FIGURE 5

BONUS APPLICATION

If you want to amplify the radio's audio signal and allow others
to hear it, you can connect it to a tape recorder.

What's Needed

- Tape recorder
- Small speaker
- 2 earphone plug ends
  (⅛-inch plugs)

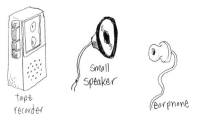

What to Do

When placed in the RECORD mode, a tape recorder will amplify
sounds from the microphone and send signals to the tape head.
It also sends audio signals to the earphone jack.

To use this function, place a cassette in the recorder. Then,
using the plug from an old earphone cable, attach its wires to a
small speaker. (Any small speaker will work; including one from
a car sound system, an old TV, a Walkman, or a nonworking radio
or tape player.) Attach the wires to the plug.

Now connect the other earphone plug end to the connections
where the radio's earphone would be (paper clips 1 and 3).

After connecting the speaker to the earphone jack, place the
cassette in the recorder and press the RECORD button. Then press
the PAUSE button. This will stop the motor from turning and will
save battery power. You will hear the radio signal emanate from
the small speaker, and everyone in the room can enjoy the
sounds from the "penny radio."

Tips

A crystal radio will usually operate best at night. Under some
combinations of conditions you may receive no stations at all.
Be patient and try again.

If no sounds are detected, not even a slight hum, check all wire connections to the paper clips and reposition the wire attached to the water pipe.

You can launch an antenna wire high up into a tree with a rock or toy dart gun. Wrap the end of a 50-foot wire to the end of a dart and shoot it toward high branches.

You can send the radio's output into the microphone input of a tape recorder and listen to it with a speaker connected to the earphone jack.

Other detector materials that can be used include a silver gum wrapper, a spring from a ballpoint pen, a rusty nail or washer, a rusty set of pliers. Remember: the detector's two parts must be two *unlike* metals.

More information on crystal radio building can be obtained from the following Web sites:

boydhouse.com/crystalradio
howstuffworks.com
midnightscience.com
scitoys.com

Con Air:
Convert Your Radio into an Aircraft Broadcast Receiver

"**F**light Four-eight-three to LAX tower . . . in need of immediate assistance. We're experiencing an emergency situation."

The VHF aircraft band is filled with fascinating and sometimes critical communications from commercial airliners, the military, and private aircraft. Many aircraft-scanner listeners enjoy the fun and excitement of tuning in tower-to-air conversations that are missed by the general public. Although aircraft radios command premium prices, there is a way to enjoy aircraft broadcasts for free. In fact, if you have an AM/FM radio, you already have an aircraft radio!

Believe it or not, you can easily convert virtually any AM/FM radio into an effective aircraft band receiver. The AM band will remain unchanged. The FM band will have limited reception after the conversion, but it can quickly be returned to its original condition with a small standard screwdriver.

This project should use a small nondigital battery-powered radio. Not too small—the ultra-tiny Walkman radios can be difficult to open and adjust. But first, some background information on how radios work and what the conversion will do.

Broadcast radio stations transmit a combination of two signals: the audio signal, which includes voice or music, and the carrier signal, which is designed to travel long distances and "carry" the audio signal with it. Voices or music affect (or modulate) the

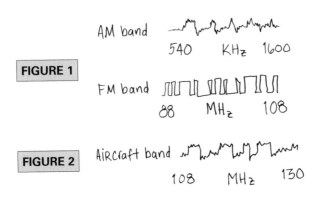

AM band

540   KHz   1600

FIGURE 1

FM band

88   MHz   108

FIGURE 2

Aircraft band

108   MHz   130

audio signal, either by varying its strength, known as *amplitude,* or its *frequency.*

Using voice and music to vary the *amplitude* of the carrier signal is called amplitude modulation—AM. Varying the *frequency* of a carrier signal is the defining feature of *frequency* modulation (FM). See Figure 1 for an illustration of these principles.

An AM radio is designed to tune to a specific range of broadcast stations, discard the carrier signal, and leave the audio signal. Then, just the strength (amplitude) of the signal is forwarded to the radio's speaker or earphone. On the other hand, in an FM radio just the varying *frequency* of the signal is sent to the radio's speaker or earphone.

Fun Fact 1: AM radios are more sensitive to static because radio interference is a result of the strength of radio waves emanating from lightning or home appliances. FM radios are designed to filter out changes in the strength of the signal, and that's why they produce superior audio quality.

Aircraft radio signals are broadcast on the AM band at a range just above the standard FM band; see Figure 2. What you'll do

is convert the FM section of the radio to AM and also allow it to
receive signals within the aircraft band. The best thing is that the
conversion is simple and does not require any parts!

Fun Fact 2: Television signals are both AM and FM; the
picture information is broadcast in AM, and the sound signal is
broadcast in FM. The two signals are combined and "ride" on
the carrier signal. The next time you experience electrical interference in your house, you'll notice that the sound of the TV set
is not affected as much as the picture.

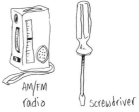

AM/FM
radio   screwdriver

What's Needed
- Portable AM/FM radio
- Small flat-blade screwdriver

What to Do
Test the AM/FM radio to ensure that the battery is strong and
that local radio stations can be received loud and clear. Open
the back of the radio so you can see the parts on the main
circuit board.

Note: Some radio cases snap or slide open while others
require you to remove a screw.

Examine the items on the circuit board and look for the part
under the tuning dial that selects the stations. This is the variable
capacitor. You'll also see two or three small square metal components. They are filter transformers. Their purpose is to filter out
noise and static on the FM band. In essence, they filter out AM
signals. Look even closer at the top of the filter transformers,
and you'll see a screw slot to allow adjustment. Also, one of the
filter transformers will have two or three small glass diodes next
to it. A diode looks like a clear slender bead with wires on each
end. This is the filter transformer that we will adjust.

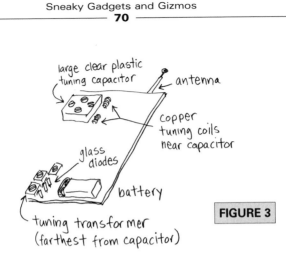

large clear plastic tuning capacitor

antenna

copper tuning coils near capacitor

glass diodes

battery

tuning transformer (farthest from capacitor)

FIGURE 3

Note: In some radios you may not see the diodes near a tuning transformer, but the adjustment can still be performed. See Figure 3 for an illustration of a typical radio and its component parts.

The first step is to turn the radio on and switch to the FM band. Tune to a spot between stations until you hear a background hiss. Now place your screwdriver in the top of the filter transformer and turn it until the hiss gets as loud as possible. When the hiss is at its highest volume, you have just converted the FM portion of the radio so it can receive AM signals.

One more step is required—you must extend the broadcast range of the FM band. To do this, look at the radio's tuning dial and notice the large square tuning capacitor on the main board. There will be two small copper wire coils next to it. With the screwdriver, spread the small coil windings apart as much as possible without letting them touch another part on the board (see Figure 4). By spreading the coils apart, you have extended the broadcast range from 88 megahertz to 108 MHz and above.

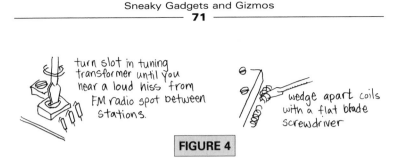

turn slot in tuning transformer until you near a loud hiss from FM radio spot between stations.

wedge apart coils with a flat blade screwdriver

FIGURE 4

Congratulations! Now your radio can receive signals within the aircraft radio band.

Next, tune the dial up and down the FM band. You should notice that the station locations have changed, now that the radio is set to receive broadcasts on the aircraft radio band. Take the radio near a local airport and tune across the band. Aircraft messages—from automatic runway signals to tower communiqués—should be audible while tuning the dial.

You can easily convert the radio back to its original state by reversing the two-step process. First, push the small wire coils that are next to the tuning capacitor back to their original positions. Second, dial the radio to a section between stations and retune the filter transformer until the hiss sound is at a minimum.

The next time you visit an airport, take your multiband radio with you and enjoy the fun and intrigue of eavesdropping on aircraft band conversations.

Part III

Security Gadgets and Gizmos

Most people like to believe that break-ins and other misfortunes won't happen to them. But ignorance is not always bliss! Nowadays, home, apartment, and hotel security matters are a fundamental concern. This section provides protection devices that can be rigged up to foil assaults on person or property using paper clips, rubber bands, and other household odds and ends.

First, you'll become skilled at using the most innocent-looking items to secure your personal things, like a letter, wallet, or purse. Next, you'll learn how to obtain "see-behind vision" and how to make devices to detect if your doors or windows have been tampered with. Also included are sneaky projects that show how to use a tape recorder to thwart intruders and how to rig a disposable camera to identify burglars by taking a thug shot.

Sneaky Ways to Thwart Break-ins:
Protect Your Fortress from a Man of Steal

Sure, traveling has its charms, but with exotic environments sometimes come mysterious and unexpected dangers. It doesn't happen often, but when you stay overnight away from home you probably worry about someone entering your room without your knowledge. The following projects provide a trio of portable and quick-to-set-up security gimmicks for use at home, on a trip, or for an unforeseen stay in a foreign location to thwart or detect window and door break-ins at a moment's notice.

What's Needed

- Rubber bands
- Bubble-wrap material
- String or wire
- Cardboard
- Small bell or chime

rubber bands

Cardboard

small bell or chime

bubble-wrap material

What to Do

To be warned when someone enters a room, place bubble-wrap material under a mat or towel near the entrance. Or place a small bell or chime on the door or window (see Figure 1).

Place an External Sneak Detector (see "Thwart Thieves" later in Part III for details) against a window handle or on a doorsill so it will produce a loud popping sound when activated (see Figure 2).

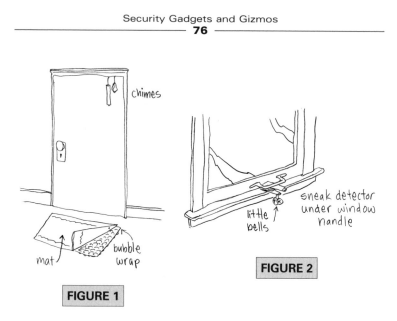

FIGURE 1

FIGURE 2

Optionally, use whatever unbreakable but noisy items are available to place against a door or window to alert you when they are displaced.

HOW TO PREVENT BREAKING AND ENTERING

What's Needed
- Wire or strong nylon thread
- Broom, mop handle, plunger dowel, or chair
- Towels
- Tape or rubber bands
- Duct tape

broom or mop handle

rubber bands

tape

wire or nylon thread

What to Do

To protect a door from opening, place a long object, like a broom, mop, or chair, under the doorknob so it's wedged in tight. If necessary, use towels or small pillows to anchor the object to the floor to prevent slippage (see Figure 1).

Even strong nylon thread can prevent a door from opening if it's wrapped tightly from the doorknob to an adjacent window handle or wall light-plate fixture screw. Apply duct tape to all corners of the door to further prevent a break-in (see Figure 2).

Similarly, a window can be secured with an object to prevent it from sliding in its track, as shown in Figure 3.

If a single long object is not available, use shorter ones, like aerosol cans or slender bottles. Position all of the objects end to end and secure them with tape or rubber bands to keep them in line (see Figure 4).

Although a determined burglar can breech these entry inhibitors, they give you valuable time to react and call for help. A chime can be taped to the windows and doors to alert you that a break-in is in progress.

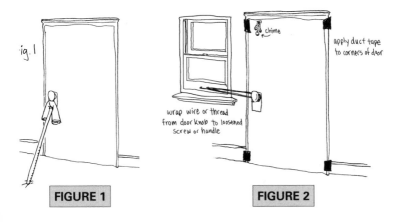

fig. 1

chime

apply duct tape to corners of door

wrap wire or thread from door knob to loosened screw or handle

FIGURE 1   **FIGURE 2**

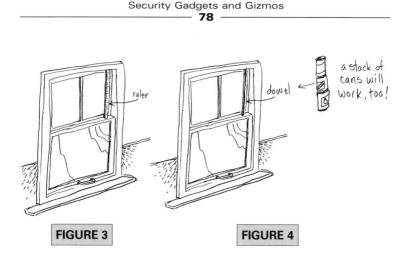

FIGURE 3   **FIGURE 4**

PHANTOM MENACE NOISEMAKERS

Your home audio/video system is probably your pride and joy.
Others might enjoy it too. But they may not spend the time and
money shopping at the places you did. They may take the direct-
theft route to aural delight.

What's Needed
- Wire
- Aluminum foil
- Cardboard
- Radio, tape recorder, or
  battery-powered clock radio
- Ballpoint pen spring

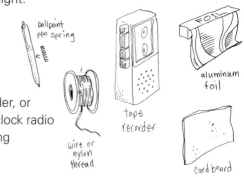

What to Do
You can cause a door or window opening to activate a battery-
powered radio, a tape player, or a battery-powered alarm clock

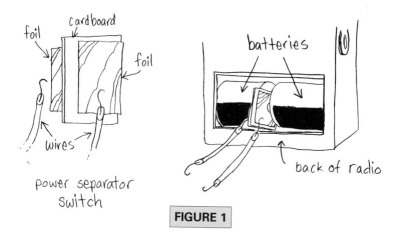

power separator switch

FIGURE 1

using a power separator switch and contact sensor. Any battery-powered toy or gadget that makes noise will work. The power separator switch, made from foil, wire, and cardboard as shown in Figure 1, is placed between batteries in a radio, tape player, or noise-making toy.

First, tape a piece of aluminum foil at the side of the door near the hinge. Then remove the spring from a ballpoint pen. Tape the spring on adjacent area, near (but not touching) the aluminum foil strip on the door. Bend and mount the spring so that the door must be open about one third of the way before it touches the foil on the door.

Next, attach wires to the spring and the foil and connect them to the wires on the power separator switch (see Figure 2). Now, when the door is opened, the spring contacts the foil, which completes the circuit, allowing the radio or tape player to obtain power from the batteries. Be sure to set the volume high enough to alert you that a door or window has been breeched.

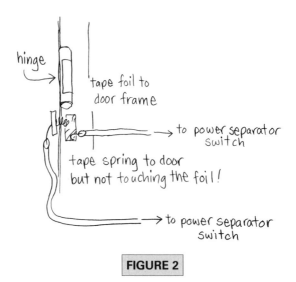

hinge

tape foil to door frame

→ to power separator switch

tape spring to door but not touching the foil!

→ to power separator switch

FIGURE 2

BONUS APPLICATION:
PHANTOM MENACE NOISEMAKER

Sure, you could install a costly and elaborate home security device that blares an ominous warning over a PA system. But you can make one with items found in virtually every household.

Using the same parts shown in the "H_2O No!" project described a little later here in Part III, you can make a cassette tape recorder protect your house or apartment in a sneaky way. By prerecording a stern, ominous message on the tape and playing it back through a large speaker, your living quarters can appear protected by an expensive alarm system and give the impression that a live security team is on the way.

Substitute a playing card (or other laminated piece of card-board) with a thin wire or nylon thread attached (see Figure 1).

Attach the other end of the wire to a window handle or door or to a TV, stereo, or other appliance (see Figure 2). When it's moved, the card will separate from the paper clips and turn on the recorder and it will play the tape.

You can have the sound emanate from the recorder's speaker or, for a greater effect, you can plug in a remote speaker (obtained from an old TV or car stereo or other entertainment device) and connect it with an earphone cable and wire; see Figure 3.

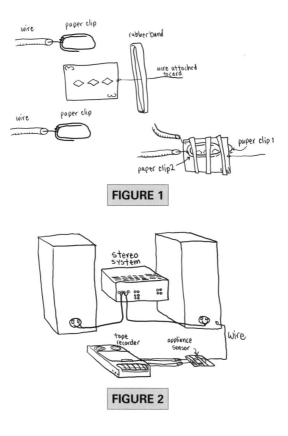

FIGURE 1

FIGURE 2

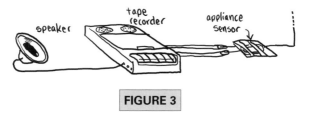

FIGURE 3

Here's a sample recorded script: *Stop. You have entered unlawfully. Security personnel have been notified and are on the way. Leave immediately.*

BONUS APPLICATION 2:
X COMMUNICATE

The sneaky alarm just described can activate an X-10® telephone dialer (or one from security system dealers). When an alarm is activated, you can be notified by pager, phone, or e-mail!

For more information about security dialers, see Resources at the back of the book.

Foam Alone:
Make a Sneaky
Fire Extinguisher

With a little planning and two items found in your kitchen, you can have a lifesaving tool available for emergencies. Having a fire extinguisher on hand gives you peace of mind and can prevent costly damage to your belongings (and possibly save a life). If you ever need a compact and portable fire extinguisher, you can make a sneaky version in just a few minutes using household materials.

What's Needed

- Baking soda
- Vinegar (or lemon juice)
- Jar or plastic soda bottle, 1 pint or larger
- Tissue
- Tape or a rubber band

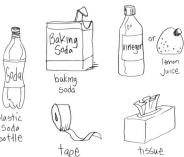

What to Do

Fill the bottle halfway with vinegar (or lemon juice). Then form the tissue into a cup shape and poke it into the mouth of the bottle, as shown in Figure 1, holding the sides of the tissue over the rim of the bottle.

Still holding the sides, pour baking soda into the tissue and then place a rubber band or tape around the bottle opening to prevent the tissue from dropping into the bottle; see Figure 2.

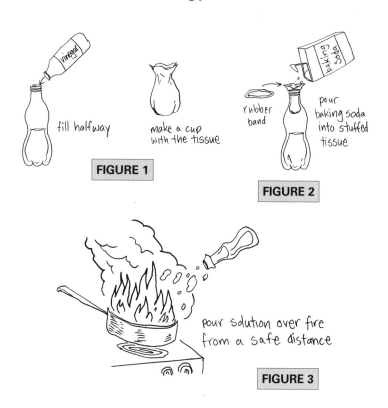

fill halfway

FIGURE 1

make a cup
with the tissue

rubber
band

pour
baking soda
into stuffed
tissue

FIGURE 2

pour solution over fire
from a safe distance

FIGURE 3

Replace the cap on the bottle or place another tissue and rubber band or tape on top of the bottle while it's in storage.

When needed, shake the bottle vigorously and remove the cap. A fire-retardant foam will bubble up, to be cautiously poured over a fire. See Figure 3.

Caution: Be particularly careful when in the presence of fire, especially an oil or grease fire.

Gain Sneaky
See-behind Vision

Forget X-ray vision, heat vision, and microscopic vision. In the real world, whether you're at an ATM or opening your car door, what counts is "see-behind" vision.

Many assaults take place when a person is distracted, and it's impossible to keep looking around while you're fiddling with keys and cards. Luckily, a sneaky remedy is at hand.

What's Needed

- Small mirror or reflective material, about 1½ inches square
- Duct tape
- Large paper clip

paper clip

mirror

tape

What to Do

Bend the large paper clip into the shape shown in Figure 1 and tape it tightly to the small mirror. If the edges of the mirror are

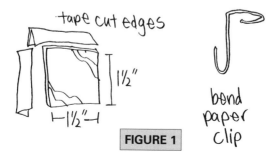

tape cut edges

1½"

—1½"—

FIGURE 1

bend paper clip

sharp, tape them carefully also. Then attach the mirror to a cap or glasses with the other end of the clip, as shown in Figure 2. Note: Adjust the position of the mirror, by bending the paper clip, to improve clarity if required.

You can use this sneaky vision device three ways: it can be carried in your hand; it can be attached to a cap; or it can be clipped to eyeglasses. Now go ahead and use your See-behind vision for safety and fun.

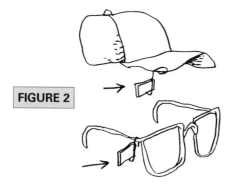

FIGURE 2

Industrious Light Magic:
Make a Sneaky Light in a Pinch

There's an irony in being caught without a light source in a car, when there are nearly twenty light bulbs in the average vehicle plus a 12-volt battery under the hood. The only thing required is some wire to connect the battery to the bulb.

Many automotive emergencies happen at night, and most people drive without a working flashlight. You could be caught without ample light to see where a problem is. Light may be needed to find a part on the ground. If you should need to leave the vehicle on a road, a light can be used to signal for help or reveal yourself to motorists so you won't be hit.

This project illustrates two methods of making a small working light from everyday things.

MAKE AN UNDER-HOOD LIGHT

What's Needed
- Small bulb
- Wire

flash light bulb

insulated wire (with stripped ends)

What to Do
Wire can be obtained from speaker wire connectors or from some other noncritical source in the vehicle. (See "Getting Wired" in Part I for more sources of emergency wire.) As shown in Figure 1, wrap the bare wire around the bulb's side and hold the other end on the battery's positive (+) terminal. Then touch the bulb's bottom to a metal part away from the battery under the hood.

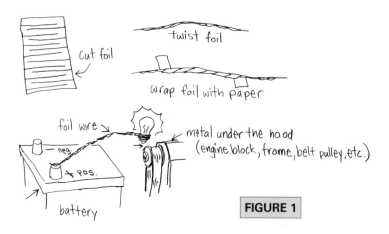

cut foil

twist foil

wrap foil with paper

foil wire

metal under the hood
(engine block, frame, belt pulley, etc.)

neg.

pos.

battery

FIGURE 1

If you have two long lengths of wire available, you can attach one end to the bottom of the bulb and the other to the side and have a more flexible light.

MAKE A PORTABLE LIGHT

There's also a way to make a sneaky light for use *away* from the vehicle. When using an automotive bulb, you can use a small 12-volt battery that some portable alarm remote controls use. Otherwise, if you have a flashlight bulb (and the flashlight batteries are depleted) you can use its bulb with batteries you may have on your person.

Note: Do not exceed the bulb's recommended voltage requirement. A, C, D, and AA batteries all supply 1.5 volts. So if a flashlight uses two D-cell batteries, the bulb requires 3 volts to operate. You can then use two C or AA or small watch batteries to light the bulb. Batteries can be found in a pager, a car alarm's remote control, a toy, a garage-door opener, or a watch. (In a remote survival situation, batteries from fruits can be used; see "More Power to You" in Part I for details.)

What's Needed

- Battery (that meets bulb voltage requirement)
- Bulb
- Wire

battery

flash light bulb

insulated wire (with stripped ends)

What to Do

You will need a small length of wire. If no standard wire is available, alternative everyday things that can be used include a paper clip, a twist-tie, a metal chain or earring, a ballpoint pen spring, keys, speaker wire, or aluminum foil from a snack bag or coffee-creamer-container lid. See Figure 2.

If more than one battery is required, you can wrap paper around them and hold the paper in place with tape, wire, a rubber band, string, or a twist-tie.

With the bulb, wire, and batteries available, attach the parts together as shown in Figure 3. If you use small batteries, try to limit your use of the sneaky light to save power.

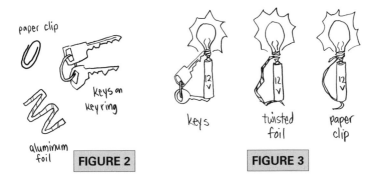

paper clip

keys on key ring

aluminum foil

FIGURE 2

keys

twisted foil

paper clip

FIGURE 3

H₂O No!:
Make a Sneaky Flood Alarm

Few events are more distressing than returning home to a flood situation. This project shows how to construct an easy-to-make sneaky flood alarm for your home from everyday things. You'll need only an inexpensive battery-powered clock or AM radio and a few other items to complete the alarm.

What's Needed
- Any fast-dissolving tablet
- Rubber bands
- Wire
- Aluminum foil
- Cardboard
- Paper clips
- Battery-powered AM radio or alarm clock

alka-seltzer
sugar cube
breath strips
fast-dissolving items

rubber bands

insulated wire (with stripped ends)

paper clip

AM/FM radio

aluminum foil

cardboard

What to Do
You can cause a seepage of water on the floor to activate a battery-powered radio, using a power separator switch and water sensor. The power separator switch, made from foil, wire, and cardboard,

is placed between batteries in a radio, as shown in Figure 1. The cardboard separates the aluminum foil contacts from completing the circuit.

The foil contacts are attached to two paper clips, which are separated by a fast-dissolving substance—seltzer tablet, sugar cube, aspirin—in the sneaky flood switch. The rubber band applies

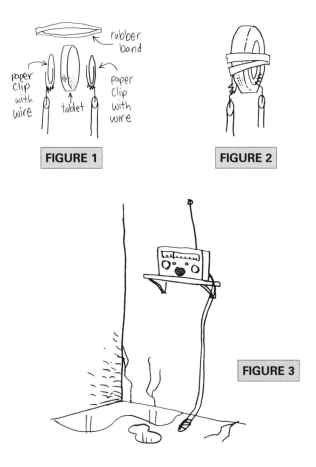

FIGURE 1

FIGURE 2

FIGURE 3

pressure (see Figure 2). When water surrounds the tablet, it will dissolve, causing the paper clips to make contact (because of the pressure from the rubber bands). This allows the radio to obtain power from the batteries. The radio, which is tuned to a strong station and set to maximum volume, will turn on with a loud roar, alerting you to the danger (see Figure 3). If you use a battery-powered alarm clock, set the alarm to activate as soon as it's turned on.

Test how fast the item you use as the water sensor will dissolve. For example, a few oral breath strips placed between the paper clips will dissolve in just a few seconds.

If necessary, use longer wires from the sneaky flood sensor so the radio can be placed where you can hear it from anywhere in the house. Another option is to connect more sneaky sensors in parallel to the first one so other areas can be protected as well.

BONUS APPLICATION:
A SNEAKY FIRE ALARM

A flood alarm isn't the only sneaky device that can be made with the power separator and paper-clip sensor. Using the same items shown in Figure 1, you can make a sneaky fire alarm too.

Construct the parts as before but, instead of a water-soluble tablet, place beeswax (or another fast-melting substance) between the paper clips (see Figure 2). Set the fire sensor as high as possible, but not near the corner of a room. Virtually any soft fast-melting substance will work (see Figure 3).

It is a good idea to place a container below the sensor so the melting substance will not collect on the floor.

Note: This device is not intended to replace a standard fire alarm. It can be used as a demonstrational device or until a standard UL-approved alarm is available.

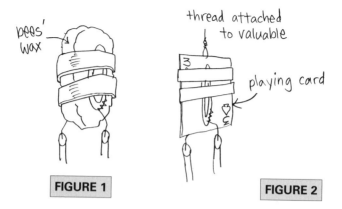

FIGURE 1

FIGURE 2

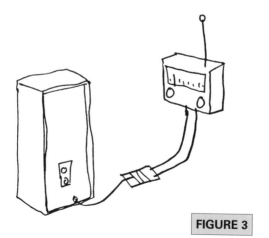

FIGURE 3

Sticky Fingers?
Keep Watch with an Internal Sneak Detector

Are you tired of people prying in your personal items? If you believe that someone is opening your mail or tampering with your belongings, you can plant an Internal Sneak Detector for verification. If you return and the device has snapped apart, you will know someone has opened the item.

What's Needed
- Standard-size envelope
- Paper clip
- Small rubber band
- Piece of strong cardboard
- Scissors
- Pen
- Pliers

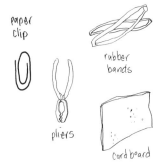

What to Do
You can use strong cardboard from a tissue box, shoe box, or videocassette box. First, cut four small pieces, 3 inches long by 1 inch wide, as shown in Figure 1.

Next, with a pen, punch small holes at the ends of the four cardboard pieces. Then straighten out the paper clip and cut it into four small pieces.

Position the four cardboard pieces and push a piece of paper clip into each hole, as in Figure 2.

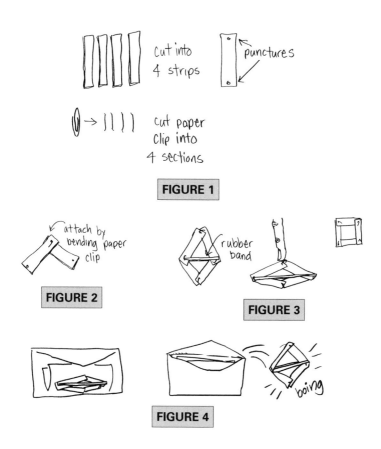

Cut into 4 strips

punctures

Cut paper clip into 4 sections

FIGURE 1

attach by bending paper clip

FIGURE 2

rubber band

FIGURE 3

boing

FIGURE 4

Attach the rubber band across two of the ends (see Figure 3).

To use the Internal Sneak Detector, push the other two ends of the rubber band together and place the device into a standard envelope. The rubber band creates spring tension. If the envelope is opened, the detector will spring out, as shown in Figure 4.

You might want to leave a small note, stating that you're aware of the tampering that's been occurring.

Thwart Thieves with the External Sneak Detector

If you use the Internal Sneak Detector, you'll undoubtedly want to try an external version for such larger possessions as a purse, briefcase, book, or laptop computer.

The External Sneak Detector can be placed under an item. It will flip and make a loud snapping sound if the item is moved. You can place a note under it to ward off future mischief.

What's Needed
- Small rubber band
- Piece of strong cardboard
- Scissors
- Glue

rubber bands

cardboard

What to Do
You can use strong cardboard from a tissue box, shoe box, or videocassette box. First, from four pieces of cardboard, cut two identical replicas each of shapes A and B, as shown in Figure 1. Glue each pair together for added strength.

Shape B is rectangular. Shape A is the same as B except for a thin notch cut into it from one end to its center; see Figure 1. The exact dimensions of A and B are not critical, but Shape A should extend to half the length of the sneak detector and be wide enough for the small rubber band to fit through easily.

Next, glue pieces A and B together along half of their length, as shown in Figure 2. Glue only the unnotched part of Shape A

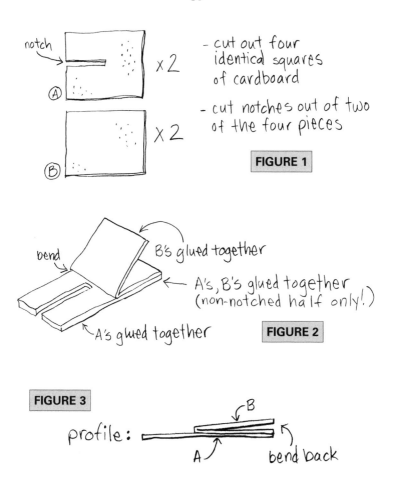

FIGURE 1

- cut out four identical squares of cardboard
- cut notches out of two of the four pieces

notch

Ⓐ ×2

Ⓑ ×2

FIGURE 2

bend

B's glued together

A's, B's glued together (non-notched half only!)

A's glued together

FIGURE 3

profile:

B

A

bend back

to Shape B. Once the pieces are glued together, bend the notched half of Shape A back and forth so it flexes (see Figure 3).

Now, with pieces A and B flattened out, attach the small rubber band. Be sure to guide the rubber band through the notch. Once it's in place, pull back on the notched half of Shape A until

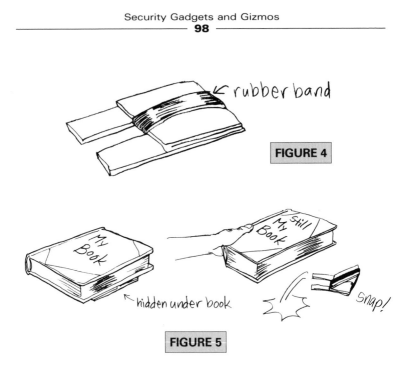

FIGURE 4

FIGURE 5

it bends all the way back. This will stretch the rubber band. If you let go, it will snap back fast and loud like a mousetrap (see Figure 4). If this does not happen, use a smaller rubber band or wrap the band around and through the notch twice.

As seen in Figure 5, the External Sneak Detector, placed under an object, will fly up and snap with a loud pop when the object is moved.

Thug Shot:
Capture Break-ins on Film

A picture can be more valuable than a thousand words . . . in court. If a break-in cannot be thwarted, the next best thing is to record it on film. This project illustrates how to set up a disposable camera so that, if a door or window is breached, you will have a "thug shot" for evidence.

What's Needed
- Disposable camera (non-flash)
- Toy dart gun, with suction-cup tips
- Strong medium-sized rubber band
- Hanger
- Thin strong thread
- Pliers
- Tape
- Cardboard
- Stick-on eyelets

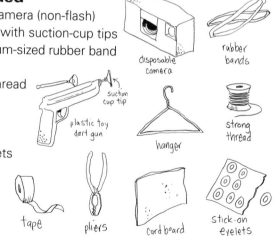

disposable camera

rubber bands

suction cup tip

plastic toy dart gun

hanger

strong thread

tape

pliers

Cardboard

stick-on eyelets

What to Do
This project works when a toy gun, triggered by a door or window opening, shoots its dart into a camera's shutter button.

Using pliers, bend the hanger into the shape shown in Figure 1 so that it secures the toy gun and the camera. You should be able to slide the gun in and out of the mount so that a dart, with the suction cup temporarily removed, can be easily reloaded.

Place the toy gun so the dart is aimed a few inches from the camera's shutter button (see Figure 2). Attach one end of the string to the toy gun's trigger and the other end to the door (or window) with stick-on eyelets or suction-cup hooks, as shown in Figure 3.

When you set up the thread and paper-clip triggering system, be sure to allow enough room for *you* to slip in and out of the room without setting off the camera. After the correct length and tension of the thread is worked out, when the door (or window) is opened, the thread will pull the toy gun's trigger, causing the dart to shoot the shutter button so the camera takes a photograph.

Since the camera has no flash—a flash would alert the burglar— the room must have sufficient ambient light so the image will be visible on film. Also, since this is a disposable camera, remember to advance the film manually so that it's ready to take a photograph when you leave the room.

Note: This project can also be used in combination with the taping of Phantom Menace Noisemakers described earlier in Part III under "Sneaky Ways to Thwart Break-ins."

bend hanger

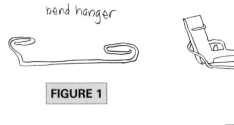

FIGURE 1

↙ suction cup
removed

FIGURE 2

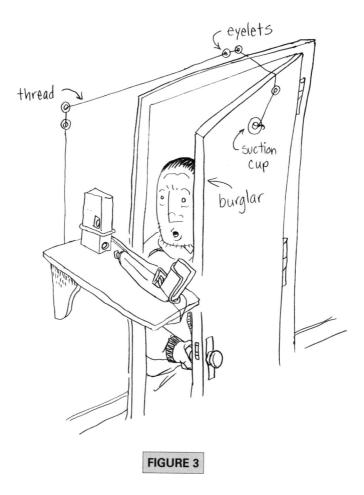

FIGURE 3

Hide and Sneak:
Secure Valuables in Everyday Things

You've seen movies where a character hides something at home and you think, That's the first place I'd look! Well, this project will illustrate how to choose sneaky locations that are the *last* places a Man of Steal would look. You don't always have access to a safe deposit box or install alarms on all of your possessions. But you can find sneaky hide-in-plain-sight places to frustrate and waste a thief's time.

Selecting this hiding place generally depends on two factors: the size of the item and the frequency of access required. From a package of soap to a tennis ball, a typical home offers a variety of clever hiding places, as shown in Figure 1. Wrapping your valuables in black plastic bags will further prevent discovery.

With enough time, a tenacious thief can eventually find virtually anything you hide. That's why you should have a room entry alarm installed in combination with sneaky hiding places to reduce the time a thief will spend searching for your valuables.

The Resources section at the back of the book provides a list of security companies marketing clever safes that appear to be soda cans, aerosol sprays, and other everyday things.

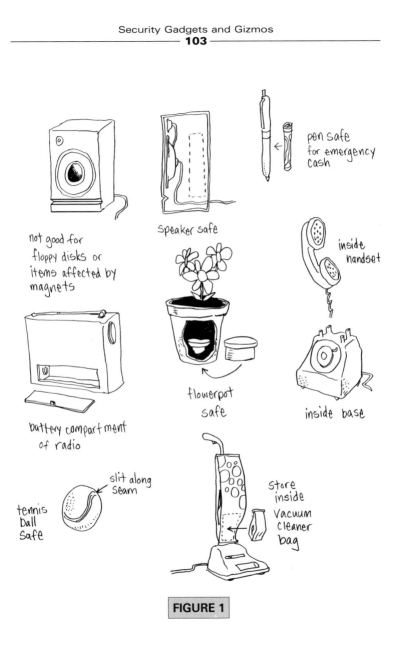

not good for
floppy disks or
items affected by
magnets

speaker safe

pen safe
for emergency
cash

inside
handset

battery compartment
of radio

flowerpot
safe

inside base

slit along
seam

tennis
ball
safe

store
inside
vacuum
cleaner
bag

FIGURE 1

Power of the Press:
Use Ordinary Objects as Sneaky Weapons

According to the Bureau of Justice, a violent crime occurs in the United States every five seconds. Being prepared can save your life. You don't have to buy a gun or a can of Mace to protect yourself from attackers. In some instances, ordinary objects can be used effectively as weapons.

First, an important warning: Don't contend with adversaries. You won't lose a fight you don't participate in. If possible, run away as soon as possible and yell for help.

In situations where there is no other way out, you will find that common objects, from a public phone to a magazine, can distract an assailant, keep distance between you, and, if you must strike, reduce injury and protect your flesh and bones. Here's how to defend yourself:

Public phone. If an assailant decides to attack you while you're on the phone, use the handset to hit your attacker on the nose or temple. In a phone booth, use the door to wedge the attacker's arm or leg.

Coins. You can throw a handful of coins at an attacker's face to stun and throw him or her off balance. See Figure 1.

Pens and pencils. Pen and pencils can be used to jab at an assailant's exposed skin and cause enough of a distraction to enable you to escape.

Magazines. By rolling up a magazine and holding it tight, you can strike the face, temple, or ear to temporarily disable an attacker. See Figure 2.

FIGURE 1

WHACK!!

Now

magazine

No

rolled up

FIGURE 2

One other technique to remember: If the attack has not occurred but is imminent, hold the ordinary object down in a nonthreatening way. The attacker may not realize that you will use it as a weapon.

If you sense that a threatening situation is escalating, look around, grab whatever you can—your shoes, a book, a cup, a package, a box, a small printer: anything you can throw and use it as if your life depends on it.

Sneaky Survival Techniques

Who hasn't seen *Gilligan's Island* or the movie *Cast Away* and thought, What would I do if I was lost or stranded somewhere? Can you imagine being marooned without fire, water, tools, weapons, or a compass? What would you do? How would you survive?

In this section you will find ways to stay afloat in sink-or-swim situations. You will learn how to make a fire and collect water, and how to build a makeshift telescope or magnifying glass, use code-signaling techniques, and make a sneaky emergency light.

You'll see how to survive in the cold and hike in deep snow, and you'll learn direction-finding techniques and how to make a compass.

Part IV concludes with crafty ways to devise makeshift weapons and tools.

Even if you feel that it'll never happen to you, review the text and illustrations. Someday your life may depend on it.

Sneaky Emergency Flotation Devices

If you find yourself in a sink-or-swim scenario, what will you do if a flotation device isn't available? Make a sneaky one from everyday things.

When floating in water, the more you try to keep your head above the surface of the water, the more likely you are to sink. Just lie back and keep your mouth above water.

When you attempt to raise parts of your body above the surface, you lose buoyancy. Luckily, however, you can add to your buoyancy with virtually any empty container that holds air. In some instances two or more may need to be secured together.

What's Needed

- Plastic bags
- Gas cans
- Large soda bottles
- Other items that will hold air
- String, wire, a belt, or cloth

plastic bags

gas can

large soda bottles

string

What to Do

To make a flotation device of plastic bags, blow the smallest one up, tie a tight knot, and place it in a larger bag (or bags, if available) as shown in Figure 1 to compensate for small holes. Use these inflated bags as water wings to help stay afloat. Rest on your back with your head up (figures 2 and 3).

Figure 4 illustrates how to connect two water-holding bottles or jars together. You can also use a log if one is available. Be sure

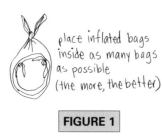

place inflated bags inside as many bags as possible (the more, the better)

FIGURE 1

plastic bags

FIGURE 2

soda bottles

FIGURE 3

tie bottles together

SODA

BLEAC

SODA

FIGURE 4

tie handles together

FIGURE 5

tie legs tight

air will be trapped up in pants

FIGURE 6

the log will float before laying your body on it (not all wood will float).

There are many other flotation devices that you can devise by using some imagination. Just make sure to test their flotation capabilities before trying to use them. Figure 5 shows how to tie bags together.

When no other items are available, your clothing can hold pockets of air to increase your buoyancy. If necessary, remove your pants or shirt, tie the ends of the pant legs or sleeves in knots and scoop air into them. Hold the other end together firmly with your hands and you should be able to ride above the water with little effort (see Figure 6).

Science Friction:
Six Fire-making Methods

Experienced campers know how to start a fire without a lighter or matches, but do you? When lost in the wilderness, being able to make a fire can be a lifesaver, both to signal your location and to use for warmth and cooking.

Everyone has heard that it's possible to make fire by rubbing two sticks together. But exactly how do you do this? What if you don't have two dry and properly shaped pieces of wood? Then what do you do?

This project will illustrate six different ways to start a small fire in an emergency. Some of the methods will work and some will not, depending on the resources available, your skill, and your luck. Review all six methods just in case you need to use them one day.

Before you attempt to start a fire, you must have tinder and kindling materials available and understand how to use them. Many people fail to start fires even when they have good matches!

A fire is built in stages. You need first to cause a small fire spark, with one of the methods shown below, to ignite your tinder: small dry items like tissue paper, dead grass, twigs, leaves, lint, or currency. Blow on the tinder carefully, so that it stays lit and grows into a larger fire. Then add kindling—sticks, branches, or thick paper—(*very* carefully, so that you do not suffocate the flame) to keep the fire going. When the kindling is burning, you can add larger logs or other fuel.

METHOD 1:
MAKE A FIRE PLOW

What's Needed
- Hard stick with a blunted tip
- Flat piece of wood
- Tinder
- Kindling
- Knife or sharp-edged rock

stick with blunted end

sharp-edged rock

flat piece of wood

kindling

What to Do
Using a knife or a sharp rock, scratch a straight indentation in the center of the flat piece of wood about the same width as

FIGURE 1

the blunt stick. Arrange the tinder so air can easily circulate and set it at the foot of the piece of wood, as shown in Figure 1.

Then, in a kneeling position, hold the flat piece of wood between your knees at an angle and move the stick rapidly back and forth in the indentation until friction ignites the fibers of tinder at the base. Mix in more tinder material and fan the smoke until a small fire starts. To keep the fire going, carefully add kindling material.

METHOD 2:
SPARK GENERATION

What's Needed
- Knife or steel
- Sharp-edged rocks
- Tinder
- Kindling

sharp-edged rock

kindling

What to Do
Use this method with very dry tinder material in a secluded nonwindy environment. Depending on what items are available, strike two rocks together to create a small spark close to tinder material (Figure 2). If a spark catches the tinder, you will see a glow. Carefully blow it so it turns into a small flame. Fan the material until it starts to smoke and burn (as in Method 1).

If you have an item made of steel, like a knife, scrape it against various rocks until a spark appears.

FIGURE 2

METHOD 3:
MAKE FIRE WITH A BATTERY

You can use the battery from a car or recreational vehicle (or batteries from a flashlight) to start a fire.

What's Needed
- Battery
- Thin wire or metal (from a twist-tie or staple, the spring from a ballpoint pen, steel wool, or a flashlight bulb filament)
- Tinder
- Kindling

auto battery

kindling

What to Do
Attach two wires to the battery terminals. With tinder and kindling material at hand, use the other two ends of the wires to create a spark near the tinder (Figure 3). Once the materials starts to burn, add kindling material to keep the fire going. If you are using flashlight batteries, put them together, as in Figure 4.

You can also use thin wire strands or other small pieces of metal to start a fire by holding them across the battery (insulate your hands because the wire will get hot) and placing them in the tinder to allow it to burn.

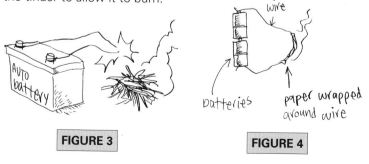

wire

batteries

paper wrapped around wire

FIGURE 3

FIGURE 4

METHOD 4:
MAKE FIRE WITH A LENS

If it's bright and sunny outside, it's possible to use a lens to focus the heat of the sun on tinder material and start a fire.

What's Needed
- Lens (from eyeglasses—reading glasses only—a magnifying glass, binoculars, or telescope)
- Tinder
- Kindling

lens

kindling

What to Do
With plenty of dry tinder available, aim the lens at it until it starts to smoke. Have other tinder material available to keep the fire going. When the tinder begins to burn, add kindling material. See Figure 5.

FIGURE 5

METHOD 5:
MAKE FIRE WITH A REFLECTOR

What's Needed

- A reflector from a flashlight or car headlight
- Tinder
- Kindling

headlight reflector

kindling

What to Do

You can use a light reflector from a flashlight or an old automobile headlight to focus the sun's rays on tinder material. If a headlight is to be used, carefully break away all the glass.

Position the tinder material in or in front of the reflector for maximum absorption of the sun's rays. With plenty of sunshine available overhead, and a little luck, the tinder material will get hot enough to catch fire. See Figure 6.

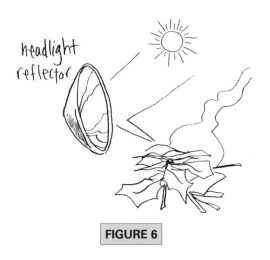

headlight reflector

FIGURE 6

METHOD 6:
MAKE FIRE WITH WATER

When positioned properly, water can act as a lens and focus enough of the sun's heat to ignite tinder.

What's Needed
- Water
- Jar or bottle
- Paper clip or twist-tie
- Tinder
- Kindling

What to Do
Pour about two teaspoons of water into a clear jar or bottle. Tilt the jar so the water rests in a corner at the bottom, position it

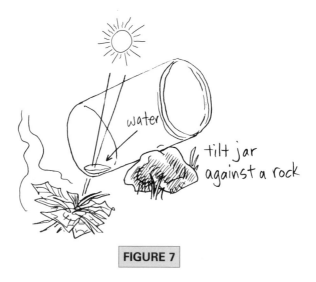

FIGURE 7

so the sun's rays shine through the water onto the tinder (see Figure 7), and ignite it.

Note: Other sneaky ways to make fire include using gunpowder from ammunition and chemicals from tablets. One of the most intriguing methods to be discovered is used by tribes in eastern Asia. They hollow out a bamboo cylinder and place small wood shavings at the bottom. When a long wooden rod is forced into the bamboo shaft (like a piston in a car engine), the rapid compression creates enough heat to ignite the wood shavings. The shavings are then poured on tinder to start a flame!

Rain Check:
Two Water-gathering Techniques

In a survival situation, finding water is crucial; without it, you can only survive a few days. Drinking water from the ocean can be dangerous because of its 4-percent salt content. It takes about two quarts of body fluid to rid the body of one quart of seawater. Therefore, by drinking from the ocean, you deplete your body's water, which can lead to death.

Fresh drinking water can be gathered from a variety of sources. This project will show how to gather rainwater and dew from the air.

COLLECTING DEW

What's Needed
- Clean towel or cloth
- Cup, bowl, or other container

What to Do
In the early morning, dew forms on grass, plants, rocks, and other large surfaces near the ground because these items have cooled and water vapor condenses on their surface. The dew can be easily gathered by laying a clean towel on the dew-covered area, dampening it, and wringing the towel out over a bowl. See Figure 1.

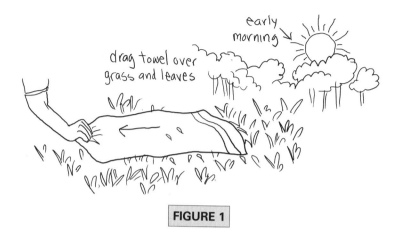

FIGURE 1

GATHERING RAINWATER

Rainwater, when available, is the preferred choice for drinking because it does not require boiling or purification. It can easily be collected by setting out items that you may already have.

What's Needed
- Cups, bowls, or other leakproof containers
- Plastic or vinyl material or a nylon jacket

What to Do
Place all available cups and containers where they can fill with rainwater. If necessary, use waterproof material—plastic, vinyl, or a waterproof article of clothing—as a substitute container, as shown in Figure 2. Or make a container from a large leaf or from coated paper, as shown in the bonus application Make a Substitute Cup in the next setting.

water-proof
vinyl sheet

rocks placed
in depression

FIGURE 2

Coming Extractions:
Get Drinking Water from Plants

Water is all around us in the air. The trick in obtaining it is to make it condense on the surface of an object and then collect it in a container.

EVAPORATOR STILL

An evaporator still can be made with a clear or translucent plastic bag and a large plant. It works by allowing the sun to shine through the bag and heat the plant, causing it to give off water vapor through its leaves. The water vapor condenses on the inside surface of the bag and drips down to the bottom. It can then be used for drinking water.

What's Needed
- Large plastic bag, preferably clear

What to Do
Gather green leaves or grass and place them in a plastic bag in a recessed area of the ground, as shown in Figure 1. Select an area where there will be plenty of sunlight. Or choose a plant or leafy tree branch, brush off any excess particles, wrap it in a plastic bag, and secure its opening with string, wire, or a tight knot; see Figure 2.

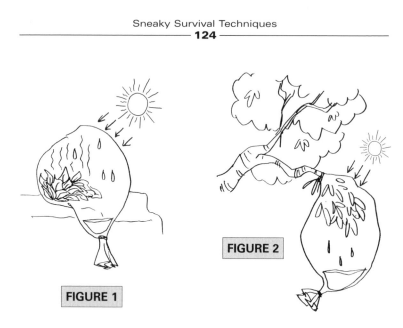

FIGURE 1

FIGURE 2

As the bag heats up, water from the leaves will evaporate and then condense in the bag as droplets that can be consumed later.

OVERGROUND SOLAR STILL

You can survive up to a month without food but only a few days without water. In the wilderness, there's always a concern about obtaining fresh drinking water. If you are near vegetation and have a large plastic bag available, you can quickly construct a solar still to acquire water.

A solar still uses heat to draw moisture from air, ground, or plants. It then collects the moisture droplets and condenses them into a container for drinking. Solar stills are easy to make, but the amount of water they produce will vary depending on their size, the amount of sunlight, and the terrain.

What's Needed

- Plastic bag, preferably clear, or plastic or vinyl material
- Cup or bowl or watertight container
- Rocks
- Stick
- Digging utensil

What to Do

The evaporator still proves that water from the air and from plant material can be trapped inside a plastic bag. With an overground solar still, you must dig out an oval or triangular trench and then another around it in an oval shape, as seen in Figure 1. Create the trench on an incline so that water will flow toward the end of the oval section.

First, place a tall stick in the center of the still and set the plant materials inside the center trench; see Figure 2. Next, cover

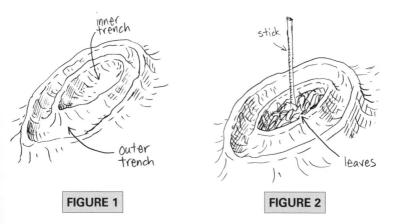

inner trench

outer trench

FIGURE 1

stick

leaves

FIGURE 2

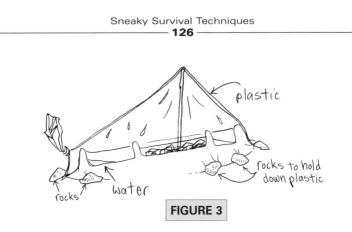

FIGURE 3

both the stick and both trenches with the plastic bag and hold it in place with rocks. Last, ensure that the bag end is closed and secure. Water from the plants will heat up in the sun, evaporate, condense on the inner surface of the plastic bag, and run down the sides and into the closed end of the bag in the outer oval trench, where it can be poured into a container later; see Figure 3.

BONUS APPLICATION:
H_2ORIGAMI—MAKE A SNEAKY CUP

Gathering or extracting condensed water from the air will be futile without a bowl or cup. You can make a sneaky cup from paper—preferably coated paper from a magazine—or from a large leaf from a tree.

What to Do
The following illustrations show a piece of paper with two sides. To clarify the folding technique, one side of the paper is shown as white and the other as gray. Each step is shown in its corresponding illustration figure number.

1. Start with a square piece of paper or large leaf.
2. Fold corner B diagonally on top of corner C.
3. Fold corner A, now point A, down as shown, forming a crease, and then unfold it.
4. Fold corner D, now point D, to the opposite edge, to the place where the first crease hits the edge of the paper.
5. Fold the paper on these two creases.
6. Fold the front (top) flap, corner B, down to cover all the layers. Fold the other flap, corner C, backward (there is only one layer to cover in the back).
7. Open the cup by pulling the front and the back apart.

The sneaky cup can be placed underneath a dripping condensation gathering area to save fresh water.

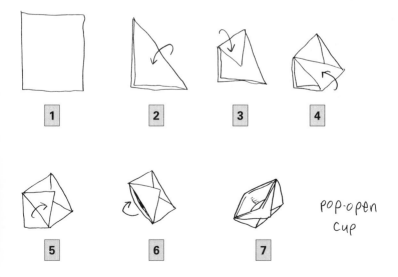

Lens Crafter:
Build a Makeshift Telescope

If you're ever lost, it would be convenient, maybe even lifesaving, to be able to see long distances. Didn't bring your binoculars with you? Don't sweat it. Make a sneaky telescope from items you already have. Usually, a telescope requires two lenses. But there is a sneaky way to make a telescope with just one lens and aluminum foil.

What's Needed

- Toilet paper roll or stiff cardboard
- Lens (from a camera, eyeglass, or watch)
- Aluminum foil
- Rubber band
- Paper clip

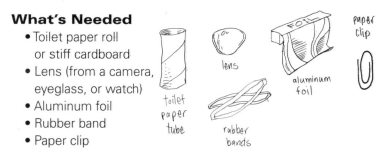

toilet paper tube

lens

rubber bands

aluminum foil

paper clip

What to Do

The aluminum foil, from a snack bag or gum wrapper, will act as the telescope eyepiece lens. To make this work, you must poke a very tiny round hole in it. To make a good pinhole, stack up several layers of aluminum foil, poke the stack with a pin, separate the layers, and choose the one with the best small round hole. The size of the hole determines whether the images are sharp, blurry, or dim. Test different sizes until you obtain a happy medium.

Wrap the foil, with the pinhole in the center, around one end of the toilet paper roll and secure it with a rubber band, as shown in Figure 1. Cut a slit in the roll at its other end. Attach the paper clip to the lens and slide the lens in the roll by using the paper clip projecting through the slot as a handle; see Figure 2.

You can now use your pinhole telescope to create a zoom-lens effect by moving the lens toward the aluminum pinhole or away. Depending on the distance from pinhole to lens, the scene you see will be either upside down or right side up. It's very complicated to build a zoom-lens telescope with real eyepiece lenses, but if you use a pinhole it becomes simple.

BONUS APPLICATION:
MAKE A SNEAKY MAGNIFYING GLASS

Need to make objects appear larger than they are? When you need to enlarge an image you can easily make a sneaky magnifier. Here are two ways to do it.

What's Needed
- Paper clip, twist-tie, or staple
- Clear window envelope or flashlight lens

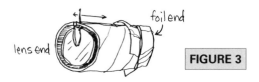

FIGURE 3

What to Do

Method 1. Bend a paper clip into the loop shape shown in Figure 3 and dip the loop in water. As long as it is not too large, the water droplet will stay bonded to the paper-clip loop because of surface tension. Look into the water droplet, and the image you see will be magnified.

Method 2. Tear off the window part of the envelope and place a drop of water on it. Now as you look through the water droplet the image will be greatly enlarged; see Figure 4. The farther away you hold the envelope from the object, the larger it will appear.

In situations where you need to see up close, a sneaky magnifier will prove useful.

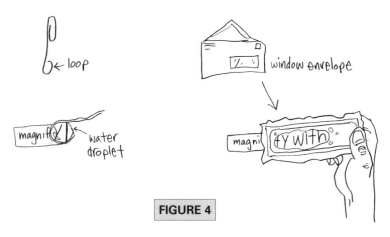

FIGURE 4

Smoke and Mirrors:
Sneaky Code Signaling

Being stranded in a remote area can fill you with fear. What's especially frustrating is seeing a plane or vehicle and not being able to get their attention to be rescued.

This chapter will supply various ways to signal for help. With a shiny object that reflects sunlight easily, you can signal to people and vehicles for assistance.

What's Needed

- Mirror, or belt buckle, metal pan or cup, or aluminum foil
- Reflective materials: canteen, watch, soda can, eyeglasses

belt buckle

mirror

aluminum foil

Soda Can

analog watch

canteen

What to Do

Using a mirror or other shiny object, point the light in one area and away in an SOS pattern (three long flashes, three short, and

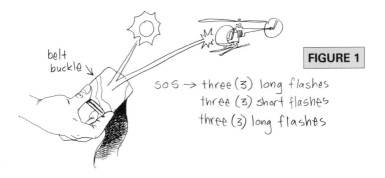

belt buckle

FIGURE 1

SOS → three (3) long flashes
three (3) short flashes
three (3) long flashes

three long). Repeat this sequence of flashes as long as possible while sunlight is available until rescued (see Figure 1).

The *U.S. Army Survival Manual* recommends:

1. Do not flash a signal mirror rapidly, because a pilot may mistake the flashes for enemy.
2. Do not direct the beam in the aircraft's cockpit for more than a few seconds as it may blind the pilot.

Haze, ground fog, and mirages may make it hard for a pilot to spot signals from a flashing object. If possible, therefore, get to the highest point in your area when signaling. If you can't determine the aircraft's location, flash your signal in the direction of the aircraft noise.

At night you can use a flashlight or a strobe light to send an SOS to an aircraft.

OTHER SNEAKY SIGNALING

When you're lost, use anything and everything as a marker to be seen by aircraft and search parties. Natural materials—snow, sand, rocks, vegetation—and clothing can be used as pointers to spell out distress signals. Follow the Ground-to-Air Emergency Code in laying out your markers.

SYMBOL	MESSAGE
I	Serious Injuries, Need Doctor
II	Need Medical Supplies
V	Require Assistance
F	Need Food and Water
LL	All Is Well
Y	Yes or Affirmative
N	No or Negative
X	Require Medical Assistance
→	Proceeding in This Direction

BODY SIGNAL	MESSAGE
Both arms raised with palms open	"I need help"
Lying on the ground with arms above head	"Urgent medical assistance needed"
Squatting with both arms pointing outward	"Land here"
One arm raised with palm open	"I do not need help"

See Figure 2 for illustrations of these signals.

To show that your signal has been received and understood, an aircraft pilot will rock the aircraft from side to side (in daylight or moonlight) or will make green flashes with the plane's signal lamp (at night). If your signal is received but *not* understood, the aircraft will make a complete circle (in daylight or moonlight) or will make red flashes with its signal lamp (at night).

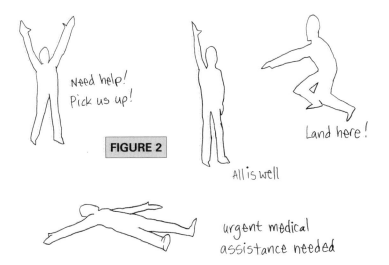

Look on the Bright Side:
Make Sneaky Snow Glasses

In daytime, bright snow can blind you and cause damage to the eyes. What's needed is an emergency visor to filter out harmful reflected rays. You can easily make snow glasses out of a variety of things around you.

What's Needed
- Cardboard or leaf
- Material from clothing

What to Do
Cut slits in a piece of cardboard or other material and mount it on your head as shown in Figure 1. This will cut down on the ultraviolet light reflecting off the snow.

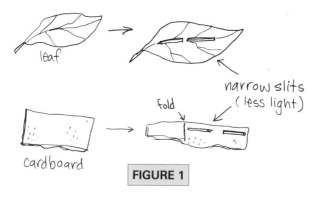

leaf

narrow slits
(less light)

fold

cardboard

FIGURE 1

Sneaky Snowshoes:
Walk on Top of the Snow

Very few of us are so prepared that we have snowshoes readily available in our house or car. In deep snow, your shoes or boots will sink and get wet. You'll waste energy and tire quickly, trying to lift your feet out of the snow to take the next steps. Also, you can't see what you are stepping on or how deep you may sink.

What's needed is a way to increase the footprint of the shoe—to spread your weight and allow more snow to provide increased support.

Snowshoes allow you to walk on the surface of the snow. If you're stranded without snowshows in the wilderness, you can quickly make a substitute set out of found items.

What's Needed
- Cardboard, or tree branches and plastic bags
- String, wire, or vine

cardboard

plastic bags

string

What to Do
Cut or tear two pieces of heavy cardboard into the shape shown in Figure 1. Cut two holes in the cardboard to feed string, vine, or wire through and wrap it around your shoes and through your laces; see Figure 2.

Making sure that the bulk of the cardboard is in front of the shoe, bend the front upward, as shown in Figure 3. Do not tie

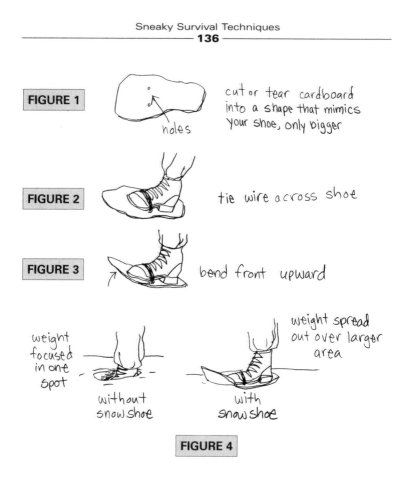

FIGURE 1 — cut or tear cardboard into a shape that mimics your shoe, only bigger

holes

FIGURE 2 — tie wire across shoe

FIGURE 3 — bend front upward

weight focused in one spot

without snow shoe

weight spread out over larger area

with snow shoe

FIGURE 4

the string too tightly. When walking in snow, your foot needs to tilt upward without gathering heavy snow.

If cardboard pieces or similar materials are not available, large tree branches encased in plastic bags can be used in a similar fashion. Now you can walk above the snow, as shown in Figure 4, and keep dry and safe.

Coldfinger:
Where There's a Chill, There's a Way

If you're like most people, you've imagined what it would be like to be stranded in a remote area in cold weather without winter clothes. If you are caught in a wintry climate without proper garments, you could get sick, injured, or worse. This project describes a sneaky way to use the things around you for comfort and safety.

What's Needed
- Leaves or paper

What to Do
If it's cold and you do not have the proper outer garments, you will rapidly lose body heat. Heat radiates and is lost from the body, especially from the head, neck, and hands. It is also lost via conduction when you perspire and touch other solid objects. Convection heat loss happens when you are directly exposed to cold winds.

You can reduce heat loss by using whatever is available to cover your head, neck, and hands. Use a plastic bag, newspaper, or undergarment to cover your head, including your mouth. (If the covering is plastic or paper, punch a hole to breathe through.) Covering the mouth as much as possible will direct some of the heat lost through breathing back toward your face as shown in Figure 1.

To create a pocket of air to trap body heat, make a sneaky cold-weather garment with leaves or paper. Assuming you are wearing a long-sleeved shirt and pants, gather leaves from trees or the ground and stuff them in your shirt, as shown in Figure 1. This will create a heat pocket to keep the air warmed by your body. Close sleeve and collar buttons securely.

Similarly, stuff your pants with leaves or paper, draw your socks over your pant legs or knot the ends to stop the leaves from falling out, and keep your hands in your pockets as much as possible; see Figure 2.

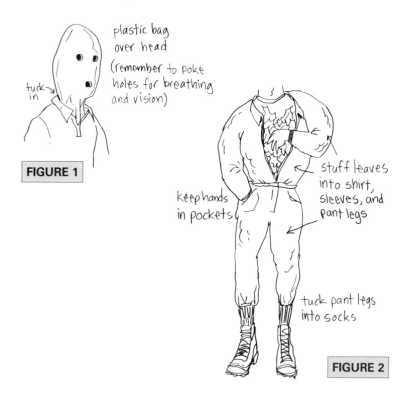

plastic bag over head
(remember to poke holes for breathing and vision)

tuck in

FIGURE 1

keep hands in pockets

stuff leaves into shirt, sleeves, and pant legs

tuck pant legs into socks

FIGURE 2

Lost in Space?
Craft a Compass

If you're ever lost, you'll find a compass is a crucial tool. When markers or trails are nonexistent, a compass can keep you pointed in the right direction to get you back to a line of reference.

A compass indicates Earth's magnetic north and south poles. For a situation where you are stranded without a compass, this project describes three ways of making one with the things around you. For each method, you will need a needle (or twist-tie, staple, steel baling wire, or paper clip); a small bowl, cup, or other non-magnetic container; water; and a leaf or blade of grass. How simple is that?

METHOD 1

What's Needed
• Magnet—from a radio or car stereo speaker

What to Do
Take a small straight piece of metal (but do not use aluminum or yellow metals), such as a needle, twist-tie, staple, or paper clip, and stroke it in one direction with a small magnet. Stroke it at least fifty times, as shown in Figure 1. This will magnetize the needle so it will be attracted to Earth's north and south magnetic poles.

Fill a bowl or cup with water and place a small blade of grass or any small article that floats on the surface of the water. Place the needle on the blade of grass (see Figure 2) and watch

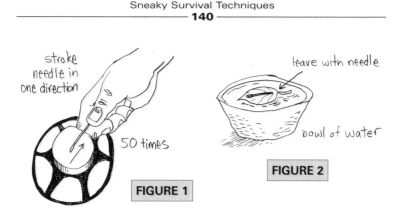

FIGURE 1

FIGURE 2

it eventually turn in one direction. Mark one end of the needle so that magnetic north is determined.

Note: To verify the north direction, see the next section, Road Scholar: Down-to-Earth Direction Finding.

METHOD 2

What's Needed

• Silk or synthetic fabric—
from a tie, scarf, or other garment

piece of silk or other synthetic fabric

What to Do

As in the first method, stroke a needle or paper clip in one direction with the silk material. This will create a static charge in the metal, but it will take many more strokes to magnetize it. Stroke at least 300 times, as shown in Figure 3. Once floated on a leaf in the bowl, the needle should be magnetized enough to be attracted to Earth's north and south magnetic poles. You may have to remagnetize the sneaky compass needle occasionally.

Note: You can also determine north and south with sneaky techniques in the "Road Scholar" chapter.

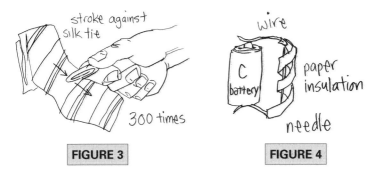

stroke against silk tie

300 times

wire

paper insulation

needle

FIGURE 3

FIGURE 4

METHOD 3

What's Needed
• Battery

What to Do
When electricity flows through a wire, it creates a magnetic field. If a small piece of metal, like a staple, is placed in a coil of wire, it will become magnetized.

Wrap a small length of wire around a staple or paper clip and connect its ends to a battery, as shown in Figure 4. (For sneaky battery and wire sources ideas, see the "Industrious Light Magic" in Part III.) If the wire is not insulated, wrap the staple with paper or a leaf and then wrap the wire around it.

When you connect the wire to the battery in this manner, you are creating a short circuit—an electrical circuit with no current-draining load on it. This will cause the wire to heat quickly so only connect the wire ends to the battery for short four-second intervals. Perform this procedure fifteen times.

Place the staple on a floating item in a bowl of water, and it will eventually turn in one direction. Mark one end of the staple so that magnetic north is determined.

Road Scholar:
Down-to-Earth
Direction Finding

If you're stranded without a magnetic compass, all is not lost. Even without a compass, there are numerous ways to find directions in desolate areas. Two methods are covered here.

METHOD 1:
USE A WATCH

What's Needed
- Standard analog watch
- Clear day where you can see the sun

analog watch

What to Do
The sun always rises in the east and sets in the west. You can use this fact to find north and south with a standard nondigital watch.

If you are in the northern hemisphere (north of the equator), point the hour hand of the watch in the direction of the sun. Midway between the hour hand and 12 o'clock will be south. See Figure 1.

METHOD 2:
USE THE STARS

What's Needed
- A clear evening when stars can be viewed

South

hour hand lines
up with sun

FIGURE 1

What to Do

In the northern hemisphere, locate the Big Dipper constellation in the sky; see Figure 2. Follow the direction of the two stars that make up the front of the dipper to the North Star. (It is about four times the distance between the two stars that make up the

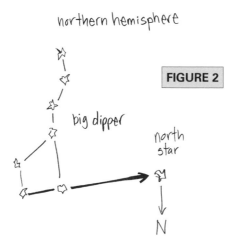

northern hemisphere

FIGURE 2

big dipper

north
star

N

front of the dipper.) Then follow the path of the North Star down to the ground. This direction is north.

In the southern hemisphere, locate the Southern Cross constellation in the sky; see Figure 3. Also notice the two stars below the Cross. Imagine two lines extending at right angles, one from a point midway between the two stars and the other from the Cross, to see where they intersect. Follow this path down to the ground. This direction is due south.

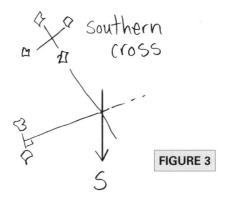

FIGURE 3

Harm and Hammer:
Devise Makeshift Weapons and Tools

Imagine being in a survival situation without any weapons, tools, or equipment except your knife. It could happen! You might even be without a knife. You would probably feel helpless, but with the proper knowledge and practice, you can improvise crude tools and weapons.

What's Needed

- Glass shards
- Thick plastic
- Rocks
- Tree branches
- Knife (if available)
- Strong vines, wire, strips of cloth, or shoelaces

glass shards

wire

What to Do

To make a club, locate a large rock with a slight indentation in the middle. If you cannot find one of this shape, you can fashion a groove in the rock by hammering the middle of the rock with another pointed rock or tool; see Figure 1. Next, find a strong stick or tree branch with a forked end and place the rock in the stick as shown in Figure 2. Last, secure the rock to the stick with the cross-wrap pattern shown in Figure 3. Test its strength by hammering an object and then check to see if it has loosened.

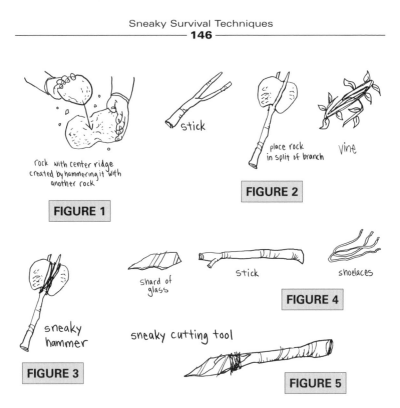

rock with center ridge created by hammering it with another rock

FIGURE 1

stick

place rock in split of branch

vine

FIGURE 2

sneaky hammer

FIGURE 3

shard of glass

stick

shoelaces

FIGURE 4

sneaky cutting tool

FIGURE 5

To make a knife, locate a sharp shard of glass or stone and a stick, as shown in Figure 4. The stick should have the short end of a branch still present so the glass or stone can be braced against it. Wrap the glass to the stick securely, and test it for strength and excess movement; see Figure 5.

Note: Sneaky weapons and tools must be used cautiously for safety reasons.

Pocket Protectors:
Sneaky Tools
and Survival Kits

How many times have you fumbled in the dark and wished you had a flashlight? Or needed a screwdriver or pliers? Many everyday situations and emergency conditions can be resolved with the proper tools, but most people do not carry a bulky toolbox with them at all times.

This project illustrates a variety of innovative and compact multitools and survival supplies you can carry around in your pocket. For trips away from urban areas, you can assemble a sneaky survival kit that can be carried inside a pen!

MULTITOOLS AND MORE

A new category of ultralight multitools is available that should be carried all the time. These novel pocket-sized items should become your everyday accessories.

To be prepared, you should always carry these items in your pocket or on your key ring: Figure 1 illustrates the usefulness of this collection.

    Multitool (includes four screwdrivers, pliers, cutters,
        and wire benders)
    Mini flashlight
    Credit card multitool (includes a compass, magnifying
        glass, and serrated blade)
    Plastic whistle

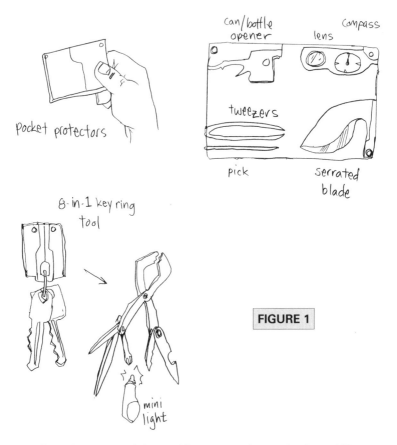

Pocket protectors

can/bottle opener

lens

Compass

tweezers

pick

serrated blade

8-in-1 key ring tool

mini light

FIGURE 1

For a low-cost mini-portable motion alarm, obtain an XP-4 Spy Pen from Wild Planet (see www.wildplanet.com). Sold in toy and discount stores for under $15 at the time of this writing, the gadget-filled pen includes a magnifying glass, telescope, flashlight, and a real working motion detector.

For information concerning multitools and gadgets, check the following company Web sites:

http://www.advanced-intelligence.com
http://www.beprepared.com
http://www.berberblades.com
http://www.colibri.com
http://www.equalizers1.com
http://www.leatherman.com
http://www.spyderco.com
http://www.swissarmy.com
http://www.swisstechtools.com
http://www.toollogic.com
http://www.topeak.com
http://www.wildplanet.com

SNEAKY SURVIVAL KITS

Why not prepare for the worst when you're traveling? Most people wouldn't want to carry a backpack full of equipment, but if there is a way always to have available the minimal items for a survival situation in a package as small as a mint box or a pen, who will argue against that?

Assuming you already have a multitool, mini flashlight, credit card multitool, and plastic whistle on your key ring, here are a few other items you should take with you when you travel outside of urban areas.

Magnetized needles
Strong nylon thread
Small safety pins (for fishing hooks)
Thin wire
2 small watch batteries, 1½ volts each
Small roll of duct tape
Small roll of aluminum foil (as a signal mirror)

Dental floss
Aspirin
Tiny multivitamins
Tiny candle
5 match heads (placed end to end and wrapped in foil)
$20 bill
Sugar

Believe it or not, you can pack all these items inside a hollowed-out mint container, cigar holder, or fat writing pen! See Figure 1. (When using a pen, remove all of the inner parts and seal both ends.) With these compact tools and supplies, you will greatly improve your odds in survival situations. For more information about assembling survival kits, see the Resources section that follows.

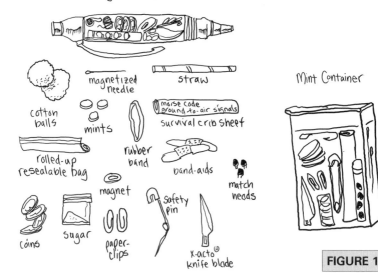

Big-wide Pen

magnetized needle

straw

Mint Container

cotton balls

mints

morse code
ground-to-air signals
survival crib sheet

rolled-up
resealable bag

rubber band

band-aids

match heads

magnet

safety pin

coins

sugar

paper-clips

x-acto® knife blade

FIGURE 1

SNEAKY NOTES

Sneakier Uses for Everyday Things

How to Turn a Calculator into a
Metal Detector, Carry a Survival Kit
in a Shoestring, Make a Gas Mask
with a Balloon, Turn Dishwashing
Liquid into a Copy Machine, Convert
a Styrofoam Cup into a Speaker,
and Make a Spy Gadget Jacket
with Everyday Things

Contents

Part I

Sneaky Science Tricks

Part II
Sneaky Gadgets

Part III
Sneaky Survival Techniques

Part IV

Gadget Jacket

Acknowledgments

Special thanks to my agent, Sheree Bykofsky, for believing in the book from the start. I'm also grateful for the assistance provided by Janet Rosen and Megan Buckley at her agency.

I want to thank Katie Anderson, my editor at Andrews McMeel, for her invaluable insights.

I'm grateful to the following people who helped me get the word out about the first "sneaky uses" book:

Gayle Anderson, Sandy Cohen, Ken Hamblin, Deborah Rowe, Ira Flatow, Steve Cochran, Christopher G. Selfridge, Timothy M. Blangger, Cherie Courtade, Charles Bergquist, Mark Frauenfelder, Phillip M. Torrone, M. K. Donaldson, Paul MacGregor, David Chang, Jessica Warren, Steve Metsch, Jenifer N. Johnson, Jerry Davich, Jerry Reno, Austin Michael, Tony Lossano, Katey Schwartz, John Schatzel, Diane Lewis, Bob Kostanczuk, Marty Griffin, Mackenzie Miller, and Rebecca Schuler.

I'm thankful for project evaluation and testing assistance provided by Bill Melzer, Sybil Smith, Isaac English, Jerry Anderson, and Raymond Moore.

And my love goes to my mother, Cloise Shaw, for giving me positive inspiration, a foundation in science, and a love of reading.

Introduction

Ever since the first tool was created, people and societies have been making sneaky uses of everyday things. Whether the adaptation is for novelty purposes or stems from a need for escape and survival, sneaky resourcefulness has produced numerous ingenious innovators. World War II, in particular, inspired many fine examples.

British Royal Air Force pilots were equipped by the Military Intelligence division (MI-9) with various concealed items, such as:

- Shoelaces with magnets in the tips and a wire saw sewn in the fabric
- Compasses and silk maps hidden in buttons and chess pieces
- Boot heels with rubber stamps for document forgery
- Cribbage game boards with crystal radios inside them
- Escape pens that hid a compass, map, currency, and dye to tint clothing

Charles Fraser-Smith—the model for Ian Fleming's character Q (for Quartermaster)—supplied equipment and gadgets for secret agents and prisoners-of-war. Some of his special designs and gadgets included:

- Flashlights with one real battery and a fake with a secret compartment
- Cigarette lighters holding tiny cameras
- Pens containing a paper-thin map, a compass, and a magnetic clip to balance it on a pin
- Buttons containing a tiny compass
- Badges and boot laces containing a Gigli's wire saw (a flexible wire with saw teeth used by surgeons)

Fraser-Smith also developed a used match containing a magnetic needle that could be dropped in water to form a compass, maps printed on handkerchiefs in invisible ink, chess pieces and tobacco pipes with hidden compartments, edible rice-paper notepaper, a cigarette-holder telescope, and fur-lined pilot boots that could be converted into ordinary shoes (to avoid detection) using a knife hidden in the leather, the removed sheepskin legging sections then being converted into a vest).

In Germany's sixteenth-century Colditz Castle, prisoners of war constructed a two-man 19-foot glider with a 33-foot wingspan using cloth from sleeping bags, nails and wood from floorboards, and other materials from their cells.

The inspiration to do this came on a snowy day in December 1943 when prisoner Bill Goldfinch looked out his window over the town and noticed that the snowflakes outside were drifting upward. He thought it might be possible to escape from the old castle in a glider, using the updraft to get airborne.

With the help of a book from the prison library, Goldfinch drew up his specifications. The glider wings would have to have enough lift to carry the glider's pilot and one passenger over the town of Colditz, more than 300 feet below, and across the Mulde River.

In one of the castle's attics, near an adjacent chapel's roof they would use for a runway, the resourceful prisoners created a workshop. With shutters and mud made from attic dust, they constructed a false wall at one end of the attic and went to work, using drills made from nails, saw handles from bed boards, and saw blades from a wind-up record player's spring and the frame around their iron window bars. To cover the glider's wooden frame they used bedsheets, which they painted with hot millet (part of their rations) to stiffen the fabric.

Takeoff was finally scheduled for the spring of 1945. The prisoners planned to assemble the glider and catapult it off the chapel's roof, using a metal bathtub filled with concrete as ballast. The tub, secured to the glider with bedsheet ropes, would fall five stories. The glider would then sail out silently over the town of Colditz, giving its occupants a good head start over the German guards, who would soon discover a bathtub in the yard and two prisoners missing. However, the flight never took place, because the prisoners were rescued by the Americans in 1945. For pictures and more details about the Colditz glider, go to www.sneakyuses.com.

Considering these ingenious contraptions, you can perform amazing feats with the materials you find around you without special knowledge or skills. *Sneaky Uses for Everyday Things* covered such adaptations as how to convert milk into plastic, extract water from air, turn a penny into a radio, and control your TV with a ring. *Sneakier Uses for Everyday Things* goes further and provides more ways to adapt things around you for novel yet practical purposes.

Did you know that you can turn a calculator into a metal detector or store a survival kit in a shoestring? Ever think you could turn a paper cup into a speaker? Adapt liquid detergent into a copy machine? Or make a gas mask out of everyday things? Now you can.

Sneakier Uses for Everyday Things includes science projects, sneaky gadgets, and resourceful survival techniques. No special knowledge or unusual tools are required. Whether your interest is in science or trivia, or you just want to make unique no-cost sneaky gadgetry, you'll undoubtedly look at everyday objects differently from now on.

Get started now—utilize what you've got to get what you want!

Part I

Sneaky
Science
Tricks

Science is sometimes difficult to understand, but with everyday things, you can make clever animated devices to demonstrate its principles. Many household items you use every day can perform other functions. Using nothing but balloons, paper clips, aluminum foil, paper cups, refrigerator magnets, and other common objects, you can quickly make innovative science projects or demonstration gadgets.

If you are curious about the way static electricity, magnetism, and basic chemistry work, you'll find plenty of project examples here, including an electroscope, a hovercraft, a rollback toy, a sneaky metal detector, an image copier, and various light transmitters and sensors.

Review the sneaky science adaptations in this section, and you'll be ready to create easy-to-make demonstrational projects with items found virtually anywhere.

How to Be Resourceful

The story of the Colditz glider is a great example of the possibilities available to us all if we can adapt everyday things. The key is to think outside the box—to see things as what they can become and not just what you think they're limited to be.

For example, a magazine is an ordinary everyday thing that provides information in printed form, but is that all it's good for? Take a few minutes and think of a periodical's every possible practical application, and then consider the following illustrated examples.

- Remove a staple from a magazine, carefully bend it into a loop shape, dip it in water so a droplet forms on the staple, and you've got a sneaky magnifier.
- Rub a straightened magazine staple ten times in the same direction across a magnet (or a few hundred times against wool cloth or silk material), and it will become magnetized. Then rest it on a floating leaf or piece of wood and one end will point north to create a mini compass.
- If you place a magazine staple across battery terminals, it will heat up enough to ignite tinder material (lint, dried grass, etc.) to start a fire in an emergency. You can also use the magazine as tinder.
- A rolled-up magazine can serve as a funnel to prevent spillage.
- Need a megaphone? Roll a magazine into a cone shape and you can project your voice by speaking into the smaller end.

- A rolled-up magazine pressed against a wall becomes a sneaky sound amplifier.
- With origami folding, a magazine page can become a cup.
- Hide your small flat valuables between pages of a magazine that are glued together.
- Need a defensive weapon? Roll a magazine tightly and jam the end against a person's temple, bridge of the nose, or throat.
- To prevent snow blindness, tear or cut a magazine page into sneaky glasses with slits to look through.
- A magazine can provide insulation when handling hot objects.
- Lost in the cold without sufficient clothing? Tear the pages from a magazine, ball them up, and stuff them in your shirt and pants to provide heat insulation.
- Stand on one end of a rolled-up magazine secured with a rubber band or tape to gain elevation in a pinch.
- Got a flat bicycle tire? Stuff torn magazine pages between the tire and rim to ride home.
- With tape, a magazine page can patch holes in an emergency.
- A very tightly rolled-up magazine can be used as a bottle opener when it is positioned near the neck of a bottle and resting on your thumb (this takes some practice).
- Make a sneaky peashooter barrel with a rolled-up magazine.
- In an extreme emergency, a staple can substitute for a small fuse (*temporarily, not permanently*!).
- If a disk is stuck in a computer CD drive, push a magazine staple into the eject hole to remove it.
- A rolled-up magazine can prop things up such as a window.

magazine

staples

Magnifier
water droplet
staple

Compass
staple
leaf
cup of water

Fire Starter
staple
battery

Tinder for Fire

Funnel

Megaphone

Hearing Aid

Cup
(origami)

Safe

Weapon

Snow Glasses

Insulation
(for heat protection)

Insulation
(for cold protection)

Elevator

Flat Tire Filler

Pea Shooter

Bottle Opener

Patch (for opening)

Window Prop

Emergency Fuse

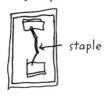

← staple

CD-ROM Drive Opener

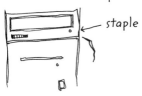

← staple

Sneaky Wire Sources: How to Connect Things

Wire is useful in many sneaky projects. You'll soon learn how it can be used to make a radio transmitter, a speaker, and more.

When wire is required for projects, try whenever possible to use everyday items that you might have otherwise thrown away and help save our natural resources. Common items like potato-chip bags, fast-food wrappers, collector-card packages, and breath-mint labels contain useful aluminum that can be carefully cut to form sneaky wire.

Even a small coffee-creamer container lid, when carefully cut in an up-down-up pattern to utilize its maximum area, can provide

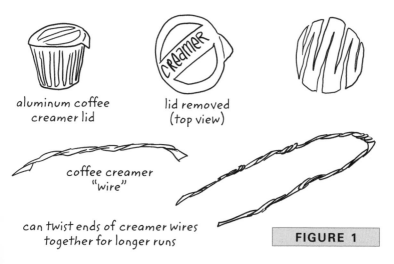

aluminum coffee
creamer lid

lid removed
(top view)

coffee creamer
"wire"

can twist ends of creamer wires
together for longer runs

FIGURE 1

a useful connecting wire. See **Figure 1**.

You can test your found wire material for electrical conductivity (to determine if it allows electricity to flow through it) with a battery and either a flashlight bulb or a light-emitting diode (LED). First place the LED leads across the battery terminals to be sure it will light. If not, reverse the direction of the leads. Then place the sneaky wire material in series (end-to-end) with the battery and LED. For example: Press one battery terminal against the "wire" and the other terminal against one of the LED leads. The other LED lead also presses against the wire material. If the LED

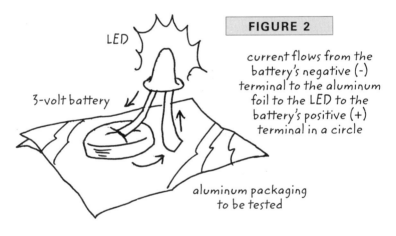

LED

FIGURE 2

3-volt battery

current flows from the battery's negative (-) terminal to the aluminum foil to the LED to the battery's positive (+) terminal in a circle

aluminum packaging to be tested

lights, it's good for using in your sneaky projects. See **Figure 2**.

To insulate your ersatz wires from each other, slip them through discarded straws or wrap paper material around them.

Figure 3 illustrates just a few of the possible items you can use, in case you do not have connecting wire available.

Figure 4 shows how to use a battery and an LED or flashlight bulb to test for electrical conductivity.

Figure 5 shows how to connect wires and LED leads

FIGURE 3

cereal liner

margarine wrapper

ketchup & other single packets

chewing gum

breath mint label

trading card package

sandwich wrapper from fast-food outlets

FIGURE 4

Sample Electrical Circuit: Current flows in circle from negative to device back to positive battery terminal.

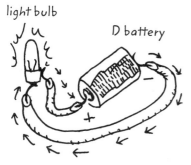

light bulb

D battery

connecting wire

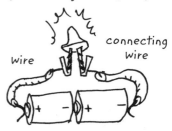

Light Emitting Diode (LED)

wire

connecting wire

2, 1.5 volt batteries in series supply a total of 3 volts

| FIGURE 5 | How to Connect Things |

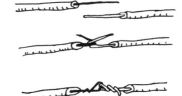

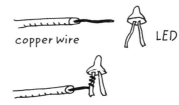

copper wire   LED

copper wire

A      watch battery

B

C

Sneaky Work Glove

Work gloves can protect your hands from harm, but they also make it difficult to access small items in your pocket that you may need. You can keep frequently used items with you for quick access with an easy-to-make set of sneaky gloves.

Sneaky gloves use Velcro pads affixed to the back of the small items and on the gloves so you can easily grab items and reattach them on the run.

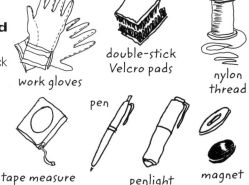

work gloves

double-stick Velcro pads

nylon thread

pen

tape measure

penlight

magnet

What's Needed
- Work gloves
- Four double-stick Velcro pads
- Nylon thread
- Tape measure
- Pen
- Penlight
- Magnet

What to Do
For this project, four common items will be attached to the gloves: a tape measure, a pen, a penlight, and a strong magnet. (The magnet allows you to hold screws, nuts, clips, and other metallic items in place until needed.)

As shown in **Figure 1**, affix half of each Velcro pad to the back of each glove near the wrist area, using its backing tape, or use nylon thread to sew it on. You may want to avoid affixing items near the palm of the glove to avoid scratching surfaces when you lay your hands down.

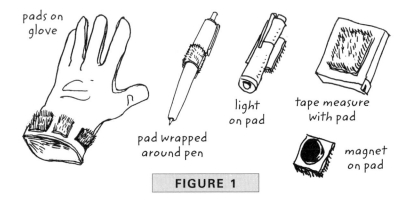

FIGURE 1

Attach the other half of each Velcro pad to one of the four items using its double-stick tape.

After the pads are securely mounted to the items, firmly press the Velcro sides against the pads on the back of the glove, as shown in **Figure 2**.

Now when you work you can take along a light, a pen, a tape measure, and a magnet that will make your next work project easier. If you stick other Velcro pads on a wall or workbench or shelf, you can place gloves and tools there for safekeeping.

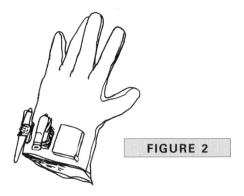

FIGURE 2

Electroscope

You've felt the presence of static electricity when the weather is dry, after receiving a shock when you walk across a carpet and touch someone or a metal object. This static discharge can be powerful enough to damage some electronic items that have sensitive memory chips inside.

You can make a homemade electroscope as a demonstrational device for science projects and for testing for harmful levels of static electricity in your environment.

What's Needed

- Large paper clip
- Two pieces of aluminum foil
- Glass jar with lid
- Quarter (optional)

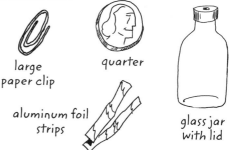

large paper clip

quarter

aluminum foil strips

glass jar with lid

What to Do

All objects, including your body, are a collection of positive and negative electrical particles. Normally there is a neutral state where the positive charges cancel the negative ones. However, in a dry environment, if a charge imbalance, called static electricity, occurs on your body, you can get shocked when you touch a large metal object (or another person). To prevent getting a static electricity shock, touch a doorknob or car door with a coin or key before grabbing it so the spark will emit from the metal instead of your fingertip.

You can make an electroscope easily enough with household items to demonstrate how static electricity charges and discharges objects.

The electroscope consists of two thin pieces of aluminum foil suspended from a metal hook made from a paper clip. When you move the top of the hook near a source of static electricity, some of the electrons in the hook are pushed to the foil and causes them to repel or attract each other.

First, cut two strips of aluminum foil, ⅓ by 1½ inches. Then bend the paper clip into the shape shown in **Figure 1**. Push the hook through the middle of the cardboard bottle cap so the **U** shape protrudes through.

Next, lay the two foil strips one on top of the other and hang them on the end of the hook; see **Figure 2**. Lower the cardboard and the paper clip with foil into the jar so the paper clip is suspended in the center of the jar.

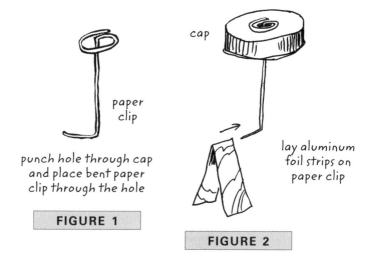

paper
clip

punch hole through cap
and place bent paper
clip through the hole

FIGURE 1

cap

lay aluminum
foil strips on
paper clip

FIGURE 2

Now hold various metallic and nonmetallic objects in your hand as you walk across the floor (preferably one that's carpeted). Bring the object near the top of the paper clip and observe what happens. You should see the foil strips move apart like little wings. See **Figure 3**.

Then see what happens when the object is moved away from the paper clip. If the strips do not fall back together, gently touch the hook with your finger. *Note:* If you affix a quarter or a large round piece of metal to the top of the paper clip, it can improve the sensitivity of the electroscope.

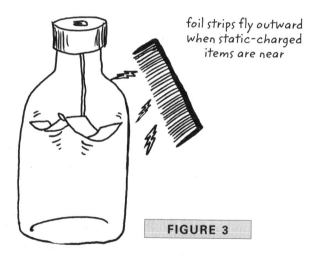

foil strips fly outward
when static-charged
items are near

FIGURE 3

Sneaky Hand-Powered Motor

As you may know, hot air rises. Rising heat can be made to move objects, and you can demonstrate this fact with a novel "hand-powered" motor. In this demonstrational science project, your hands will actually provide the heat to demonstrate how moving air currents can move an object in a rotary motion.

All it takes is an ordinary piece of paper, scissors, a needle, a cardboard box, and your hands.

What's Needed

- Paper
- Scissors
- Sewing needle
- Small cardboard box

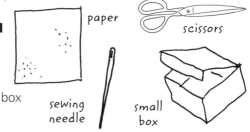

paper

scissors

sewing needle

small box

What to Do

Cut a piece of paper into a 2-inch square. Fold it in half diagonally; then unfold it and fold it in half on the other diagonal, as shown in **Figure 1**. This should create a cross-fold with a center point.

You can use a paper-clip box or similar small box as a mount

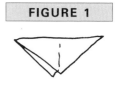

| **FIGURE 1** |

fold paper in half   unfold paper   fold over other way

for the needle. Hold the needle on its side with your fingers and carefully twist it into the top of the box (or use a thimble) until it punctures a hole in the top. Place the piece of paper on top of the needle so its center point allows the paper to turn freely.

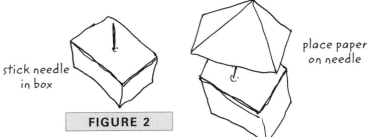

stick needle in box

place paper on needle

FIGURE 2

See **Figure 2**.

To make the sneaky "motor" turn, rub your hands together back and forth about twenty times to generate heat and place them near the sides of the paper. After a few seconds, the paper will begin to spin (**Figure 3**).

The paper spins because the heat on your hands causes a temperature increase in the air around the paper. As the heated air rises and cooler air takes its place, the air movement pushes the paper sides, causing it to rotate like a motor.

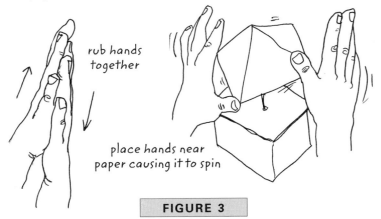

rub hands together

place hands near paper causing it to spin

FIGURE 3

Sneaky Hovercraft Toy

Ever wonder how a hovercraft can ride on air? It floats over surfaces by forcing air underneath its chassis. It also uses large air fans to propel and steer it across the terrain.

Using everyday objects, you can easily demonstrate how compressed air can lift and propel a toy hovercraft vehicle.

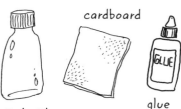

cardboard

glue

plastic bottle

What's Needed
- Plastic bottle with top
- Cardboard or CD
- Glue
- Large balloon
- Coffee stirrer
- Tape (plastic or duct)
- Twist-tie

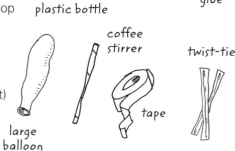

coffee stirrer

twist-tie

tape

large balloon

What to Do
The hovercraft will use compressed air stored in a balloon to lift and propel the "vehicle."

Cut off the top of the bottle one-third of the way from the top.

Punch a small hole in the top of the plastic bottle top and tape it to the top of the vehicle and either cut a hole in the center of the cardboard or use a CD and glue the vehicle to the bottle top, as shown in **Figure 1**. The balloon's air will be forced to exit from the bottle top's small hole and provide lift underneath the CD.

Blow up the balloon and place it on the mouth of the bottle. Hold it tight to prevent air from escaping, or wrap a twist-tie around it.

As shown in **Figure 2**, place a coffee stirrer under the lip of the balloon facing the rear of the "hovercraft." Air escaping from the stirrer tube will propel the craft forward.

When you let go of the balloon or unwrap the twist-tie, the air will escape under the hovercraft, causing it to float, and the air from the stirrer will propel it forward, as shown in **Figure 3**.

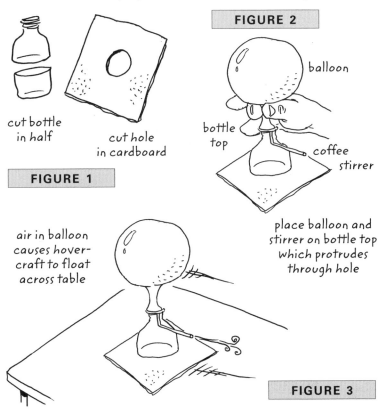

cut bottle
in half

cut hole
in cardboard

FIGURE 1

FIGURE 2

balloon

bottle
top

coffee
stirrer

place balloon and
stirrer on bottle top
which protrudes
through hole

air in balloon
causes hover-
craft to float
across table

FIGURE 3

Sneaky Metal Detector

You've seen metal detectors used in businesses, in public buildings, and in the movies. Believe it or not, you can make a working device using everyday things that can actually detect hidden metal objects.

Many everyday electronic devices—calculators, digital watches, TV remote controls, small video games—emit radio waves that can be detected with an AM radio. This project illustrates the reflective properties of radio waves, using a carefully positioned calculator and an AM radio to detect the radio waves bouncing off a metallic object.

What's Needed
- Small AM radio
- Calculator, solar or battery-powered (or a TV remote control or hand-held video game)
- CD case
- Velcro pads
- Metal object (spoon or tool)
- Aluminum foil
- Tape

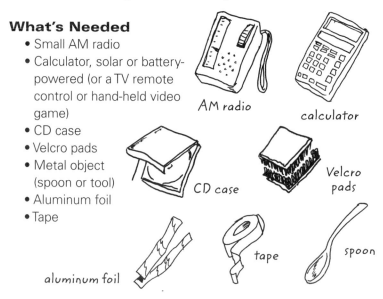

AM radio

calculator

CD case

Velcro pads

aluminum foil

tape

spoon

What to Do

This project requires a radio and a calculator that are small
enough to fit on a plastic CD case. Instead of holding the radio
and calculator with both hands (and having your body affect the
reception), the cover of a CD case allows you to mount them for
ease of use. *Note:* You do not need to close the case.

To assemble the sneaky metal detector, affix Velcro pads on
the inside cover of the CD case and on the backs of the calculator
and the radio. Press the calculator and the radio onto the Velcro
pads that are mounted side by side in the CD case. See **Figure 1**.
Since CD cases are hinged, you can vary the distance between
the radio and calculator.

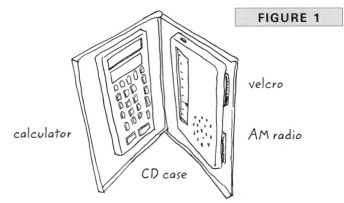

FIGURE 1

velcro

calculator

AM radio

CD case

First, tune the radio near the high end of the AM band, but not
directly on a broadcast station. Adjust the volume to the maximum
level so you can hear static. Turn on the calculator and position
it close to the radio until you hear a loud tone. The tone is the
calculator's electronic circuit producing a radio frequency signal.
Note: Most portable calculators will turn off if no buttons are
pressed within a few minutes. If it turns off simply press a key
periodically to keep it turned on.

Next, move the radio back until you can barely hear the calculator's tone. While holding the CD case so that the radio and calculator are at about a 90-degree angle, move the case close to a metal object. The tone in the radio should get louder as you get within a few inches of the object. As you move away or to the side, the tone should disappear. Congratulations. You've just made a sneaky metal detector!

With practice, you'll discover the angle position of the CD case that always allows you to hear a tone when it's close to a metallic object, as shown in **Figure 2**.

GOING FURTHER

Test your new sneaky metal detector using other items that emit radio waves, like remote controls and small hand-held electronic games (the kind that are given away at fast-food restaurants).

Also, see if placing aluminum foil between the radio and other items causes the detector to be more (or less) sensitive to the position of metallic objects. Tape the aluminum foil to the back of the CD case to see if it reduces interference from your body and improves performance.

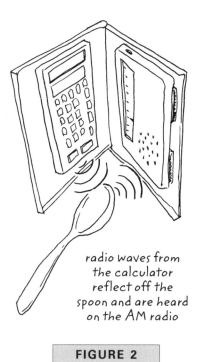

radio waves from
the calculator
reflect off the
spoon and are heard
on the AM radio

FIGURE 2

Sneaky Light Sensor

With a few easy adjustments, a portable cassette recorder (which includes microphone and earphone jacks) can provide you with an audio signal amplifier. You will be able to boost low-level electrical signals and use their increased output for a variety of sneaky applications. All you need is a ⅛-inch plug, the kind you can cannibalize from an old microphone or earphone, and an earphone or speakers.

This project, and the next three, uses a tape recorder to allow you actually to "listen" to light. With a tape recorder's microphone input as an amplifier, you can hear changes in the light around you as sound.

What's Needed

- Cassette recorder
- Solar cell (from an old calculator or other toy; also available at electronic parts stores)
- Cable with ⅛-inch plug
- Earphone or speakers
- Wire
- Flashlight

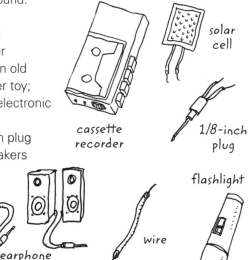

cassette recorder

solar cell

1/8-inch plug

earphone or speakers

wire

flashlight

What to Do

By connecting a solar cell to the recorder's microphone input and an earphone or speaker to the microphone jack, you'll be able to hear changes in light levels.

First, using connecting wire, attach the leads from a solar cell to a cable with an ⅛-inch plug (using an input plug end from an old microphone or earphone). Plug the cable into the microphone input jack of the tape recorder as shown in **Figure 1**.

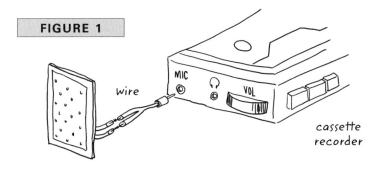

FIGURE 1

wire   MIC   VOL

cassette recorder

Next, with a blank tape inside the recorder, press the RECORD button and then the PAUSE button. Placing the recorder in RECORD/PAUSE mode will activate its amplifier but prevent the tape reels from spinning to save power.

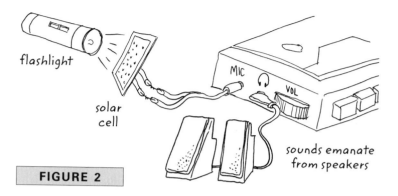

flashlight

solar
cell

MIC

VOL

sounds emanate
from speakers

FIGURE 2

Last, connect an earphone or portable speakers to the
recorder's earphone jack. Move the solar cell around or shine a
flashlight on it, and you will hear various tones. Light from the
solar cell will produce varying voltages and create sounds that
you can hear from the recorder when listening with an earphone
or portable speakers, as shown in **Figure 2**.

Sneaky Light Sensor II

This project will show the versatility of everyday things in science experiments. Light-emitting diodes (LEDs) are found in most electronic devices. They are the little lights that indicate that a device, or function, is enabled.

LEDs, unlike lightbulbs, do not have filaments that heat up to produce light. Instead, an LED is a special diode: an electronic component that conducts electricity through it better in one direction than the other. Unlike regular diodes, LEDs emit light when a low-voltage electrical signal (normally about 2 to 3 volts) passes through it. It operates very quickly, runs cool, and, since it has no filament, theoretically will never burn out.

A little-known fact about LEDs is that they can not only emit light but also sense it. Although this seems similar to a solar cell, an LED, when exposed to a light source, will vary (not produce) an electrical voltage. This will allow you to use an LED for the following sneaky light detection project.

What's Needed
- Cassette recorder
- LED
- Cable with ⅛-inch plug
- Earphone or speakers
- Wire
- Flashlight

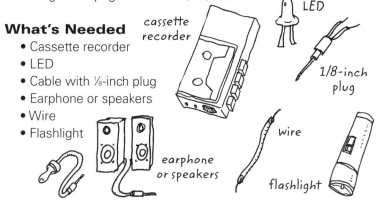

cassette recorder

LED

1/8-inch plug

earphone or speakers

wire

flashlight

What to Do

First, using connecting wire, attach an LED to a cable with an ⅛-inch plug. Plug the cable into the microphone input jack of a cassette recorder. Then connect an earphone or portable speaker cable into the earphone jack of the recorder, as shown in **Figure 1**.

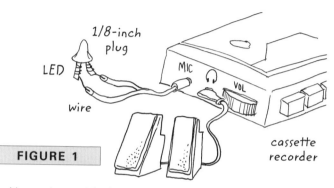

1/8-inch plug

LED

wire

MIC

VOL

FIGURE 1

cassette recorder

Next, place a blank tape in the recorder, press the RECORD and PAUSE buttons, and set the volume level to maximum. Darken the room and shine a light on the tip of the LED with the flashlight. You will hear the static and tone signals from the recorder change according to the light intensity on the tip of the LED. Test the sneaky LED sensor near both fluorescent and neon lamps.

GOING FURTHER

Test your sneaky LED light sensor with all the different-color LEDs you can obtain.

If you place your finger near the tip of the LED, you may find it will detect the nearness of your body. (Some diodes, even LEDs, are also sensitive to nearby electrical charges, including those stored in the human body.)

Sneaky Flashlight or Laser Beam Communicator

Laser beams and LEDs can be used in amazing ways. Most people know that compact discs, DVD players, and bar-code scanners use laser beams to detect and decode electronically encoded digital signals. With special equipment, law enforcement agencies can hear sounds in a room by aiming a laser beam at a window to detect its vibrations.

Now you'll discover how an LED and a battery can be used like a laser beam to transmit and receive sound on a beam of light.

What's Needed

- Cassette tape recorder
- Radio
- Solar cell
- Two AA batteries or one 3-volt watch battery
- Two LEDs, preferably white or yellow
- Flashlight
- Wire
- Tape
- Two cables with ⅛-inch plugs
- Earphone or speakers

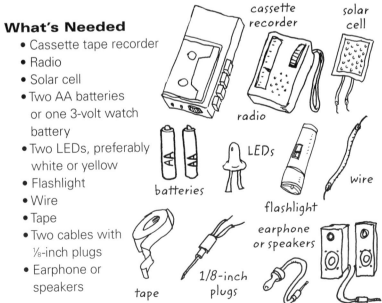

cassette recorder

solar cell

radio

LEDs

batteries

flashlight

wire

tape

1/8-inch plugs

earphone or speakers

What to Do

This project requires a sound transmitter and an amplifying receiver device. All necessary parts can be found in discarded toys or purchased at an electronics parts store.

You can build a light transmitter using the parts from an ordinary key ring LED light or by using separate LEDs, batteries, and wire. The sound source can be from a radio or tape player.

This project works best with a white or yellow super-bright LED.

SNEAKY TRANSMITTER

The transmitter consists of a simple battery and LED light circuit connected to a sound source, in this case a radio.

First, connect a wire to both leads of an LED. Then connect the other ends of the wires to the ends of an ⅛-inch plug cable. Next, tape two wires to the ends of the battery and attach them to the LED leads. See **Figure 1**.

Now, plug the ⅛-inch plug cable into the earphone jack of a radio, as shown in **Figure 2**. When tuned to a strong broadcast station, the radio's audio signal will alter (modulate) the light emitting from the LED. This signal can be detected by a light-sensitive device, like a Sneaky Light Sensor receiver device.

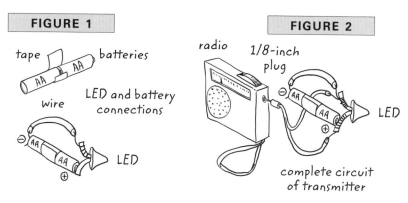

FIGURE 1

tape   batteries
AA AA
wire   LED and battery
connections
⊖ AA AA LED
⊕

FIGURE 2

radio   1/8-inch
plug
⊖ AA
AA   LED
⊕
complete circuit
of transmitter

SNEAKY RECEIVER

The light-beam receiver uses the same parts and design as shown in the earlier Sneaky Light Sensor receiver project.

First, connect a solar cell or a white LED to a cable with an ⅛-inch plug and plug it into the microphone jack of the cassette recorder. Then connect the earphone (or speakers) to the earphone jack of the recorder. See **Figures 3 and 4**.

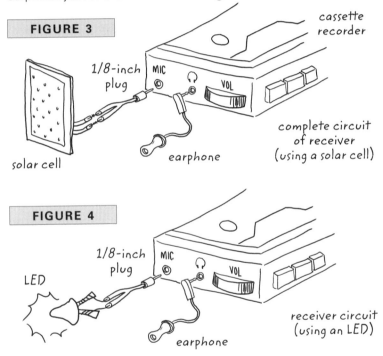

FIGURE 3

cassette
recorder

1/8-inch
plug   MIC

VOL

complete circuit
of receiver
(using a solar cell)

solar cell   earphone

FIGURE 4

1/8-inch
plug   MIC

LED   VOL

receiver circuit
(using an LED)

earphone

Next, place the cassette recorder in RECORD/PAUSE mode to activate the internal amplifier yet prevent the reels from turning to save battery power.

Last, turn up the radio's volume level and position the LED in front of the receiver's solar cell (or LED).

Figure 5 illustrates how to position the receiver's solar cell in front of the transmitter's LED. You can then hear the radio's audio signal from an earphone or speakers plugged into the tape recorder. If necessary, adjust the position and distance of the receiver in relation to the transmitter until a strong signal is detected.

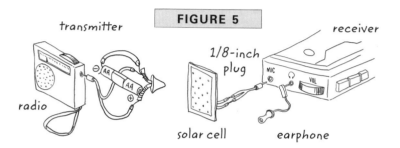

transmitter

FIGURE 5

receiver

1/8-inch plug

radio

solar cell

earphone

GOING FURTHER

This sneaky light-beam sound-transmitter project allows for plenty of sneaky adaptations for experimentation. See the list below and the illustrations in **Figure 6**.

- On the transmitter, connect an additional LED across the first one to increase its range.
- Aim the transmitter through the lens of a magnifying lens or reading glasses to increase the operational distance.
- Set up small mirrors or aluminum foil to see how far you can transmit and receive sound.
- Roll aluminum foil into a tube and test the receiving range.
- Aim a TV remote control at the receiving LED and push its buttons. Can you hear tones from the earphone?

- Perform the same remote control test with the solar cell and compare the distance achieved.
- "See what you can hear" by aiming the receiver at TV and PC screens, fluorescent lights, and other light sources.

FIGURE 6

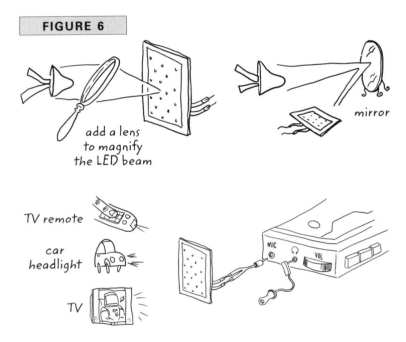

add a lens
to magnify
the LED beam

mirror

TV remote

car
headlight

TV

MIC   VOL

Sneaky Speaker

If you think you need a big woofer and tweeter or fancy headphones or earphones to hear electronic audio, think again. Speakers convert electrical signals into rapid vibrations to make sound. A typical speaker consists of a coil of wire attached to a paper cone with a magnet mounted close by. When an audio signal travels through the wire, it creates a magnetic field. Since magnets (and magnetic fields) attract and repel each other, the speaker's magnet causes the coil to push in one direction against the paper cone. This rapid motion vibrates the air and creates sound.

This project will show you how to use an ordinary paper or Styrofoam cup, wire, and a magnet to create a sneaky speaker.

What's Needed

- Thick pen or felt-tip marker
- Paper or Styrofoam cup
- Thin wire
- Magnet
- Tape
- Cable with ⅛-inch plug
- Cassette recorder

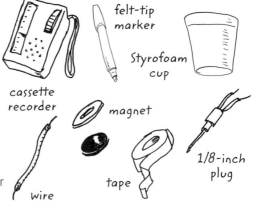

felt-tip marker

Styrofoam cup

cassette recorder

magnet

1/8-inch plug

tape

wire

What to Do

To create a sneaky speaker, wrap ten turns of thin wire around a thick pen or felt-tip marker and use tape to keep it in the shape of a coil. Slide the coil off the pen and tape it to the back of a paper or Styrofoam cup. Tape a small magnet on the back of the coil as shown in **Figure 1**.

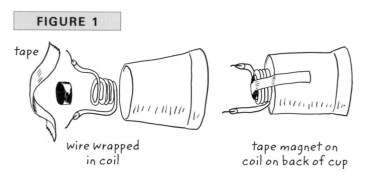

tape

wire wrapped
in coil

tape magnet on
coil on back of cup

Next, connect the coil wires to the cable with an ⅛-inch plug. Insert the plug into the earphone jack on the cassette recorder and turn the volume to maximum, as shown in **Figure 2**. You should be able to hear sounds from the cup. If not, reposition the magnet on the wire coil. For a louder volume, use a larger magnet.

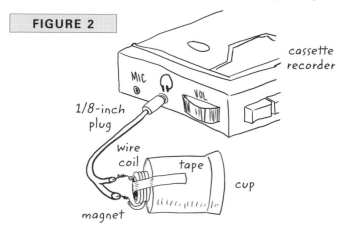

cassette
recorder

MIC

VOL

1/8-inch
plug

wire
coil

tape

cup

magnet

Sneaky Speaker II

In the first Sneaky Speaker project, you learned that a speaker consists of a coil of wire attached to a paper cone with a magnet mounted close by. Believe it or not, another common everyday item can become a sneaky speaker, further demonstrating the amazing versatility of wire and magnets.

What's Needed

- Electric motor (from a toy car)
- Paper or Styrofoam cup
- Cable with ⅛-inch plug
- Cassette recorder
- Wire

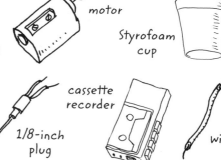

motor

Styrofoam cup

cassette recorder

1/8-inch plug

wire

What to Do

Electric motors convert electrical power into motion using a coil of wire and magnets. Normally you supply battery power to get a mechanical spinning motion from it. You can obtain a different effect by feeding the audio output of a radio or tape player into it and using a paper cup to "amplify" the vibrations for you to hear.

You can remove a motor from a discarded toy car for this project demonstration. As shown in **Figure 1**, connect the two wires of an electric motor from a toy car to an ⅛-inch plug cable. Insert the plug into the earphone jack on the radio, and turn the volume to its maximum level.

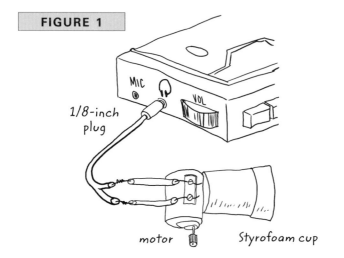

FIGURE 1

motor   Styrofoam cup

The audio signal from the radio creates a magnetic field in the motor's coil windings that repel against the motor's internal magnets, causing it to vibrate. With the motor lying on a table, rest a paper or Styrofoam cup on it so it's positioned at a near-45-degree angle. The cup will vibrate when resting on the motor and allow you to hear sounds from the radio. If not, reposition the cup on the motor until the sound is audible.

Sneaky Earphone

Your outer ear is always collecting air vibrations for your inner ear to process into sound. Using the same items in the Sneaky Speaker project, without the cup, you can turn your outer ear into a "speaker" and experience more of the sneaky versatility of a simple piece of wire.

What's Needed
- Magnet
- Thin wire
- Tape
- Cable with ⅛-inch plug
- Pen or felt-tip marker
- Cassette recorder

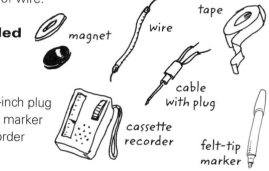

What to Do

First, wrap about ten turns of thin wire around a thick pen or felt-tip marker and use tape to keep it in the shape of a coil. Slide the coil off the pen and tape and connect the coil wires to the ⅛-inch plug cable wires.

Next, insert the plug into the earphone jack on the radio, as shown in **Figure 1**, and turn the volume to maximum. Press the wire coil to the back of the cup of your ear and press the magnet near the coil.

The magnet will cause the coil to vibrate your outer ear, and you'll actually hear the audio from the radio. *Note:* Even with the radio at high volume, there is no harm to your ear in performing this project because of the very weak signal from the coil of wire.

FIGURE 1

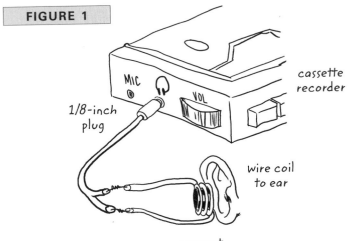

1/8-inch plug

MIC

VOL

cassette recorder

wire coil to ear

magnet

Sneaky Microphone

The Sneaky Speaker and Sneaky Earphone projects have demonstrated how speakers convert an electrical signal into sound by vibrating the air. This project shows how to reverse this effect to make a Sneaky Microphone.

What's Needed

- Cassette recorder
- Paper or Styrofoam cup
- Magnet
- Thin wire
- Tape
- Cable with ⅛-inch plug

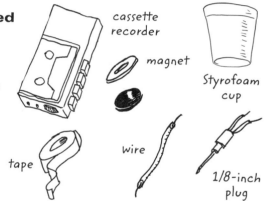

cassette recorder

magnet

Styrofoam cup

tape

wire

1/8-inch plug

What to Do

Just as an electrical signal in a coil attached near a magnet can vibrate a cup and produce sound, so can you reverse the effect and create a Sneaky Microphone using the same parts and setup as the Sneaky Speaker.

By speaking loudly into the cup, you will vibrate the coil. When the coil vibrates near the magnet, it produces an electrical signal that corresponds to your voice. The electrical signal is detected and amplified by the tape recorder.

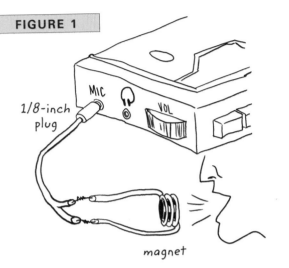

FIGURE 1

1/8-inch plug

MIC

VOL

magnet

Plug the ⅛-inch plug cable into the microphone input jack on the cassette recorder. With a blank tape in the recorder, you can record your voice (press just the RECORD button) and listen to it by playing back the tape or press the RECORD and PAUSE buttons and listen with an earphone or speakers connected to the earphone jack.

Sneaky Current Tester

Here's a sneaky fact: Small motors and even fruits can generate electrical power. You can make a current tester with everyday things to see this phenomenon.

What's Needed

- Wire
- Compass
- Clear tape
- Two paper clips
- Small electric motor
- Lemon, battery, or solar cell (optional)

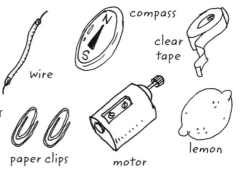

What to Do

First wrap eight turns of connecting wire around the compass and secure it with tape, as shown in **Figure 1**. Remove a motor from a small motorized toy and disconnect its two wires from the toy's main board. Connect the two motor wires to the wires around the compass.

FIGURE 1

wrap wire
around compass

Then bend a paper clip in the crank shape shown in **Figure 2** and attach it to the motor's gear. The paper clip allows you to turn the gear like a crank. By rotating the crank you can produce an electrical current strong enough to cause the compass needle to move.

Besides the electric motor, the Sneaky Current Tester can also detect other sources of electrical power—obtained from a lemon or battery or solar cell—as shown in **Figures 2 and 3**.

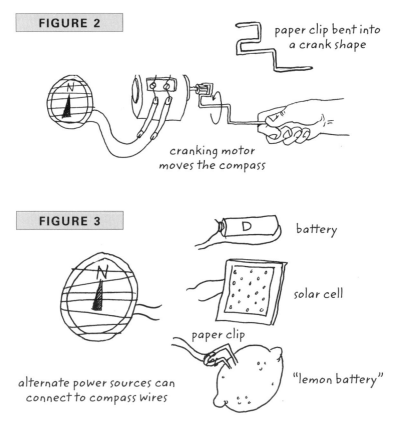

FIGURE 2

paper clip bent into a crank shape

cranking motor moves the compass

FIGURE 3

battery

solar cell

paper clip

alternate power sources can connect to compass wires

"lemon battery"

Antigravity Rollback Toy

If you've wondered how hybrid cars can boast such impressive mile-per-gallon ratings, this project will show you how. You will demonstrate the principle that allows hybrid cars to store and release energy by using a simple-to-build rollback toy.

What's Needed

- Small container with plastic lid
- Extra plastic lid
- Thick rubber band 3–4 inches long
- Two paper clips
- Bolts or large lug nuts
- Scissors

container

plastic lids

rubber band

paper clips

bolts or nuts

scissors

What to Do

First, obtain a small cardboard container and remove the bottom. Cut slits through the center of the can's plastic lid and the extra lid. Take the lids off the container. See **Figure 1**. Thread a rubber band through the bottom of the container and pull it through the lidless top of the container.

Tape the washers or lug nuts together and connect them to the middle of one section of the rubber band (do not tape the

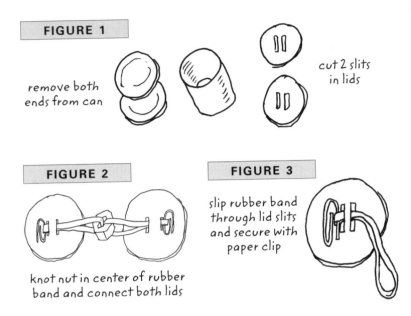

FIGURE 1

remove both ends from can

cut 2 slits in lids

FIGURE 2

knot nut in center of rubber band and connect both lids

FIGURE 3

slip rubber band through lid slits and secure with paper clip

strands of the rubber band together). See **Figure 2**.

Put the end of the rubber band through the container lid. Use a paper clip to secure the band so it does not slip inside the container (put the paper clip through the end loop of the rubber band that remains outside the hole). See **Figure 3**. Put the lid on the container, making sure the rubber band is still sticking out the other end.

Carefully pull on the rubber band until it comes through the hole. Secure the band with the second paper clip. Be sure to situate the weight so it is in the center of the container and does not touch the sides. Put both lids on the ends of the container. See **Figure 4**. Your rollback toy is ready to go!

Roll the toy and watch as it stops and returns to you. See **Figure 5**. This sight is more amazing when you roll it downhill

FIGURE 4

bend and push one
lid through can and
put lids on both ends

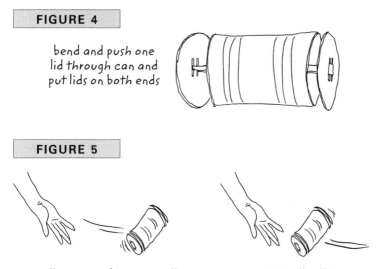

FIGURE 5

rolling away from you will store energy and it will roll back

and it stops and returns to you uphill, seemingly defying gravity.

The weight holds one end of the rubber band stationary while the free side twists around. The farther the toy rolls, the more potential energy is stored. Release and watch the toy roll back toward you, demonstrating its conversion into kinetic energy.

Hybrid vehicles use this principle to store energy in a flywheel to power an electric motor. The motor is used when you take off from a standing stop to save engine fuel.

Sneaky Copier

Have you ever found yourself needing to make a copy of a drawing and no copy machine is around? Using household items you can make a sneaky copy machine of your own

What's Needed

- Teaspoon
- Vanilla extract
- Liquid dish detergent
- Small bowl
- White paper
- Ink pens of various colors
- Paintbrush (optional)
- Comic strip or newspaper picture (optional)

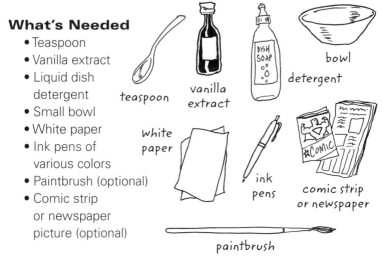

teaspoon

vanilla extract

detergent

bowl

white paper

ink pens

comic strip or newspaper

paintbrush

What to Do

First, draw a picture on a sheet of paper, using a black pen. Go over the lines to thicken them. (Thicker lines allow you to make more copies from the original.)

Next, mix equal parts of vanilla extract and liquid dish detergent together in a small bowl; one teaspoon of each should be enough. Using your finger or a small paintbrush, completely cover the drawing with a thin layer of your Sneaky Copier solution, as shown in **Figure 1**.

FIGURE 1

mix extract and dishwashing
liquid in bowl

rub "copier" liquid
mix on original

Now place a clean sheet of white paper on top of the picture. Rub the back of the paper firmly with the bowl of the teaspoon until the picture begins to show through the paper. Peel the paper off the picture to see your copier creation; see **Figure 2**. You should be able to make multiple copies this way if your original drawing has thick dark lines.

Last, test the Sneaky Copier technique with other ink colors. Try to make a copy of a newspaper page or a comic strip. Keep in mind that the images on the copy will be reversed.

FIGURE 2

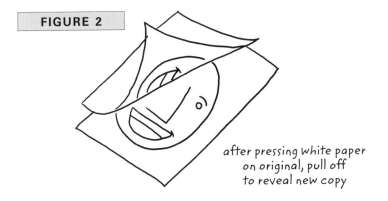

after pressing white paper
on original, pull off
to reveal new copy

Sneaky Tracer

Some items cannot be copied using a chemical transfer technique (shown in the preceding Sneaky Copier project), because their images are printed on coated paper or, in the case of text, the image will be reversed.

Another way to make a duplicate of an original image is to use a Sneaky Tracer.

What's Needed

- Four cardboard strips
- Hole punch or nail
- Paper clips
- Paper-clip box
- Tape
- Two pencils

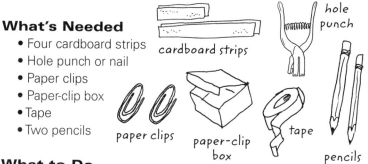

cardboard strips

hole punch

paper clips

paper-clip box

tape

pencils

What to Do

First, cut two pieces of cardboard, each measuring 2 by 8 inches. Then cut another two pieces, each 2 by 4 inches.

Arrange the cardboard pieces in the pattern shown in **Figure 1** and then punch holes in the corners of the shape. Bend paper clips into **C** shapes and push them through the holes to secure the pieces, yet still allow them to move freely.

Next, punch pencil-sized holes in the cardboard at points A and B, just large enough so a pencil can fit through snugly, and insert a pencil in each (see **Figure 2**). Now place the copier device so one end rests on the top of the paper-clip box and secure it with tape. The box acts as an elevated mounting

FIGURE 1

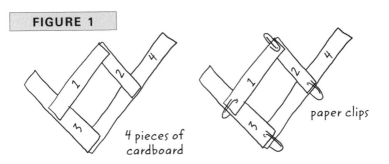

4 pieces of
cardboard

paper clips

platform to keep the pencils balanced and stable yet free to
move about.

Last, select an original drawing that you want to trace and set
it under the pencil in hole A. Place a blank sheet of paper under
hole B. Use pencil A to trace the drawing and you'll see another
picture being created by pencil B. If necessary, secure the
pencils to the cardboard and the paper to the table with tape.
See **Figure 3**.

Now you can easily trace complex drawings and make copies
for your needs. Experiment with the lengths of cardboard, and
you'll see that you can easily enlarge or reduce the size of the
drawings made.

FIGURE 2

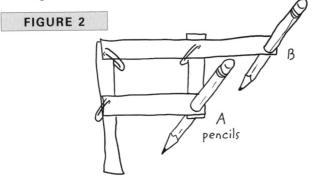

pencils

FIGURE 3

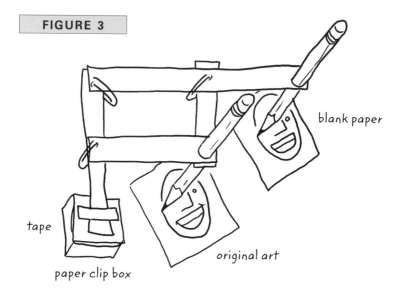

blank paper

tape

paper clip box

original art

Part II

Sneaky Gadgets

If you're curious about the sneaky adaptation possibilities of household gadgets, you have the right book. People frequently throw away damaged gadgets and toys without realizing they can serve unintended purposes.

It's hard to believe, but such common household items as broken tape recorders, LED flashlights, key-chain voice memo recorders, radios, walkie-talkies, and toy car motors can be used to create a novel ID card, a radio transmitter made with only a piece of wire, inventive radio-controlled car applications, sneaky walkie-talkie uses, and more.

All these projects are tested safe, and you can make them in no time. If you enjoy the idea of high-tech resourcefulness, the following chapters will undoubtedly provide plenty of resourceful ideas.

Sneaky Radio-Control Car Projects

Radio-controlled cars have many sneaky adaptation possibilities that can increase their usefulness. This project uses the inexpensive single-function type of radio-controlled toy car; this model will travel forward continuously, once its ON/OFF switch is placed in the ON position, until you actuate the remote control button, causing it to back up and turn. When you release the control, the vehicle goes forward in a straight line again.

The instructions and illustrations that follow will show you how to modify the transmitter to a more compact size, to use it as an alarm trigger. You'll also see how to modify the receiver to activate other devices, such as lights and buzzers.

What's Needed

- Radio-controlled car
- Three 3-volt watch batteries (or fewer, depending on transmitter)
- LEDs
- Buzzer
- Tape
- Wire
- Rubber band
- Playing card
- Strong thin thread

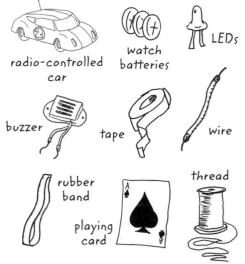

radio-controlled car

watch batteries

LEDs

buzzer

tape

wire

rubber band

playing card

thread

What to Do

How a radio-controlled car works. Pressing the transmitter button closes an electrical switch, which turns on the transmitter. This sends electromagnetic waves through the air that are detected by the radio receiver in the vehicle. The receiver detects the radio signal from the transmitter and reverses the electrical polarity (direction of current flow) of the power applied to the motor. This causes it to run in the reverse direction.

Adapting the car's transmitter. The first sneaky adaptation to the transmitter is to make it as small as possible, for concealment inside other objects or clothing.

Since the transmitter is always in the OFF mode until its activator button is pressed, it can operate using tiny long-life watch batteries.

If the transmitter uses one AA or AAA battery, it can be replaced by one small watch battery with the same voltage output. *Note:* Each AA or AAA battery supplies 1½ volts of power.

If the transmitter operates on two AA or AAA batteries, you can substitute either two 1½-volt watch batteries or a single 3-volt watch battery. If a 9-volt battery was in use, you will need to use three 3-volt watch batteries. When stacking batteries, place the positive side of one battery against the negative side of the other.

Figure 1 shows how to replace regular AA or 9-volt batteries in the transmitter with 3-volt watch batteries.

If you connect two wires across the transmitter's activator button, you can have another sensor or switch activate the transmitter to alert you of an entry breech or that your valuables are being removed. Place a piece of tape over the transmitter button so that when the device is activated it will be on. See **Figure 2**.

Adaptating the car's receiver. You can also modify the car's radio receiver, which is on a circuit board in the car's body, for use as an alarm trigger. See **Figure 3**.

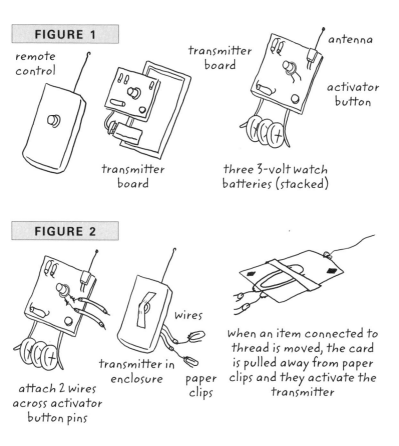

FIGURE 1

remote control

transmitter board

transmitter board

antenna

activator button

three 3-volt watch batteries (stacked)

FIGURE 2

attach 2 wires across activator button pins

transmitter in enclosure

wires

paper clips

when an item connected to thread is moved, the card is pulled away from paper clips and they activate the transmitter

Unlike the transmitter, the receiver must stay ON to be able to operate, and this produces a small constant drain on the batteries. **Figure 4** illustrates how to modify the receiver for use with watch batteries using the same technique described for the radio transmitter.

If desired, the toy car motor can be used in an application of your own design. (*Sneaky Uses for Everyday Things* illustrated

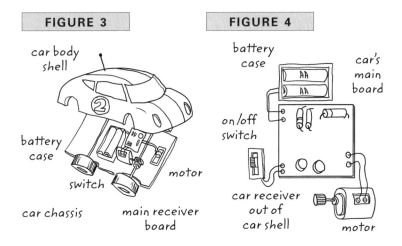

FIGURE 3

car body shell

battery case

switch

car chassis

main receiver board

motor

FIGURE 4

battery case

car's main board

on/off switch

car receiver out of car shell

motor

a Door Opener using a toy car.) The car motor is attached to the receiver with two connecting wires. If you physically remove the motor from the car body (either by unclipping or unscrewing it), you can use the receiver for more project applications. It's easy to connect the receiver's motor wires to other devices to activate them remotely.

Figure 5 shows how the wires in the receiver that previously connected to the motor can be connected to other devices, like an LED or a buzzer for remote control.

FIGURE 5

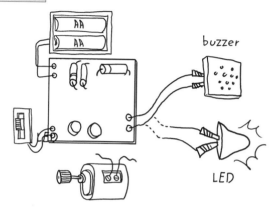

Sneaky Radio Transmitter and Receiver

Have you ever seen movie characters rig a radio transmitter to save the day? What does it take to make a radio transmitter— transistors? integrated circuits?

Believe it or not, there's an easy, sneaky way to transmit audio privately from a radio, TV, cassette, or MP-3 player to a nearby person's radio or tape recorder, with just a loop of wire!

What's Needed

- Thirty to 100 feet of wire
- Cables with two ⅛-inch plugs
- Portable radio or audio player
- Cassette recorder
- Earphone or Walkman speakers
- Blank tape

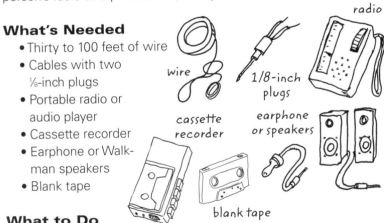

wire

radio

1/8-inch plugs

cassette recorder

earphone or speakers

blank tape

What to Do

A wire loop creates a magnetic field when an audio signal is connected to it. Another wire loop, located within or near the original wire loop, can detect the magnetic field from the other wire loop.

When the smaller wire loop, acting as a Sneaky Receiver, is connected to the microphone input of a tape recorder, you can hear the original sound signal.

SNEAKY RADIO TRANSMITTER

The transmitter consists of a single loop of wire. Use a small loop of wire, about 4 feet in length, to start and experiment with longer wire lengths later.

First, connect the two ends of the wire loop to the ends of the ⅛-inch-plug cable.

Next, plug the ⅛-inch plug cable into the earphone jack of a radio or other audio device, as shown in **Figure 1**. When tuned to a strong broadcast station, the radio's audio signal will alter (modulate) a magnetic field in the wire loop. This signal can be detected by another wire loop connected to an amplifier.

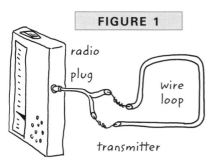

FIGURE 1

radio

plug

wire loop

transmitter

SNEAKY RECEIVER

The light-beam receiver uses a design similar to the earlier Sneaky Light Sensor project, but, instead of a solar cell, a wire loop is used as an input device.

First, connect the ends of a 2-foot length of wire to both ends of a cable with an ⅛-inch plug. Plug the cable into the microphone input jack of the tape recorder and connect an earphone or portable speakers to the recorder's earphone jack, as shown in **Figure 2**.

Next, with a blank tape inside the recorder, press the RECORD button and then the PAUSE button. Placing the recorder in RECORD/PAUSE mode will activate its amplifier but prevent the tape reels from spinning to save power.

Last, turn up the radio's volume level and move the wire loop close to the radio transmitter's larger loop, and you will hear the radio's broadcast station. See **Figure 3**.

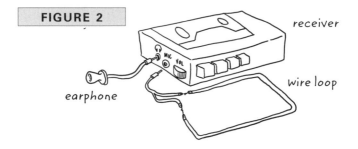

FIGURE 2

receiver

wire loop

earphone

GOING FURTHER

If necessary, adjust the position and distance of the receiver
in relation to the transmitter until a strong signal is detected.
Experiment with a larger loop and see how far away you can get
from the transmitter and still receive a signal.

Use a 50-foot length of wire for the transmitter and lay it around
the perimeter of a room. Test to see if you can walk around the
room and listen to the radio using the portable tape recorder.

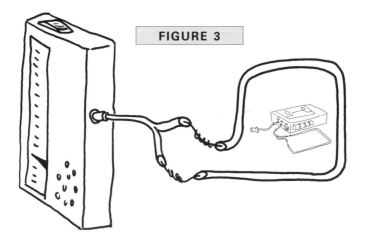

FIGURE 3

Sneaky Walkie-Talkie Uses

A pair of compact walkie-talkies lends itself to a variety of sneaky applications. Some models are so small, they are now mounted in toy wristwatches. This project illustrates methods to use walkie-talkies as an intercom, as an alarm sensor, and as a sneaky listening device.

What's Needed

- Pair of walkie-talkies
- Tape
- Nylon thread
- Coated business card or bookmark
- Nine-volt battery eliminator (optional)

What to Do

First, test the walkie-talkies with fresh batteries and note their maximum reliable operating distance. Follow the directions in the categories below for your desired application.

SNEAKY INTERCOM

This is the easiest project application to set up. It takes the place of an intercom system when wires cannot be placed between locations. For example, you can place one walkie-talkie in one room of the house and the other in the basement, the garage, a bedroom, or at the front door (mounted securely with screws or glue underneath a protective awning).

Simply mount the first walkie-talkie in a remote area (possibly under a cover to protect it from the elements) and listen with the second unit as shown in **Figure 1**.

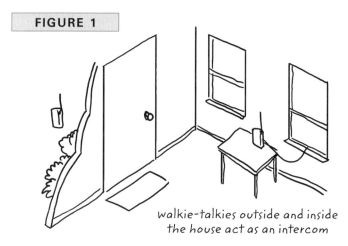

FIGURE 1

walkie-talkies outside and inside
the house act as an intercom

For constant monitoring applications, (e.g., as a baby monitor), apply a piece of strong tape across the TALK button so the unit is always in transmit mode. This application will eventually drain the battery, so you may want to use walkie-talkies that use 9-volt batteries. Then you can attach an AC battery eliminator to the battery clip (available at electronic parts stores), so it can always be in the ON or STANDBY mode without requiring frequent battery replacement. See **Figure 2**.

SNEAKY LISTENER

Use the Sneaky Listener application, similar in operation to the Sneaky Intercom, when you want to monitor a remote location

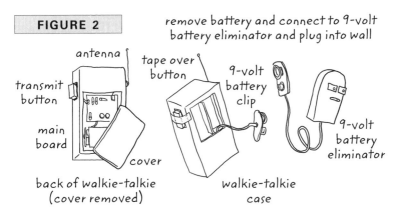

FIGURE 2

remove battery and connect to 9-volt
battery eliminator and plug into wall

antenna

tape over
button

9-volt
battery
clip

transmit
button

main
board

cover

9-volt
battery
eliminator

back of walkie-talkie
(cover removed)

walkie-talkie
case

secretly. Simply place one walkie-talkie out of sight, within or
under an object. Place the power button in the ON position and
put tape across the TALK button to keep it transmitting.

As shown in **Figure 3**, you can monitor the audio in the area
with the other walkie-talkie (and retrieve the remote one later).
Or, as shown in the Gadget Jacket project (Part IV), a walkie-
talkie can be placed in a jacket (that's left in a room) to monitor
nearby sounds from afar.

SNEAKY ALARM TRIGGER

A walkie-talkie set provides an inexpensive quick-to-set-up option
for a sneaky wireless alarm system. One walkie-talkie set up
with tape across its TALK button, to keep it in the transmit mode,
can broadcast a warning signal to the remote unit. The trick is to
place an insulator strip, from a coated business card or a bookmark, between one battery terminal and its clip. Connect a thin
strong nylon thread or wire to the other end of the insulator strip
and wrap it around the item you want to protect.

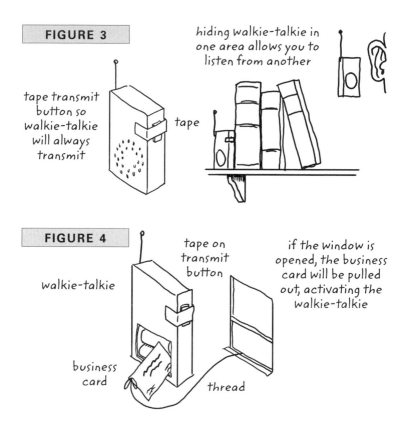

FIGURE 3

hiding walkie-talkie in one area allows you to listen from another

tape transmit button so walkie-talkie will always transmit

tape

FIGURE 4

walkie-talkie

tape on transmit button

if the window is opened, the business card will be pulled out, activating the walkie-talkie

business card

thread

First, open the first walkie-talkie and remove one side of the 9-volt battery clip so that it rests on top of the battery terminal. Then poke a small hole in the insulator strip and tie the thread through it into a knot. Attach the other end to a window handle, door knob, or other object that you want to keep from being moved.

Next, place the insulator strip between the battery terminal and the battery clip. The battery clip should still be attached to the other battery terminal and should keep pressure on the insulator. If the insulator is pulled away from the battery, the battery clip should rest on the top of the battery terminal and turn on the walkie-talkie. If not, wrap a small rubber band around the battery and the battery clip, to apply more pressure. See **Figure 4**.

Turn on the walkie-talkie's power button and tape the transmit or TALK button so it stays on. Place it out of sight from the window or object that it will be connected to with the thread.

When someone opens the window, the thread will pull the insulator away from the battery clip, turning on the walkie-talkie, which will transmit to the other walkie-talkie.

Note: If the walkie-talkie includes a signal button or a Morse code signaler, it can be taped in the ON position too.

Sneaky Buzzer

A buzzer is a fairly common item. Actually, it's a simple electromagnet with a clever modification that demonstrates a very elegantly designed circuit. You can make your own Sneaky Buzzer with found items like paper clips, wire, and a battery.

What's Needed

- C- or D-size battery
- Twenty-five feet of wire
- Magnet
- Fifteen paper clips
- Cardboard
- Tape

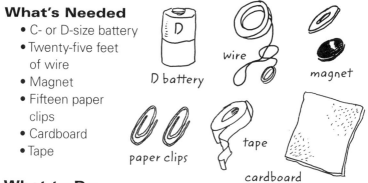

D battery

wire

magnet

paper clips

tape

cardboard

What to Do

When electricity flows through a wire, it creates a magnetic field around it. Winding wire in a coil and placing a piece of metal inside the coil increases the strength of the field and creates an electromagnet.

A buzzer consists of an electromagnetic circuit with a piece of metal close by that is pulled onto another piece of metal and creates a tapping sound. The metal is actually a part of the wire coil circuit; when it is pulled toward the second piece, it turns off the electromagnet.

The metal then returns to its original position because of spring tension. Once in place again, the electromagnetic field is

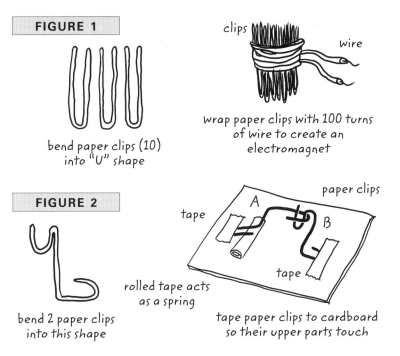

FIGURE 1

bend paper clips (10)
into "U" shape

clips

wire

wrap paper clips with 100 turns
of wire to create an
electromagnet

FIGURE 2

bend 2 paper clips
into this shape

rolled tape acts
as a spring

tape

A

paper clips

B

tape

tape paper clips to cardboard
so their upper parts touch

activated and the cycle restarts. The rapid tapping of the metal on the second metal piece is what causes the buzzing sound.

To make an electromagnet, wind a coil of wire around **U**-shaped paper clips, as shown in **Figure 1**.

Then bend two paper clips into the shape shown in **Figure 2** and mount them on the cardboard with tape so they touch. Notice that paper clip A rests on a roll of tape, which acts as a spring to keep it in contact with paper clip B.

Next, tape one coil wire to paper clip A and the other to one battery terminal with tape. Connect the other battery terminal to paper clip B. See **Figure 3**. In this arrangement, the battery's

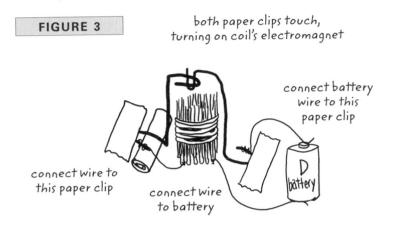

FIGURE 3

both paper clips touch,
turning on coil's electromagnet

connect battery
wire to this
paper clip

connect wire to
this paper clip

connect wire
to battery

D
battery

power flows from one of its terminals to the wire coil, through both paper clips, and back to the second battery terminal. In this circuit it does not matter which direction, positive or negative, the battery terminal is connected to the other parts.

Once the battery is connected, the wire coil electromagnet will attract paper clip A toward it and move away from paper clip B. This disconnects the electromagnetic circuit, and the electromagnet turns off. The rolled-up tape "spring" pushes the paper clip up toward the second paper clip and makes a tapping sound. When the two paper clips are in contact again, the coil turns on and the cycle begins again. See **Figure 4**.

FIGURE 4

when the wire coil has power, it attracts
paper clip and disconnects battery

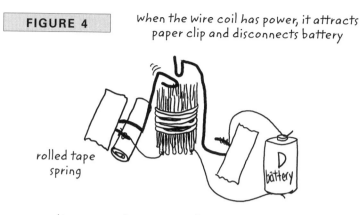

rolled tape
spring

once disconnected, the paper clip is pushed back up by the
"spring" tension; this connects both paper clips, turning on the
electromagnet

Sneaky ID Card

If you want the safety and convenience of a "card-swiping" security system in your home (like the ones used at many businesses), you can use a few household objects to achieve your dream.

With a few components, you can create a sneaky personal ID card, allowing you to identify your friends through walls and doors.

What's Needed

- Cardboard
- Wire
- Two paper clips
- Two C-size batteries
- LED or buzzer
- Glue
- Tape
- Two business cards

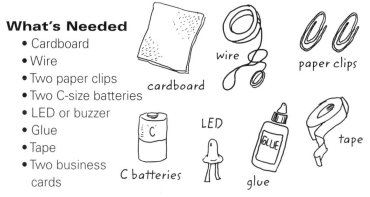

cardboard

wire

paper clips

C batteries

LED

glue

tape

What to Do

The Sneaky Card ("Don't sneak around without it") is designed to activate a complementary signal circuit that will properly identify you as a "friendly" carrier.

The Sneaky Access Card is made of two ordinary business cards, or a card of your own design, with two bent paper clips inside. Two small loops of the paper clips will protrude through the back of the card so they can make contact with the signal circuit.

To make the card, simply straighten the paper clips into a **U**
shape and poke them through one card about two inches from
each other. Bend the paper clips back onto the card so they rest
flat and touch each other. See **Figure 1**. Then glue the second
card over the first so it conceals the paper clips connections,
as shown in **Figure 2**.

FIGURE 1

front   back

punch 2 paper clips through card and bend back

FIGURE 2

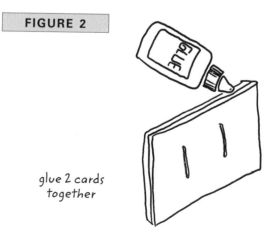

glue 2 cards
together

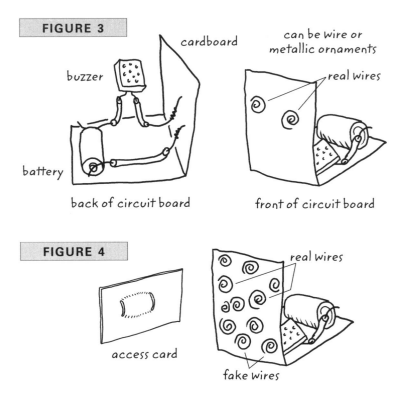

FIGURE 3

cardboard

can be wire or metallic ornaments

buzzer

real wires

battery

back of circuit board

front of circuit board

FIGURE 4

real wires

access card

fake wires

The signal circuit consists of a battery and a buzzer, with two coils of wire acting as a switch. When a piece of metal contacts both wire coils, the buzzer will turn on. The items are easily mounted and assembled on a piece of cardboard and are secured with tape. The front of the signal circuit stands vertically with the small wire coils protruding through the front. See **Figure 3**. Additional wire coils can be placed on the front of the signal circuit board for subterfuge. See **Figure 4**.

When you place the Sneaky Access Card on the surface of

the signal circuit in the correct position, it completes the circuit and activates the buzzer. See **Figure 5**. For your own applications you can extend the wires going to the signal-circuit front panel so it's on the other side of a door or other partition.

FIGURE 5

access card

pressing access
card against wires
turns on buzzer

Sneaky Survival Techniques

We prefer to believe that misfortunes won't occur, but why take chances? Why not prepare for the worst when you're traveling? With the proper knowledge, you can improvise sneaky gear that may save you and others from harm.

Most people would object to carrying a full array of emergency equipment, but you can have the most fundamental items available in a package as small as a shoelace. Who can argue against that?

After reviewing this section, you'll be equipped, among other things, to assemble a shoestring survivor kit; make a sneaky breathing device; hide security devices in a ring, pen, or watch; construct animal traps and fishing lures with items in your pocket; and make a whistle with a blade of grass.

Living on a Shoestring

When you take a hiking or camping trip, it's wise to bring emergency provisions. Despite such preparations, sometimes you might leave your main camp and get separated from your bag or backpack. If you get lost, what will you do? Why not carry the most essential items on your person, so even if you get separated from your group, you'll always have basic equipment with which to save your life.

You can make a sneaky survival kit that fits into the most un-likely places, including a jacket patch, a pen, a watch, even your shoestrings! Even if you never have to remove your Sneaky Survival Kit while hiking or camping, you will never be without it.

What's Needed

The list below contains the most essential items you should have in case of emergencies. The quantity of items depends on the amount of room that's available in your desired storage compartment.

- Two aspirins
- Penlight bulb
- Watch battery
- Wire (to connect bulb and battery for flashlight)
- Three-inch square of aluminum foil (as signal mirror)
- Dental floss (for fishing)
- Multivitamins
- Duct tape

aspirin

penlight bulb

watch battery

dental floss

tape

- Wooden match heads
- Paper clip
  (to hold match heads)
- Small Baggie
- Antibacterial tablet
  (to treat water in Baggie)
- Survival information sheet
  (semaphore signals, Morse
  code, etc.)
- Pencil lead (for notes on
  survival sheet)
- Mints (for emergency
  sugar source)
- Needle
- Magnet (to make compass
  from a needle or paper clip)

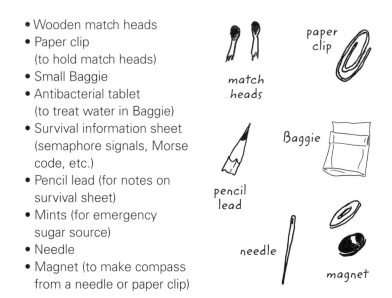

What to Do

As shown in **Figure 1**, you can remove the inner parts from a large pen or an inexpensive watch and carefully position all these items inside. Roll the aluminum foil, survival instruction sheets, and plastic Baggie tightly into a very small size.

FIGURE 1

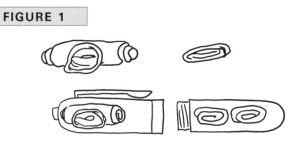

   Or you can very carefully sew all of the items between two jacket patches and sew the patch onto your jacket. It's also possible to arrange all the survival items carefully between two athletic shoestrings and then sew them together with the items in between as shown in **Figure 2**. This saves the space in your pen or watch for larger essentials: currency, coins—and balloons and rubber bands for Sneaky Water Wings!

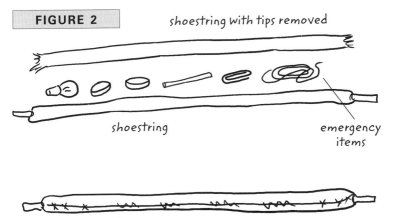

FIGURE 2   *shoestring with tips removed*

shoestring   *emergency items*

shoestrings sewn together with emergency items inside

Ink or Swim

Who among us has not feared for our small companions, children and pets alike, when they're near a body of water? With a few everyday items, you can prevent a possible drowning. Just bring this easy-to-make lifesaving gadget with you when traveling over or near water with your little ones.

What's Needed

- Large wide-barreled pen
- Four large balloons (two for each arm)
- Four large rubber bands

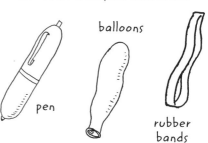

What to Do

You can store emergency sneaky water wings available for nonswimmers inside a large hollow pen barrel. When tightly wrapped, the balloons and rubber bands will easily fit inside a pen, as shown in **Figure 1**. Just slip the pen in a pocket or purse before a trip for added peace of mind.

Figure 2 shows how to affix the sneaky water wings to a child's arms in case of an emergency swim. If the rubber bands are too large for the arms or legs of the child (or pet), just wrap them around multiple times for a snug fit.

FIGURE 1

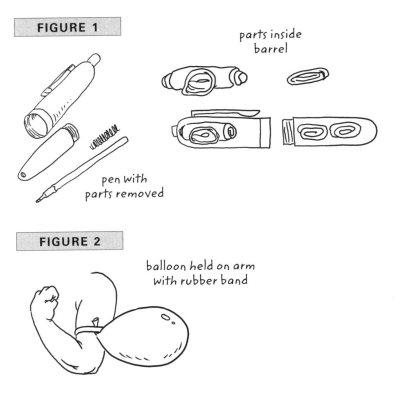

parts inside
barrel

pen with
parts removed

FIGURE 2

balloon held on arm
with rubber band

Sneaky Breathing Device

Did you know that smoke inhalation causes more fire-related deaths than flames or heat? The smoke uses up oxygen required for breathing and replaces it with toxic gases that can quickly make you drowsy and disoriented.

If you must enter an area clouded with thick smoke, you need to continue breathing clean air as long as possible. Most people can hold their breath for just under a minute. Here is an inexpensive and easy way to have clean air for another five to ten minutes, long enough for you to move to safety or for rescuers to arrive.

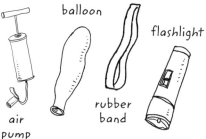

What's Needed
- Compact air pump
- Large balloons
- Rubber bands (optional)
- Flashlight (optional)

What to Do

First, always keep a flashlight with fresh alkaline batteries handy in your house or office in case of emergencies. Let everyone know its location for easy access. Attach several balloons and a compact air pump to the flashlight with a large tightly wrapped rubber band. This will allow you to grab all three items quickly, even in the dark. In case the lights go out, the flashlight will allow you to signal for help at a window.

If you must remain in a room that is slowly filling with smoke or if you absolutely must enter a smoke-filled hall, pump up the balloons with clean air and wrap the ends tight around your finger or wrap rubber bands around them to prevent air from escaping. See **Figure 1**. Take a deep breath, hold it as long as possible, and exhale. Inhale clean air from the balloons as needed.

FIGURE 1

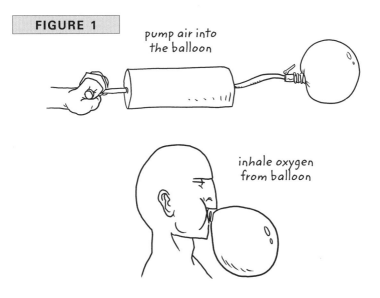

pump air into the balloon

inhale oxygen from balloon

How to Make Invisible Ink

If anything is a prime example of a Sneaky Use project, it's using everyday things to make invisible ink. (Sneaky fact: Casinos now use cards marked with symbols that are only visible when viewed with a special lens.) You can use a large variety of liquids to write secret messages. In fact, some prisoners of war used their own saliva and sweat to make invisible ink.

What's Needed

- Milk *or* lemon juice *or* equal parts baking soda and water
- Small bowl
- Cotton swab or toothpick
- Paper

bowl

cotton swabs

lemon juice

paper

What to Do

Use a cotton swab or toothpick to write a message on white paper, using the milk or lemon juice or baking soda solution as invisible ink. The writing will disappear when the "ink" dries.

To view the message, hold the paper up to a heat source, such as a lightbulb. The baking soda will cause the writing in the paper to turn brown. Lemon or lime juice contain carbon and, when heated, darken to make the message visible.

You can also reveal the message by painting over the baking soda solution on the paper with purple grape juice. The message will be bluish in color.

Sneaky Invisible Ink II

Here's another sneaky method to write and view invisible messages that stay invisible (unless you know the trick), this time using common laundry detergent and water.

What's Needed

- Cotton swab or towel
- Small bowl
- Liquid detergent
- Water
- Black light
- Piece of white cardboard

What to Do

In a small bowl, mix a teaspoon of liquid laundry detergent with one cup of water and use a small towel or cotton swab to write a message on a white piece of cardboard. See **Figure 1**. The message will not be visible at this point.

To view the secret message, darken the room and shine a black light—invisible ultraviolet light—on the board. The previously invisible message will become visible, as shown in **Figure 2**.

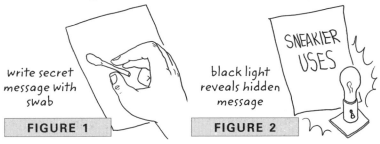

write secret message with swab

FIGURE 1

black light reveals hidden message

FIGURE 2

More Hide and Sneak

When you think of sneaky you usually think of something that is secret or hidden from you. Actually, the most common sneaky-use application is hiding your valuable belongings from others.

The following figures show how to keep your things to yourself, even if they are in plain sight. Most likely a thief or nosy houseguest will briefly examine the item and then ignore it as a possible safe. See **Figure 1** for examples.

- Hollowed-out candle
- Figurine
- Tissue container
- Trash container base
- Video or audio cassette shell
- Pen
- Watch case
- Inner pocket
- Shoestring
- DVD case
- Between magazine pages
- Inside a candy box
- Ironing board padding
- Bag within a bag

FIGURE 1

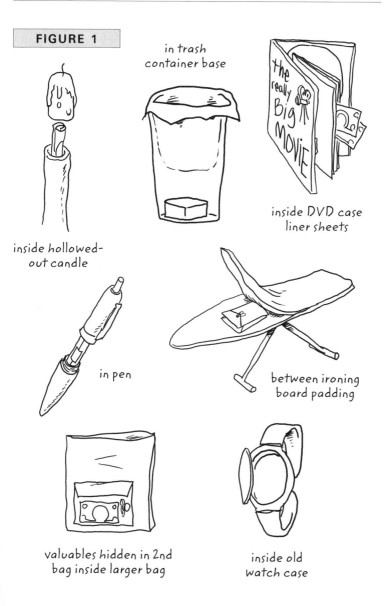

in trash
container base

inside DVD case
liner sheets

inside hollowed-
out candle

in pen

between ironing
board padding

valuables hidden in 2nd
bag inside larger bag

inside old
watch case

Sneaky Repellent Sprayer

If you're wary of a predator (animal or human) approaching you, you can carry your own concealed defense device made with household items. The Sneaky Sprayer provides you with a safe deterrent that wards off potential attackers.

You can carry the sprayer in your pocket or bag. Or you can attach it to the Gadget Jacket's Sleeve Device (see Part IV).

What's Needed
- Small squeeze bottle
- Baby powder
- Ground cayenne pepper

squeeze bottle

cayenne pepper

baby powder

What to Do
When you perceive a potentially dangerous situation, it's always best to leave the area. But in some situations you may need a deterrent to keep others away and give you precious moments to escape. (It's also important not to cause any harm to anyone in the process.)

The Sneaky Repellent Sprayer uses a combination of two safe ingredients: baby powder and pepper.

First, find a small squeeze bottle (the kind that trial-size shampoos and hand sanitizers come in) with a flip-up top. Empty the container, rinse it thoroughly, and allow it to dry.

Next, unscrew the top and fill the bottle one-quarter full of baby powder, another quarter with pepper, and a third quarter

with baby powder. See **Figure 1**. Replace the top, and you're
ready.

FIGURE 1

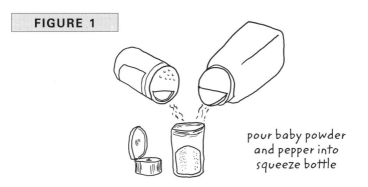

pour baby powder
and pepper into
squeeze bottle

You may want to test the Sneaky Repellent Sprayer outside
to see how hard you should squeeze and how far the repellent
mixture will travel, as shown in **Figure 2**.

Let's hope you never need this deterrent, but you can be prepared without spending a dime, using these household items.

FIGURE 2

sprayer in action

Sneaky Security Pen

When you are away from home, you may need a quick way to set up sneaky security devices to alert you to unauthorized entry into your room via door or windows. You may be in a hotel or at a friend's house and want to have sneaky noisemakers go off to alert you when you're sleeping or in another room.

Using everyday items stored inside a pen, you can sleep soundly, knowing your windows and doors cannot be tampered with without your knowledge.

What's Needed
- Large wide-barreled pen
- Two large rubber bands
- Two small chimes
- Fifteen feet of dental floss
- Duct tape
- Piece of thin bubble wrap, 2 by 4 inches

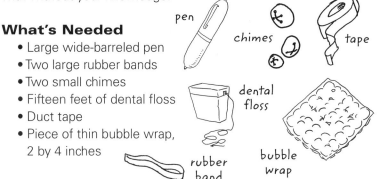

What to Do
First, unscrew the pen and remove its inner parts. Then carefully insert the rubber bands, chimes, and floss into the pen. You can also put a small sheet of bubble wrap (the thin type used to protect small objects) around the other items, tape it, and insert it into the pen. **Figure 1** shows the essential parts.

To set your sneaky booby trap, attach one end of the floss around a door or window handle (or both) and wrap the other end around a chair or desk leg. Then tape one chime in the

FIGURE 1

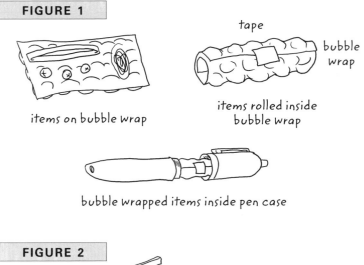

items on bubble wrap

tape

bubble wrap

items rolled inside bubble wrap

bubble wrapped items inside pen case

FIGURE 2

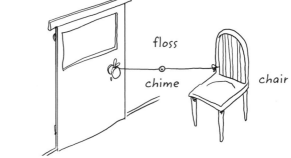

floss

chime

chair

middle of the length of dental floss, so that it will alert you if the door or window is opened. See **Figure 2**.

Next place rubber bands, linked if necessary, around the doorknob and a nearby object, like a window handle, to impede entry and tape a chime to it. It won't prevent someone from entering the room but it will cause the chime to ring repeatedly. See **Figure 3**.

FIGURE 3

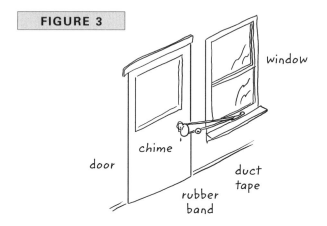

Last, set the small piece of bubble wrap near the door (or under a mat if there is one) to alert you by popping if someone enters and walks on it. See **Figure 4**.

FIGURE 4

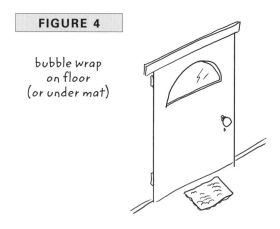

Sneaky Wristwatch

Some situations require a rapid response and quick access to the proper tools to be effective. The most convenient place to store a sneaky gadget is in a wristwatch. Because it's always at hand, you don't have to waste time fumbling for it in a pocket or bag. Also, wristwatches are so common they don't attract unnecessary attention, and devices hidden inside can be used secretly.

This project explains how to assemble a Sneaky Wristwatch to store covert devices for a variety of applications.

What's Needed

- Wristwatch
- Voice recorder
- Siren
- Radio-control transmitter
- Retractable key ring
- Mini-light
- Watch batteries

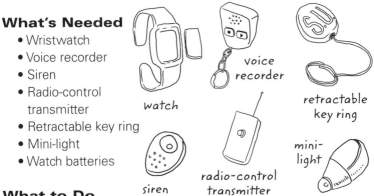

voice recorder

watch

retractable key ring

siren

radio-control transmitter

mini-light

What to Do

First, obtain the largest toy wristwatch you can find that looks real. Depending on your needs, you can remove the watch parts and install a miniature voice recorder, a simple radio transmitter (from a radio-controlled car), an electronic mini-siren, a retractable key ring, or any other small gadget that will fit in the watch case. See **Figure 1**.

Next, locate the smallest version available of the item you will mount in the case. Most drugstores, department stores, and toy stores sell miniature inexpensive versions of the foregoing devices for just a few dollars.

A compact device like a voice recorder usually uses tiny watch batteries for power. But a device like a radio-control transmitter may require two AA batteries. If the device uses AA or AAA batteries, you can substitute tiny watch batteries with the same voltage output. *Note:* Each AA or AAA battery supplies 1½ volts of power.

For instance, if the device uses one AA battery, use one 1½-volt watch battery in its place. If two AA or AAA batteries are needed, you can substitute either two 1½-volt watch batteries or a single 3-volt watch battery.

Figure 2 shows how to remove a tiny voice recorder from its original case and exchange its large 6-volt battery for two smaller 3-volt watch batteries, stacked together. (When stacking batteries, place the positive side of one battery against the negative side of the other.)

FIGURE 1	FIGURE 2

cover

watch with
cover removed

voice recorder with
cover removed

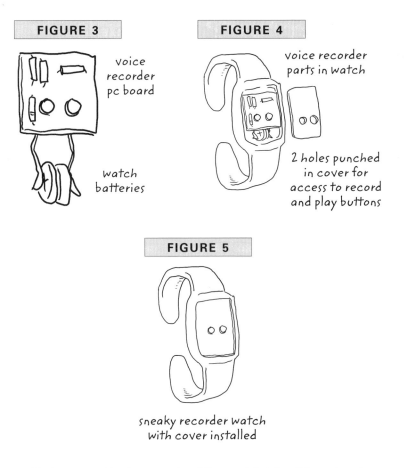

FIGURE 3

voice recorder pc board

watch batteries

FIGURE 4

voice recorder parts in watch

2 holes punched in cover for access to record and play buttons

FIGURE 5

sneaky recorder watch with cover installed

First remove the inner parts of the watch (circuit board and batteries) and put them aside. Then carefully position the desired device inside the case. In the example shown in **Figures 3 and 4**, a small voice-recorder device is placed inside of the empty watch case and small holes are punched in the watch face for access to the recorder's PLAY and RECORD buttons. See **Figure 5**.

| **FIGURE 6** | **FIGURE 7** | **FIGURE 8** |

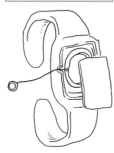

hole punched in
watch case; key ring
placed in watch case

connect 2 extra
ultra-bright
LEDs to mini-
lights battery

parts inside
watch case

GOING FURTHER

The sneaky technique of emptying the watch case and punching
appropriate holes in its front face allows for innumerable items
to be secreted inside, including:

- A retractable key cord (**Figure 6**)
- A mini-keychain light, with additional LEDs across its watch
  battery for almost blinding brightness (**Figures 7, 8, and 9**)
- A radio-control transmitter (from a toy car) or mini-siren
  (shown in **Figures 10, 11, and 12**)

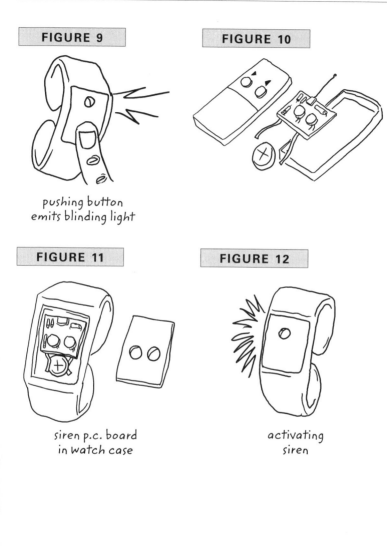

FIGURE 9

pushing button
emits blinding light

FIGURE 10

FIGURE 11

siren p.c. board
in watch case

FIGURE 12

activating
siren

Defense or Signal Ring

Here's a compact gadget you can make that will serve three practical purposes. It's a mini-flashlight or an emergency safety beacon, and it can act as a sneaky self-defense device.

What's Needed
- Large toy ring with a tin band and bubble top
- Ultra-bright LED key-ring light
- Two extra ultra-bright LEDs
- Three-volt watch battery
- Wire
- Glue
- Paper
- Transparent tape

toy ring   light

watch battery   wire

LED

glue   paper   tape

What to Do
Select an adjustable toy ring that has a clear case mount so the LED light can shine through. Or obtain a clear bubble top from another ring, toy, or ornament and glue it to your ring later.

Remove the battery and ultra-bright LED from the key-ring light. See **Figure 1**. Connect the LED from the toy and the two other LEDs to one piece of wire as shown in **Figure 2**.

Next, position the other LED leads to one side of the watch battery, as shown in **Figure 3**. Ensure that all the LEDs light when you touch the other end of the wire to the other side of the battery. If not, reverse the leads and test them again.

Place insulated material, like tape or vinyl or paper, on the

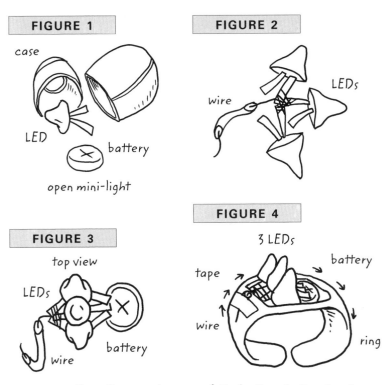

FIGURE 1

case

LED

battery

open mini-light

FIGURE 2

wire

LEDs

FIGURE 3

top view

LEDs

wire

battery

FIGURE 4

3 LEDs

tape

wire

battery

ring

current flows from the bottom of the battery to the ring, to the wire, then to the LEDs and back to the top of the battery

surface and on one side of the ring. Then set the battery and LEDs on top of the ring's surface. Lead the other end of the wire to the outside of the ring (**Figure 4**). In this manner the insulating material prevents the bottom of the battery from contacting the ring's metal surface and inadvertently turning on the LEDs.

Last, when all parts are positioned properly, glue the toy bubble top back on and press the wire end against the tin band.

FIGURE 5

vinyl covered ring

pressing wire on side activates ultra-bright light

This will connect the wire to the battery and turn on the LEDs, causing them to emit blinding light. See **Figure 5**.

Your sneaky ring can now serve as a convenient flashlight, as an emergency safety blinker (when walking at night in unlit areas), and as a self-defense device to temporarily blind and disorient an attacker.

Safety Measure

Traveling brings a sense of adventure, discovery—and, some-times, danger. While staying away from home you can gain a sense of security easily by setting up a sneaky safety alarm, using just one or two everyday things.

What's Needed
- Retractable mini tape measure or key cord
- Tape
- Small chime (optional)

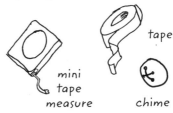

mini tape measure

tape

chime

What to Do
Since they both extend and recoil with a noticeable sound, a retractable compact tape measure or key cord provides a versatile sneaky tool for sensing when a door or window has been breeched. It can also alert you when an item has been inappropriately moved from the surface of a desk.

Simply extend the tape measure and carefully place its end tab under a window handle or a doorknob. See **Figures 1 and 2**. If it won't stay in position, use tape to secure it properly.

Want to know if someone moves one of your valuables? Simply place the tape measure's end underneath it and let it extend down the other side of a table, as shown in **Figure 3**. When the item is lifted, the tape measure will retract with a loud snap, alerting you and catching the person off guard.

For an extended measure of safety, you can set up a tape measure to turn on a noisemaker, like a portable battery-powered

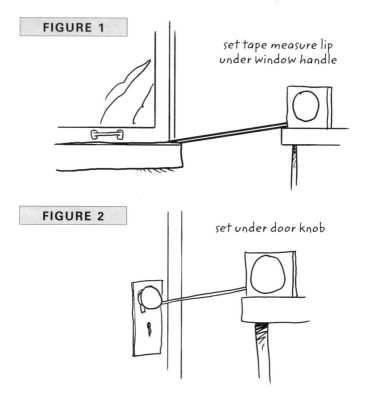

FIGURE 1

set tape measure lip
under window handle

FIGURE 2

set under door knob

radio. As shown in **Figure 4**, place a piece of tape between a
battery and its connector in the radio. Simply attach the tape to
one end of the tape measure and secure the radio and tape
measure so they will not move.

When the window is opened, the end of the tape measure
slides back to its case, pulling the tape away from the battery
and causing the radio to turn on and alert you.

FIGURE 3

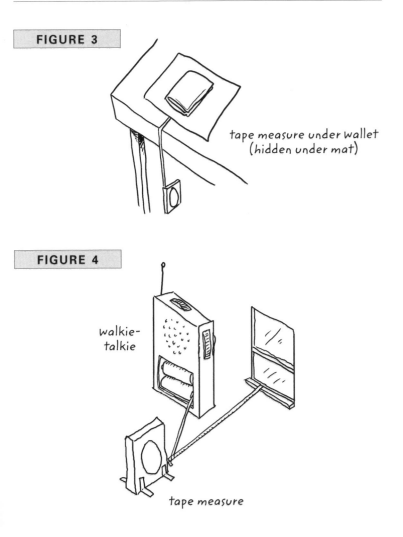

tape measure under wallet
(hidden under mat)

FIGURE 4

walkie-
talkie

tape measure

Animal Traps

If you're ever trapped in the wilderness, capturing small animals for food can prove to be energy-wasting and very difficult. Using items you may already have in your pocket, along with rope, twigs, string, twine, and wire, you'll be able to set small sneaky traps to catch emergency food.

By setting several traps, you'll have the ability to catch much more potential food than by chasing animals with a weapon (which you probably don't have anyway!).

What's Needed

- Box
- Sticks
- Wire
- Strong threads
  from clothing
  or string
- Belt
- Vines
- Tree branches
- Small bits of food
  or worms
- Bottle
- Small rocks
- Large rock

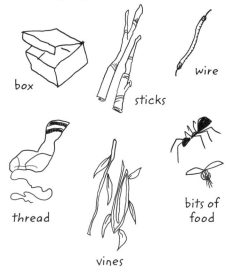

box

sticks

wire

thread

vines

bits of
food

What to Do   BOX TRAP

First, locate a cardboard box or use wood branches tied together with vines or strings to make a sneaky box shape. The box must have a door that can be propped open with a small branch in order to close behind the animal.

Next, position some small food or worms or a shiny item to lure the animal into the box opening. Set the stick so that it is positioned to keep the box door open gently, not rigidly. This allows the animal to bump into it and inadvertently close the door, thereby trapping the animal inside as shown in **Figure 1**.

FIGURE 1

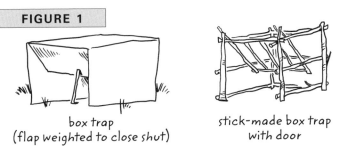

box trap
(flap weighted to close shut)

stick-made box trap
with door

If the box has an open top or no door flap, place the branch so that it props the box up off the ground. Set the bait near the base of the branch so when the curious animal moves about, it will bump into the stick and cause the box to drop on him. See **Figure 2**.

SNARE TRAP

First, locate items like long vines, thread from clothing, string, twine, or wire to make into a sneaky rope. Braid the material for strength and tie knots in both ends.

Next, tie one end of the rope around the base of a tree and secure it with a knot. Make a loop with the other end; this will become the snare. See **Figure 3**.

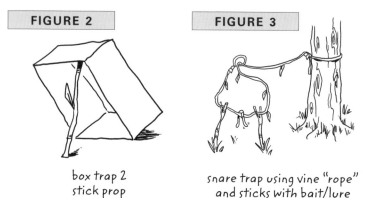

box trap 2
stick prop

snare trap using vine "rope"
and sticks with bait/lure

Hide the loop with grass and twigs placed on top of it. Place small bits of food or worms to attract an animal into the snare's loop. When a small animal runs into the loop, it will attempt to escape and pull it tighter, thus becoming trapped more tightly.

ROCK TRAP

If no box is available, use a large rock to trap a small animal.

As for the box trap, place a branch so it props up the rock. Position the stick very delicately, because it should fall at the lightest touch.

Place bait material next to the base of the branch so that the animal will knock over the stick while investigating and become trapped by the weight of the rock, as shown in **Figure 4**.

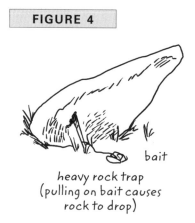

heavy rock trap
(pulling on bait causes
rock to drop)

Sneaky Fishing

Experienced outdoorsmen know the value of being able to lure and trap fish. In an emergency survival situation, when you're near water and cannot get back to your campsite, you can use everyday items to make sneaky fishing rigs.

A sneaky fishing rig consists of a line, a hook, and a lure. The line extends the hook and lure deep into the water. The lure attracts the fish, and, with a little luck, the hook ensnares it, allowing you to pull it in for a meal. If the hook and lure stay too close to the water's surface, tie a small rock to the line so it will sink deeper into the water.

What's Needed
- Foil or other shiny object
- Bait (worms, insects, food bits, or feathers)
- Wire
- Strong threads from clothes or string
- Dental floss
- Paper clip
- Vine
- Plastic bottle
- Tree branches

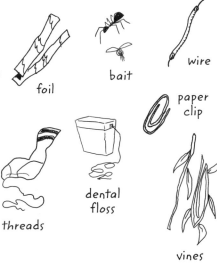

foil

bait

wire

paper clip

threads

dental floss

vines

What to Do
FISHING RIGS

Lines. Fashion your fishing line from items you have on or around you, such as dental floss, clothing thread, or wire. Nature provides tree vines that, when flattened with a rock and braided together, can make a good makeshift fishing line.

Hooks. You can make sneaky fishhooks using pins, needles, wire, small nails—even a thorny branch. Paper clips, a straightened key ring, stiff wire, shells, and bones can also be used.

Lures. Just because a hook is dangling from a line, you can't depend on a fish to investigate it, so some sort of bait is required. Use whatever you can find in your area that can be stuck on the end of the hook. Insects, worms, and small bits of food will do the trick. If you're out of real food, objects like a button, a shiny chain or foil wrapper, a feather, a small key, or even a fish-shaped leaf will increase the odds that you'll lure a fish to swallow the hook.

Simply wrap the line around the hook, place the bait item on the hook, and extend the line as far out and into the water as you can as shown in **Figure 1**. If possible, prop up the line with a forked branch to allow it to extend farther into the water.

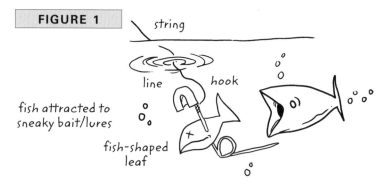

FIGURE 1

string

line   hook

fish attracted to
sneaky bait/lures

fish-shaped
leaf

FISH NETS

If you're near a stream, you may be able to catch fish with a net, which is easy enough to make.

First, find a long tree branch that splits off into a fork and remove all the leaves on the branch. Take a spare shirt and tie the sleeves and collar area into a knot.

Then place the shirt upside down into the forked branch so it produces a makeshift net. Secure the shirt to the branch using whatever you have—paper clips, a key ring, wire, or smaller forked branches—to keep the shirt tight on the branch ends. See **Figure 2**.

FIGURE 2

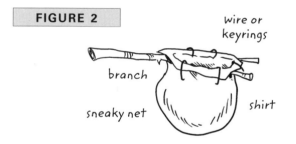

Last, lay the branch and shirt into the water, and you can ensnare aquatic creatures in your Sneaky Net.

AQUA TRAPS

A spare plastic bottle can provide another sneaky method to trap small fish if you're near a stream or pond.

First, use a knife or sharp rock to cut off the top of the bottle. Then place some sort of bait material in the bottom of the bottle. You can use insects, worms, small food bits, a button, a shiny chain, a foil wrapper, or a feather.

FIGURE 3

sneaky trap

bottle cut
in half

bait

place bottle top inside
bottom to trap small fish

Next, turn the bottle top upside down and push it, mouth down, into the bottom section so it's wedged tight. See **Figure 3**. Now place the bottle near the edge of a stream or pond. Curious fish will swim through the mouth of the bottle looking for the bait but will not be able to get out. Leave as many of these aqua traps as you can in the water, and with a little luck you will find a fish dinner waiting for you on your return.

Sneaky Whistle

If you're trapped in the wilderness and need to signal for assistance, especially during daylight hours, a whistle is far more noticeable then a visual signal. It can mean the difference between being found or left behind.

If you neglected to bring a whistle with you, you can make a sneaky version from things around you easily enough.

What's Needed
- Long blade of grass
- Hollowed-out acorn
- Small pebble

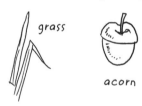

grass

acorn

What to Do
To make a whistle with a long blade of grass, hold it between your thumbs, as shown in **Figure 1**. Blow through the gap between your thumb knuckles. After some practice, and adjustments when necessary, you'll be able to produce a loud whistle with this nature-provided adaptation.

Similarly, you can blow into a variety of small shells, like an acorn, with your cupped hands and achieve a loud piercing sound that will surely be heard by anyone nearby. See **Figure 2**.

If no whistle sound is produced, place a small pebble in the shell and try again. Another method is to cut a tiny hole in the shell with a knife or sharpened rock and then cup your hands to produce a whistle effect.

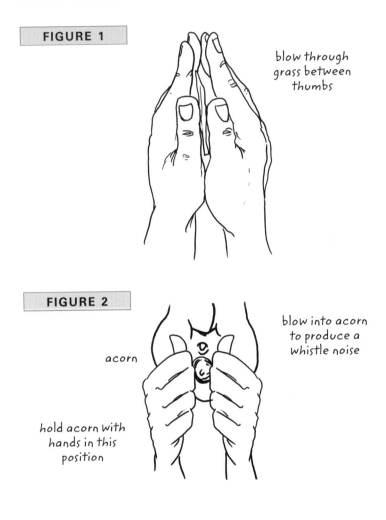

FIGURE 1

blow through
grass between
thumbs

FIGURE 2

acorn

blow into acorn
to produce a
whistle noise

hold acorn with
hands in this
position

Part IV

Gadget Jacket

With so many sneaky project possibilities available here, and in *Sneaky Uses for Everyday Things,* you'll want a way to keep them hidden and handy. The most practical way is to make a portable home for them in your own gadget jacket.

The following projects illustrate how to adapt a favorite jacket to make your sneaky devices instantly available for a variety of purposes. You can mix and match different gadgets according to your "mission," limited only by your imagination and the availability of your devices.

The examples that follow were selected for practicality. For example, typically you can outfit your gadget jacket with a mini remote-control transmitter, a voice recorder, a retractable magnet (to verify currency), and a mini-camera. When traveling, the gadget jacket can be outfitted with a compass, mini-poncho, pocket heater, mini survival kit, telescope, and a defensive repellent sprayer.

Sneaky Interior Pockets

The interior of the gadget jacket has a modular design to allow for both easy expansion and quick removal of the added items (for cleaning, inspection, and while traveling). Don't use the jacket's original pockets for your sneaky devices; they may clink against other personal items. Also, you should know the locations of operational buttons and controls for all the gadgets without having to peer into your exterior pockets. That's only possible when your gadgets are specifically arranged in custom-made pockets.

What's Needed

- Jacket
- Cloth to match jacket lining
- Nylon thread
- Velcro strips

jacket

cloth

nylon thread

velcro strips

What to Do

The areas where interior pockets can be added without unsightly bulges are alongside the upper back, near the underarms, and on the lower back and front. The upper side near the underarm is perfect for longer tube-shaped items, like the safety light stick and the mini air pump.

Custom pockets that provide a perfect fit for easy access and reinsertion of devices can be quickly made with cloth material that matches the jacket lining. Velcro strips that also match the jacket's interior color allow for easy installation and quick removal of the pockets.

FIGURE 1

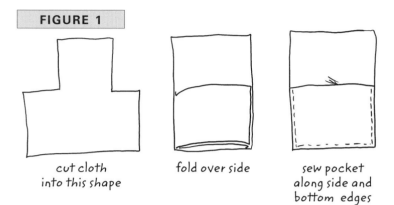

cut cloth
into this shape

fold over side

sew pocket
along side and
bottom edges

You should carefully plan which device or group of devices you will place in each particular pocket. Measure the cloth material for a snug fit (but not so snug that it is difficult to insert and remove an item). **Figure 1** shows how to cut a piece of material into a **T** shape and sew it together to create a mini-pocket with flap. Simply sew two Velcro strips to the back of the pocket and to the desired area in the jacket for mounting. See **Figure 2**.

FIGURE 2

pocket (rear view)

jacket

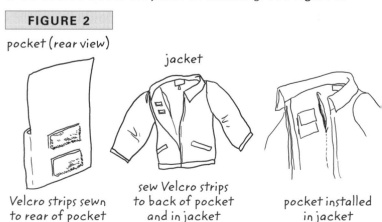

Velcro strips sewn
to rear of pocket

sew Velcro strips
to back of pocket
and in jacket

pocket installed
in jacket

FRONT INTERIOR POCKETS

The lower front interior pockets can store various sneaky items that come in handy in everyday life.

The list includes—but is not limited to—a mini pocket multi-tool, a telescoping antenna with magnet (when the mirror with magnet is attached, it acts as an around-the-corner sneaky viewer), a whistle or siren, mini-telescope, key finder, a mini–universal remote control, and a mini-camera.

Sneaky Camera Cozy. In order to store and use the mini-camera secretly, hide it inside a long candy box, along with a shorter box that's filled with candy.

To build the Sneaky Camera Cozy, position the camera inside a long candy box. Note where the camera shutter is located in relation to the box (if necessary, mark it with a pencil) and cut a hole in the front of the box for the lens to receive light. See **Figure 1**.

Then place a smaller candy box with candy inside in front of the camera. This will fill up the space in the larger box; you can even take candy from it occasionally so as not to raise suspicion. When needed, you can carry the box and position it properly to take a sneaky snapshot. See **Figure 2**.

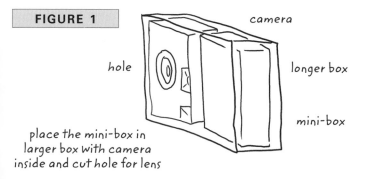

FIGURE 1

camera

hole

longer box

mini-box

place the mini-box in larger box with camera inside and cut hole for lens

FIGURE 2

press shutter to take
secret, sneaky snapshots

SIDE INTERIOR POCKETS

The lower side interior pockets are perfect for slightly bigger
items that need not be frequently accessed, such as the mini-fan
and hand warmer.

Other items for side pockets include balloons, a mini air pump
(for emergency flotation), and an air breather (for protection in a
smoked-filled environment). See **Figure 4**.

BACK INTERIOR POCKETS

The lower back pockets provide storage space for emergency
items such as an ultra-thin poncho, an emergency foil blanket,
a safety light stick, and various sneaky pens that include survival
and security implements. See **Figure 5**.

SHOULDER

To obtain the best long-range distance for your walkie-talkie or
radio-control transmitter, sew a thin wire, the same color as the
jacket's interior, into the upper shoulder area. See **Figure 6**. Then
attach the wire to the antenna connector on the component board
of the walkie-talkie or radio-control transmitter.

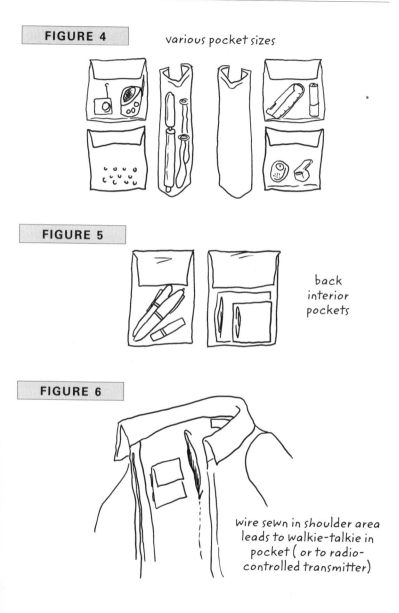

FIGURE 4   various pocket sizes

FIGURE 5

back
interior
pockets

FIGURE 6

wire sewn in shoulder area
leads to walkie-talkie in
pocket (or to radio-
controlled transmitter)

Sneaky Sleeve Pockets

Want instant access to a small defense item (like a repellent sprayer or other device) secretly propelled in the palm of your hand? Once you've made your own sneaky sleeve gadget for just a few everyday items, you'll never want to be without it.

What's Needed

- Jacket
- Cloth
- Nylon thread
- Paper clips
- Woven elastic strip
- Elastic band
- Velcro strips
- Scissors

jacket

cloth

nylon thread

paper clips

scissors

velcro strips

What to Do

By now you should have created and mounted a few pockets in the gadget jacket for your devices. The Sneaky Sleeve Pocket will use a similar design with one difference: The sleeve pocket is mounted upside down with an elastic band and thread for a sneaky release mechanism. If desired, the sneaky pocket can be mounted at the jacket's waist area for storing larger objects.

For this project, the sleeve pocket hides a mini-bottle, as described in the Sneaky Repellent project, but you can substitute another compact device or tool of your choice. Be sure to use cloth material, Velcro strips, an elastic strip, and strong nylon thread that match the jacket's color.

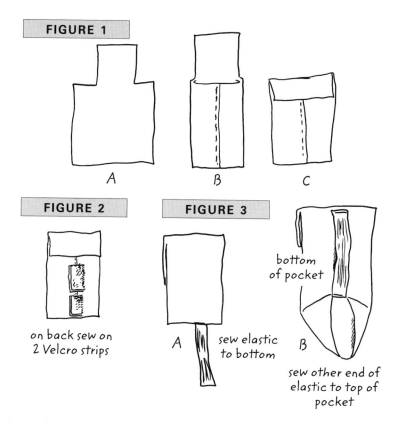

FIGURE 1

A

B

C

FIGURE 2

on back sew on
2 Velcro strips

FIGURE 3

A   sew elastic
to bottom

bottom
of pocket

B

sew other end of
elastic to top of
pocket

First, cut a piece of cloth into a **T** shape and sew it together to create a mini-pocket with flap that will house the bottle. The pocket should fit the bottle but not be so tight as to keep it from easily sliding out of the pocket's bottom hole. Sew two Velcro strips to the back of the pocket and a matching pair of strips inside the jacket's sleeve area. See **Figures 1 and 2**.

Then sew a strip of woven elastic (that is half the pocket's length) to the bottom and top of the pocket, as shown in **Figure 3**.

FIGURE 4

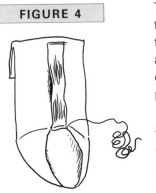

sew nylon thread
to band of elastic

The elastic will cause the bottom of the pocket to curl up, which prevents the bottle from falling out. Next, sew a 6-inch length of nylon thread to the elastic strip at the bottom of the pocket. See **Figure 4**.

Now you can test the quick-release action of the threaded pocket opener. As shown in **Figure 5**, hold the pocket and pull the thread downward. Slip the bottle in the pocket. Let the thread go and the bottom of the pocket curls up, keeping the bottle from falling out. Pull the thread and the bottle should easily slip out. If not, make adjustments to the size of the pocket for a better fit.

FIGURE 5

pulling down elastic
with thread opens
bottom

side view
of pocket

bottle drops out of
bottom of pocket

FIGURE 6   **FIGURE 7**

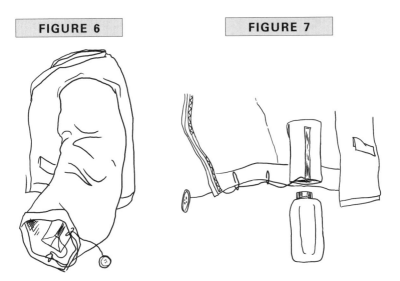

Last, remove the jacket's sleeve button and, using scissors, poke a small hole in the sleeve for the thread to fit through. Place the sneaky pocket on the Velcro strips sewn into the jacket sleeve. Lead the thread through the sleeve hole and cut it so it just reaches the button. Sew the end of the thread to the button. As shown in **Figure 6**, you can sew a paper clip or two in the sleeve as a guide for the thread. This will ensure a proper fit and a smooth release when you pull the button. With the bottle in the pocket and your arm positioned downward, you can pull the sleeve button and the bottle will slide right into the palm of your hand.

Figure 7 illustrates the same sneaky pocket design mounted at the lower side area of the jacket near the waist. Pulling on the jacket's front button causes the thread to open the bottom; your hand should be ready to grab the bottle when it falls.

Sneaky Buttons

Virtually every area of a garment can be used for sneaky subterfuge. Even the gadget jacket's buttons can be used to hide sneaky devices.

What's Needed

- Magnet
- Retractable key fob
- Buttons
- Button caps
- Velcro strips (optional)
- Paper currency

magnets

buttons

Velcro strips

What to Do

You can use the jacket's existing buttons or sew on a different type, depending on your needs. Or you can sew cloth over an item, like a compass or magnet, and sew it on an existing button as shown in **Figure 1**.

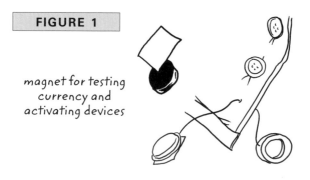

FIGURE 1

magnet for testing currency and activating devices

FIGURE 2

retractable
key fob

For an added sneaky effect, use Velcro strips to attach a mini-retractable key fob to the inside of the jacket and connect its cord to a button on the jacket's exterior, as shown in **Figure 2**.

Whenever you doubt the authenticity of paper currency, simply pull your button magnet and perform the magnetic attraction test: Fold the bill in half and set it upright on a table, as in **Figure 3**. Point the button magnet near the edge of the bill but do not touch it. A legitimate bill will move toward the magnet. See **Figure 4**.

FIGURE 3

fold bill and
set upright
on table

FIGURE 4

real bill
moves toward
button magnet

button
magnet

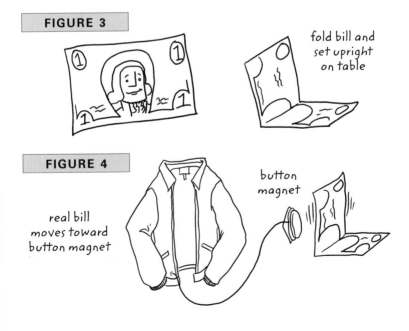

Sneaky Listener

Even when you're not wearing the gadget jacket, it can provide you with valuable information. A pair of mini walkie-talkies can be used to provide your gadget jacket with a sneaky communications system.

What's Needed

- Jacket
- Pair of mini walkie-talkies
- Candy box
- Tape (plastic or duct)

jacket

tape

walkie-talkies

What to Do

First, apply tape to cover the walkie-talkie's TALK button so it is always in the TRANSMIT mode. Then position the walkie-talkie in a candy box, punch a small hole at the location of the ON/OFF button, and put the candy box in your jacket pocket. In this manner, you can reach in and turn on the walkie-talkie while it's in the candy box. (**Figures 1 and 2**).

As shown in **Figure 3**, once you activate the ON/OFF switch and leave the jacket in a suitable location, you can use the other walkie-talkie (stored on your belt clip or in your pocket) to monitor conversations in the jacket's vicinity.

FIGURE 1

FIGURE 2

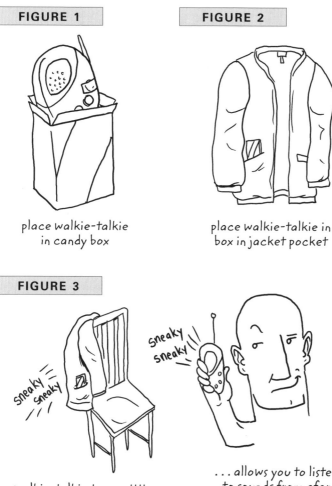

place walkie-talkie
in candy box

place walkie-talkie in
box in jacket pocket

FIGURE 3

walkie-talkie transmitting
in jacket pocket...

sneaky
sneaky

sneaky
sneaky

...allows you to listen
to sounds from afar

Sneaky Collar

The gadget jacket's collar provides a mounting location for a couple of useful sneaky devices.

What's Needed
- Jacket
- Velcro strips
- Flexible mini-light
- Two small magnets
- Small compact mirror
- Mini voice recorder

What to Do
First, sew two small Velcro squares on each side of the jacket under the collar area. This will allow you to quickly position and mount a variety of miniature devices that are available for your eyes and ears. Simply apply the other half of the Velcro squares, with its double-stick tape material, to the items of your choice. See **Figure 1**.

For example, as shown in **Figure 2**, you can mount a compact light with a flexible end to have hands-free access to a light source when required.

Want to see behind you while walking down the street or at an ATM? Glue a small magnet on the side of the flexible light's end and to a small compact mirror. Mount the mirror on the end of the shaft. This will provide you with an adjustable mount for a sneaky rearview mirror. See **Figure 2**.

Figure 3 illustrates how a mini voice recorder can be mounted under the collar, allowing you the ability to secretly record important conversations. Or you can mount the voice recorder in another location in the jacket, such as the front pocket or sleeve.

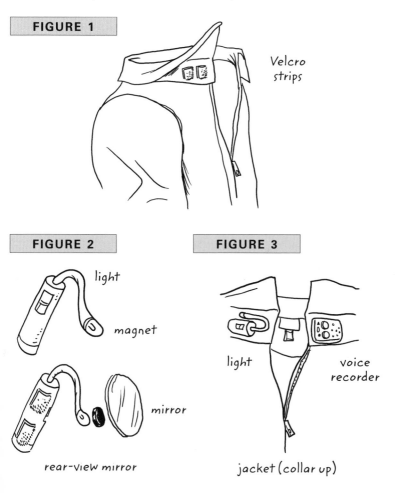

FIGURE 1

Velcro strips

FIGURE 2

light

magnet

mirror

rear-view mirror

FIGURE 3

light

voice recorder

jacket (collar up)

Portable Heater

If you've ever wished for a portable heater in a cold-weather situation, wish no longer. Using everyday items, you can make a compact portable heater that will distribute warm air to every part of your gadget jacket (and optionally your pants too).

What's Needed

- Hand-warmer heat pack (sold at drug and sporting goods stores)
- Motor from toy car or battery-powered mini-fan
- Wire
- Cardboard
- Tape

heat pack

mini-fan

wire

cardboard

tape

What to Do

Remove a motor from a toy car and tape a cardboard-made fan to its shaft. See **Figure 1**. While the fan is in the jacket, you'll need to protect its blades so they can spin freely without touching other items.

To make a fan blade protector, cut out a triangular cone shape from the cardboard and tape it to the body of the fan as shown in **Figure 2**. Turn on the fan and, if necessary, position it so the blades spin freely without touching the cardboard.

Then cut small holes in an interior pocket of the jacket (or sew another pocket inside the lining) for ventilation and place the hand warmer and fan inside. When you're cold, activate the hand

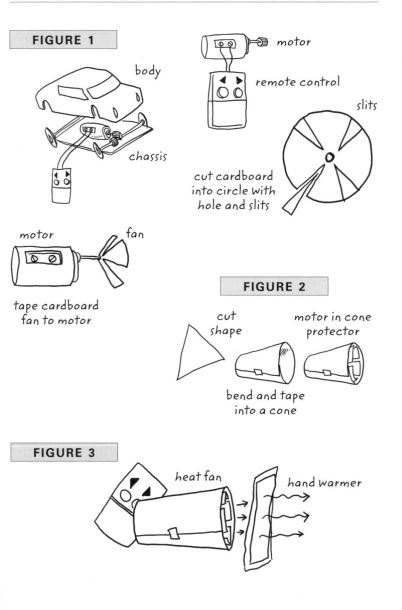

FIGURE 1

body

chassis

motor

remote control

slits

cut cardboard
into circle with
hole and slits

motor

fan

tape cardboard
fan to motor

FIGURE 2

cut
shape

motor in cone
protector

bend and tape
into a cone

FIGURE 3

heat fan

hand warmer

FIGURE 4

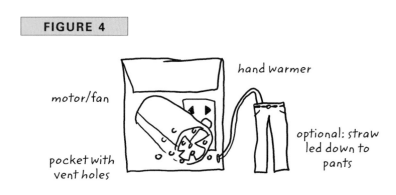

hand warmer

motor/fan

optional: straw
led down to
pants

pocket with
vent holes

warmer (follow the manufacturer's instructions) and position it near the ventilation holes so the fan will blow on it and the heat will travel from the holes to the jacket's interior, as shown in **Figure 3**.

Additionally, a long flexible straw or tube can be attached to the fan enclosure and led down the back of your pants to warm up your lower extremities. See **Figure 4**.

GOING FURTHER

The gadget jacket projects will undoubtedly provide you with sneaky fun ideas for your own personal design. **Figure 5** illustrates how all of the items will appear when installed in the jacket, along with other devices that complement the jacket's devices (like an additional walkie-talkie, sneaky pen, power ring, defense ring, sneaky watch, and sneaky shoestrings) from projects in this book and the earlier *Sneaky Uses for Everyday Things.*

Have fun devising and making your own sneaky jacket adaptations and be sure to check for additional ideas (and post your own) at www.Sneakyuses.com

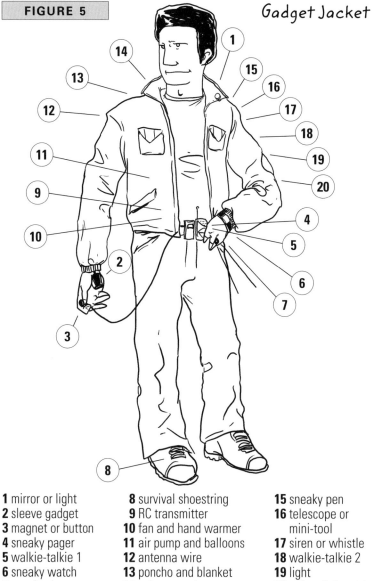

FIGURE 5

Gadget Jacket

1 mirror or light
2 sleeve gadget
3 magnet or button
4 sneaky pager
5 walkie-talkie 1
6 sneaky watch
7 sneaky ring

8 survival shoestring
9 RC transmitter
10 fan and hand warmer
11 air pump and balloons
12 antenna wire
13 poncho and blanket
14 voice recorder

15 sneaky pen
16 telescope or mini-tool
17 siren or whistle
18 walkie-talkie 2
19 light
20 safety light stick

SNEAKY NOTES

Sneakiest Uses for Everyday Things

How to Make a Boomerang with a
Business Card, Convert a Pencil into
a Microphone, Make Animated Origami,
Turn a TV Tray into a Giant Robot,
and Create Alternative Energy
Science Projects

Contents

PART I

Sneaky Science Tricks . . . 323

PART II
Sneaky Gadgets . . . 367

PART III

Part IV

Science and Technology Resources . . . 483

Acknowledgments

Special thanks to my agents, Sheree Bykofsky and Janet Rosen, for believing in the book series from the start. I want to also thank Katie Anderson, my editor at Andrews McMeel, for her invaluable insights.

I'm also grateful to the following people who helped spread the word about the first two Sneaky Uses books:

Gayle Anderson, Ira Flatow, Susan Casey, Sandy Cohen, Katey Schwartz, Cherie Courtage, Mike Suan, John Schatzel, Mark Frauenfelder, Melissa Gwynne, Steve Cochran, Christopher G. Selfridge, Timothy M. Blangger, Charles Bergquist, Phillip M. Torrone, M. K. Donaldson, Paul MacGregor, David Chang, Jessica Warren, Steve Metsch, Jenifer N. Johnson, Jerry Davich, Jerry Reno, Austin Michael, Tony Lossano, Diane Lewis, Bob Kostanczuk, Marty Griffin, Mackenzie Miller, Rebecca Schuler, Larry Elder, Dennis Prager, Carlos Daza, Paul Scott, Ronald Mitchell, and Bruce Pasarow.

I'm thankful for the project evaluation and testing assistance provided by Bill Melzer, Sybil Smith, Isaac English, and Jerry Anderson.

And a special thanks to Clyde Tymony, Helen Cooper, and my mother, Cloise Shaw, for giving me positive inspiration, a foundation in science, and a love of reading.

Introduction

"Life is what you make it."

People rarely think about the common items and devices they use in everyday life. They think even less about adapting them to perform other functions.

You can easily learn how to become a real-life MacGyver using nothing but everyday items at your disposal. It doesn't hurt to have the smarts of Einstein or the strength of Superman, but they're not necessary with *Sneakiest Uses for Everyday Things.* When life puts you in a bind, the best solution is frequently not the obvious one. It'll be the sneaky one.

Thousands of you have bought the first two books in the series, *Sneaky Uses for Everyday Things* and *Sneakier Uses for Everyday Things,* and I am immensely grateful. I've asked for feedback and listened to your requests. Some parents wanted more nontechnical, easy-to-make projects using just paper and cardboard, which they could construct with their children. Others requested updates to projects in the first two books. In addition, the desire for more science projects was made clear.

I've kept your requests in mind while writing *Sneakiest Uses for Everyday Things.* It not only has a new assortment of sneaky gadget projects but includes 30 percent more material, including the aforementioned additions. Plus, a bonus "Science and Technology Resources" section provides the information you need to further explore science experimentation and education. You'll find links to city, state, and national science fairs, camps, schools, organizations, scholarships, inventor resources and contests, grants and awards, free government programs, educator lesson plans, and science projects Web sites.

Did you know that you can turn a screw into a motor? Or a bookmark into a boomerang? Want to know what common kitchen items can be turned into a modular 6-foot robot? It's in here. Want to know how oil is refined? Or how fuel cells work or nuclear energy is produced? That's here, too. *Sneakiest Uses for Everyday Things* avoids projects or procedures that require special or expensive materials not found in the average home. No special knowledge or tools are needed.

For lovers of self-reliance and gadgetry, *Sneakiest Uses for Everyday Things* is an amazing assortment of more than fifty-five fabulous science tricks, build-it yourself projects, alternative energy experiments and simulations, updates to projects from the previous *Sneaky Uses* books, and more.

Sneakiest Uses for Everyday Things can be used in many ways. Perhaps you like to conserve resources, or the idea of getting something for nothing. You can use the book as a practical tool, a fantasy escape, or a trivia guide; it's up to you. "Things" will never appear the same again. Let's start now.

You can do more than you think!

PART I

Sneaky Science Tricks

Science is sometimes difficult to understand but you can demonstrate its principles with household items you use every day. Using nothing but paper, cardboard from product packaging, paper clips, aluminum foil, paper cups, and refrigerator magnets, you can quickly perform sneaky science tricks.

In this part of *Sneakiest Uses for Everyday Things,* you'll learn sneaky sources for wire and how to connect things. You'll be shown how to make clever center-of-gravity balancing designs, a handheld Sneaky Boomerang, and a palm-size Sneaky Mini-Boomerang.

You'll also learn how to make additional Sneaky Flyers, including a paper plate flyer, a Styrofoam glider, and a hoop ring/straw flyer; an intercom with just speakers and no power source; a pencil that acts as a microphone, a tornado in a bottle, and more.

If you have an insatiable curiosity for sneaky secrets of everyday things, look no further. You can begin demonstrating clever resourcefulness right here.

Sneaky Wire Sources

Ordinary wire can be used in many sneaky ways. You'll soon learn how it can be utilized to make a radio transmitter, a speaker, and more.

When wire is required for sneaky projects, whenever possible try to use everyday items that you might otherwise have thrown away. Recycling metal will help save our natural resources.

Getting Wired

In an emergency, you can obtain wire—or items that can be used as wire—from some very unlikely sources. **Figure 1** illustrates just a few of the possible items that you can use in case connecting wire is not available.

Ready-to-use wire can be obtained from:
    Telephone cords
    TV/VCR cables
    Headphone wire
    Earphone wire
    Speaker wire
    Wire from inside toys, radios,
        and other electrical devices

Note: Some of the sources above will have one to six separate wires inside.

Wire for projects can also be made from:
    Take-out food container handles
    Twist-ties
    Paper clips
    Envelope clasps
    Ballpoint pen springs
    Fast-food wrappers
    Potato chip bag liners

You can also use aluminum from the following items:
    Margarine wrappers
    Ketchup and condiment packages
    Breath mint container labels
    Chewing gum wrappers
    Trading card packaging
    Coffee creamer container lids

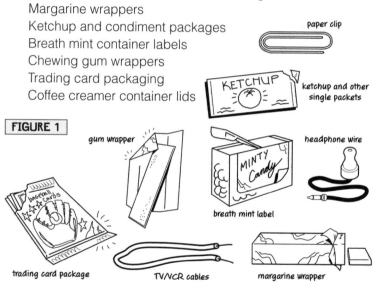

FIGURE 1

paper clip

ketchup and other single packets

gum wrapper

headphone wire

MINTY Candy

breath mint label

trading card package

TV/VCR cables

margarine wrapper

Note: The wire used from the sources above are only to be used for low-voltage, battery-powered projects.
    Use special care when handling fragile aluminum materials. In some instances, aluminum may be coated with a wax or plastic coating that you may be able to remove.

You can cut strips of aluminum material from food wrappers easily enough. With smaller items—such as aluminum obtained from a coffee cream container—use the sneaky cutting pattern shown in **Figure 2**.

Making resourceful use of items to make sneaky wire is not only intriguing, it's fun.

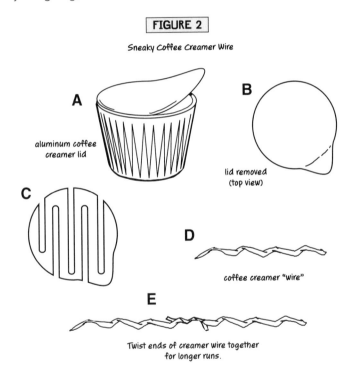

FIGURE 2

Sneaky Coffee Creamer Wire

A aluminum coffee creamer lid

B lid removed (top view)

C

D coffee creamer "wire"

E Twist ends of creamer wire together for longer runs.

How to Connect Things

The "Getting Wired" project illustrated how to obtain wire from everyday things. Now you'll learn how to connect the wires to provide consistent performance. (A tight connection is crucial to the operation of electrical projects, otherwise faulty and erratic result may occur.)

Figure 1 shows a piece of insulated wire. The insulation material must be stripped away to make a metal-to-metal connection to other electrical parts. Strip away about one to two inches of insulation from both ends of the wire. See **Figure 2**.

To connect the wire to another wire lead, wrap both ends around each other, as shown in **Figure 3**.

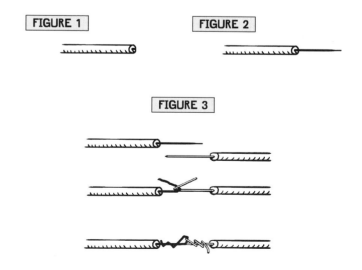

When connecting the wire to the end of a stiff lead (such as the end of an LED), wrap the wire around the lead and bend the lead back over the wire. See **Figure 4**.

To connect wire to the end of a small battery, bend the wire into a circular shape, place it on the battery terminal, and wrap the connection tightly with tape, as shown in **Figure 5**.

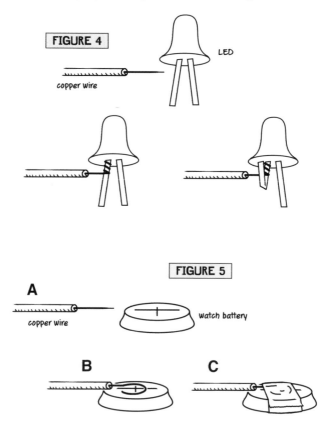

Electricity Fun-damentals

Many forms of alternative energy, including wind, thermal, hydro, even nuclear, are used to generate electrical power. This is accomplished by moving blades (wind or hydro) or heating water into steam (thermal or nuclear) to turn an electrical generator. The following projects illustrate how electrical power is produced and the relationship between electricity and magnetism.

What's Needed
- Transparent tape
- Two D-size batteries
- Wire
- Compass
- Two small, strong magnets
- Bolt
- Paper clips

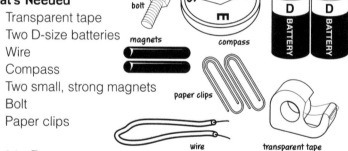

bolt
magnets
compass
D-size batteries
paper clips
wire
transparent tape

What to Do

When electricity flows through a wire, a magnetic field is produced around it. To test this, first tape the two D-size batteries together and place them near a length of wire. Next, set the compass near the wire and hold the ends of the wire to both battery terminals (only for a few seconds), and you'll see the compass pointer move. See **Figure 1**.

Position the wire vertically in a small loop shape and touch the battery terminals. Bring a magnet close to the wire as you connect and disconnect the wire, and you'll see the wire move because it has become an electromagnet. See **Figure 2**.

If you wrap wire thirty times around a bolt and connect it to the battery terminals, it will become an electromagnet. **Figure 3** shows how it can attract and lift paper clips.

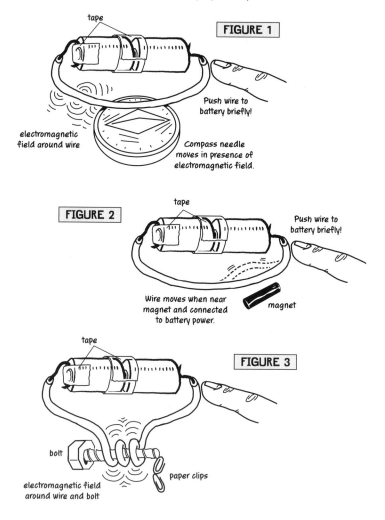

tape

FIGURE 1

Push wire to battery briefly!

electromagnetic field around wire

Compass needle moves in presence of electromagnetic field.

tape

FIGURE 2

Push wire to battery briefly!

Wire moves when near magnet and connected to battery power.

magnet

tape

FIGURE 3

bolt

paper clips

electromagnetic field around wire and bolt

Simple Electrical Circuits

To test an item's conductivity (the ability to let electricity to flow through it), use a flashlight bulb or an LED (light emitting diode). An LED is used in most electronic devices and toys as a function indicator because it draws very little electrical current, operates with very little heat, and has no filament to burn out.

Lay a 3-volt watch battery on the item, as shown in **Figure 1**. If the lightbulb or LED lights, then the item can be used as wire for battery-powered projects.

Note: If the bulb or LED does not light, reverse the connections of its leads and test it again. LEDs are polarity (direction) sensitive.

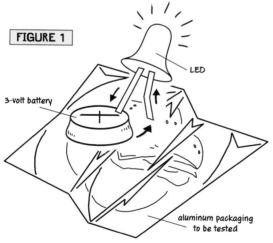

FIGURE 1

LED

3-volt battery

aluminum packaging
to be tested

Current flows from the battery's negative (-) terminal to the aluminum foil to the LED to the battery's positive (+) terminal in a circle.

Figure 2 shows a simple electrical circuit that consists of a battery, connecting wire, and a lightbulb. Power flows in a circle (*circuit* means "circle") from the negative battery terminal to the light and back to the positive battery terminal.

When using one 1 1/2-volt battery in a circuit, you must use a lightbulb rated the same voltage. This applies to whatever else you may want to turn on, such as a buzzer or motor.

LEDs generally require two to three volts (unless otherwise noted) to turn on, so connect two 1 1/2-volt batteries in series (end to end) to activate an LED.

Figure 3 illustrates how to do this. If the LED does not turn on, reverse its leads and test it again.

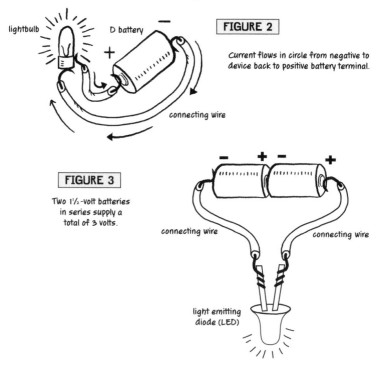

lightbulb   D battery   —

FIGURE 2

Current flows in circle from negative to device back to positive battery terminal.

connecting wire

FIGURE 3

Two 1 1/2-volt batteries in series supply a total of 3 volts.

—   + —   +

connecting wire

connecting wire

light emitting diode (LED)

Sneaky Balance Tricks

You can make everyday things balance in sneaky ways when you know the secret to determining the center of gravity. The center of gravity is the point in an object at which its mass is in equilibrium. Where this point is depends on the object's shape and weight distribution, and you can produce some attention-getting creations with this knowledge.

The following four projects are easy to do with items found just about everywhere.

Sneaky Balancer I

Knowing how to lower the center of gravity of an object allows you to produce figures that seemingly defy gravity (or make you seem like a skilled magician). This project demonstrates what happens when two similar cardboard figures have their center of gravity in different positions.

What's Needed

    Scissors
    Cardboard, a piece 8 1/2 by 11 inches
    Optional:
    Sewing thread

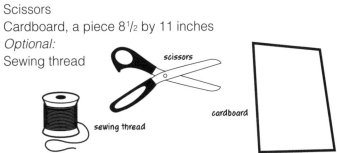

What to Do

Cut out the small shape shown in **Figure 1** from the piece of cardboard. Follow the dimensions shown. Next, try to balance the head of the figure on your fingertip, as shown in **Figure 2**. It's almost impossible to keep it upright without its tipping over.

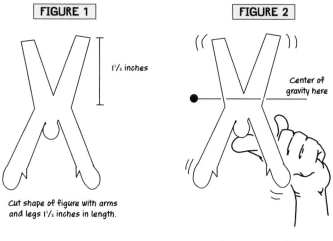

FIGURE 1

1¹/₂ inches

Cut shape of figure with arms and legs 1¹/₂ inches in length.

FIGURE 2

Center of gravity here

Try to balance the figure's head on your finger, and the figure falls.

Next, cut out the figure shown in **Figure 3**. The only difference is the legs are much longer. Try to balance this larger figure on your hand. It's easy now, because the center of gravity is below your finger. See **Figure 4**. You should be able to walk around the room and the figure will not fall.

Going Further

To demonstrate how acrobats keep their balance, cut a small slit in the head of the figure. See **Figure 5**.

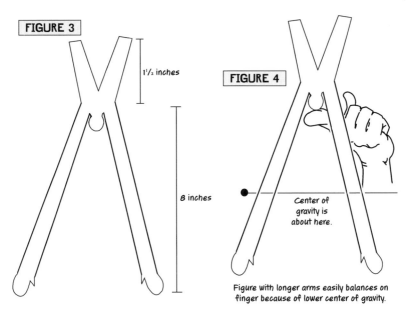

FIGURE 3

1¹/₂ inches

8 inches

FIGURE 4

Center of gravity is about here.

Figure with longer arms easily balances on finger because of lower center of gravity.

Then, tie a length of thread from a chair to a lower object, such as another chair or table, and set the figure on the thread. The figure should rest on the thread in its slit and, with a slight push, slide across without falling. See **Figure 6**.

FIGURE 5

Cut slit in head.

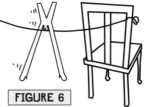

FIGURE 6

The figure can slide down inclined thread without falling off thread.

Sneaky Balancer II

This sneaky balancer can rest horizontally on the tip of a paper clip and will surely astonish onlookers.

What's Needed

Scissors
Cardboard
Paper clip

scissors

cardboard

large paper clip

What to Do

Cut out the figure shown in **Figure 1** from the piece of cardboard. Be sure to include the spiked hair, with a long center spike. Try to adhere to the dimensions shown but, if desired, you can produce a larger or smaller figure as long as you keep the arm and body lengths in proportion.

Bend the figure's arms down at the shoulder and elbows. See **Figure 2**.

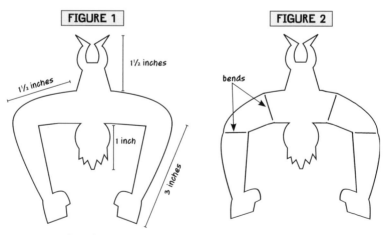

| FIGURE 1 | FIGURE 2 |

1½ inches

1½ inches

1 inch

3 inches

bends

Cut out figure from cardboard box.

Bend down the arms of the figure.

Next, bend a paper clip, as shown in **Figure 3**, so one end stands up vertically.

Last, place the figure on the paper clip with the spiked hair resting on the tip. If necessary, bend the arms down so it won't fall. The figure should balance on the tip of the paper clip. You should be able to carefully push its legs to the right or left and it will stay aloft. See **Figure 4**.

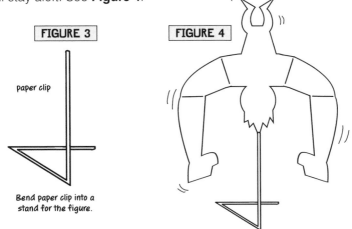

| FIGURE 3 |

paper clip

Bend paper clip into a stand for the figure.

| FIGURE 4 |

Gently rest head of figure on tip of paper clip and it will magically balance.

Sneaky Balancer III

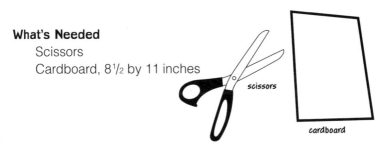

What's Needed
   Scissors
   Cardboard, 8½ by 11 inches

scissors

cardboard

What to Do

Cut out the shape shown in **Figure 1** from the cardboard. Be careful to follow the dimensions shown.

You should be able to easily balance the figure on the tip of your finger, elbow, or nose, because its center of gravity is at the large circular area. See **Figure 2**.

You can create similar figures and, using paper clips or coins secured with tape, add weight to an area near the bottom section of the figure so it balances effortlessly.

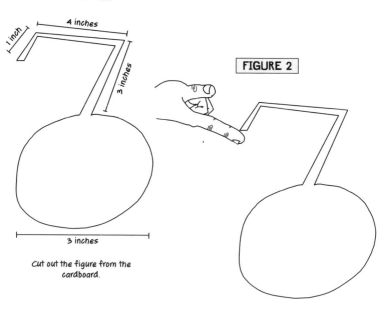

FIGURE 1

4 inches

1 inch

3 inches

3 inches

Cut out the figure from the cardboard.

FIGURE 2

Since the center of gravity is low, the figure will balance easily.

Sneaky Balancer IV

What's Needed
   One quarter
   Two metal forks
   Drinking cup

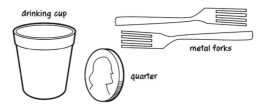

What to Do
Place the quarter between the teeth of the two forks as shown in
Figure 1.

   If a lightweight cup is used, you must fill it with water so
it will not tip over. If a heavy cup or jar is used, water is not
required.

   Carefully rest the edge of the quarter on the lip of the cup.
You should be able to let go and the forks will stay aloft. If
they don't, adjust the angle of the forks until they balance. See
Figure 2.

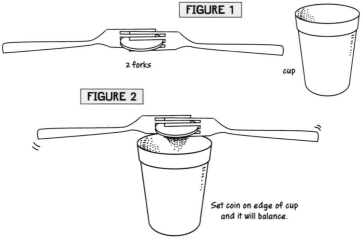

FIGURE 1

2 forks

cup

FIGURE 2

Set coin on edge of cup
and it will balance.

Sneaky Flyers

Sneaky Demonstrations of Air Pressure and Wing Lift
Have you ever wondered how airplanes and helicopters are able to fly? If you have, and want to demonstrate this principle, all you need are such ordinary items as straws, postcards, and strips of paper.

Air Pressure Demonstration I

An ordinary straw can be used to demonstrate that air pressure is all around us (15 pounds per square inch, to be exact). You can demonstrate this easily enough with everyday items.

What's Needed
    Straw
    Glass filled with water

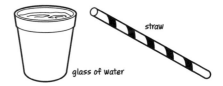
glass of water   straw

What to Do
Insert a straw into the glass of water, as shown in **Figure 1**. Next, place a finger over the top of the straw and lift it out of the water. See **Figure 2**.

You'll see that the water stays in the straw and doesn't flow out because air pressure from the bottom is keeping it in, as shown in **Figure 3**. When you lift your finger from the top of the straw, air pressure flows from the top and pushes against the water, forcing it out.

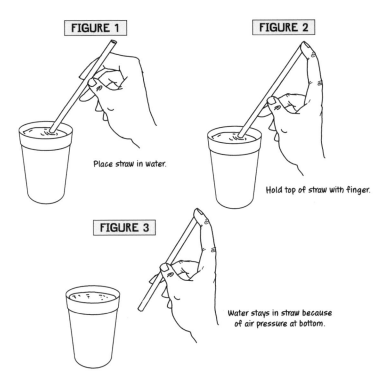

FIGURE 1

Place straw in water.

FIGURE 2

Hold top of straw with finger.

FIGURE 3

Water stays in straw because
of air pressure at bottom.

Air Pressure Demonstration II

You can demonstrate the power of air pressure in a more
dramatic way with the following project, again using everyday
items.

What's Needed
    Glass filled to the brim with water
    Plastic-coated postcard

postcard

glass of water

What to Do

Working over a sink, hold up the glass of water. Place a postcard over the mouth of the glass and turn the glass upside down, holding the postcard in place with your finger under it, as shown in **Figure 1**.

Carefully remove your finger from the postcard and you should see that the postcard will not fall. With no air in the glass to push against the postcard, the air outside presses against the postcard, keeping it in place, even with the weight of the water upon it. See **Figure 2**.

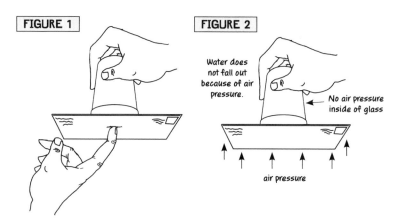

FIGURE 1

FIGURE 2

Water does not fall out because of air pressure.

No air pressure inside of glass

air pressure

Air Pressure Demonstration III

What's Needed
    Paper (preferably a paper
       towel or napkin)
    Scissors

paper towel

scissors

What to Do

Cut a paper strip ½ inch wide by 4 inches in length as shown in **Figure 1**. Hold the paper strip up to your face above your mouth and blow. The paper naturally moves upward. Now hold the paper strip just below your lips and blow above the strip. As shown in **Figure 2**, the paper will also rise and move upward!

This occurs because of Bernoulli's principle, which states that fast-moving air has less pressure than nonmoving air. The air under the strip has more pressure than the air above it and pushes the strip upward.

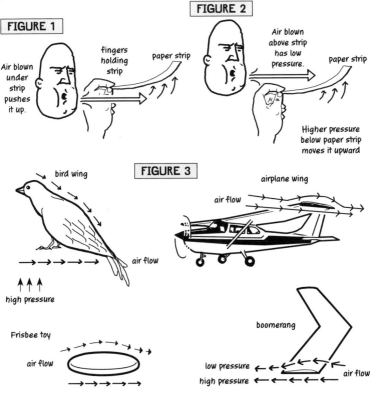

FIGURE 1

Air blown under strip pushes it up.

fingers holding strip

paper strip

FIGURE 2

Air blown above strip has low pressure.

paper strip

Higher pressure below paper strip moves it upward

FIGURE 3

bird wing

air flow

high pressure

airplane wing

air flow

Frisbee toy

air flow

boomerang

low pressure

high pressure

air flow

Figure 3 illustrates a side view of a bird's wing, an airplane wing, a Frisbee flying disk, and a boomerang. Notice the top of the wing curves upward and has a longer surface as compared to the bottom. When the airplane moves forward, air moves above and below the wing. The air moving along the curved top must travel farther and faster than the air moving past the flat bottom surface. The faster-moving air has less pressure than the air at the bottom and this provides lift.

Baseball pitchers can take advantage of Bernoulli's principle by releasing the ball with a forward spin. The ball produces a lower pressure below it, causing it to dip when it reaches the plate. Hence, a curveball. See **Figure 4**.

Sailboats apply Bernoulli's principle to use the wind, regardless of its direction, to propel the boat in any desired direction. **Figure 5** shows how altering the shape of the sail into a curve produces an effect similar to that of an airplane wing. The wind moves at a faster rate over the curved side, with a lower pressure, and the higher pressure on the other side of the sail pushes the boat laterally. A centerboard, attached to the boat hull, prevents the boat from moving sideways while allowing it to use the wind thrust to move forward. See **Figure 6**.

Automobile bodies are similar to an airplane wing because they are flat on the bottom and curved on top. They can lose stability at high speeds since they tend to achieve lift from the higher air pressure below, as shown in **Figure 7**. To reduce the Bernoulli effect, automakers have incorporated improvements in vehicle design, such as lowering the body height, adding special front bumper and fender contours, and installing rear spoilers. See **Figure 8**.

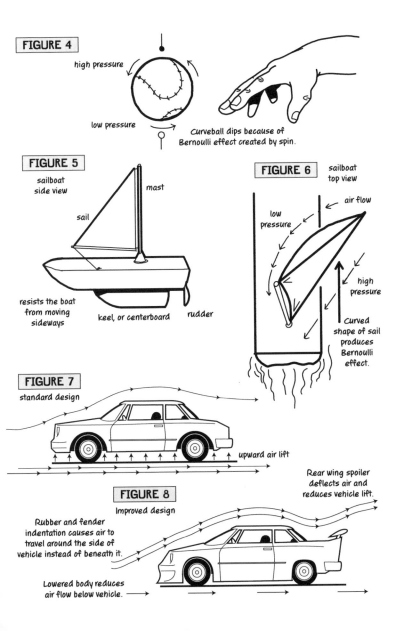

FIGURE 4

high pressure

low pressure

Curveball dips because of
Bernoulli effect created by spin.

FIGURE 5

sailboat
side view

mast

sail

resists the boat
from moving
sideways

keel, or centerboard   rudder

FIGURE 6   sailboat
top view

air flow

low
pressure

high
pressure

Curved
shape of sail
produces
Bernoulli
effect.

FIGURE 7

standard design

upward air lift

Rear wing spoiler
deflects air and
reduces vehicle lift.

FIGURE 8

Improved design

Rubber and fender
indentation causes air to
travel around the side of
vehicle instead of beneath it.

Lowered body reduces
air flow below vehicle. ⟶

Air Pressure Demonstration IV

What's Needed

Scissors
Paper (preferably a paper
    towel or napkin)
Two empty soda cans
Magazine

scissors

paper towel

magazine

soda cans

What to Do

Cut two paper strips ½ inch wide by 4 inches in length and
hold them about 2 inches apart, as shown in **Figure 1**. Blow air
between the paper strips and watch what occurs. You would
expect the strips to blow apart but they actually come together,
as shown in **Figure 2**.

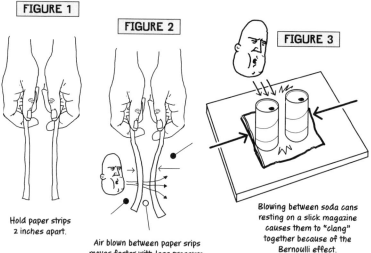

FIGURE 1

Hold paper strips
2 inches apart.

FIGURE 2

Air blown between paper srips
moves faster with less pressure,
causing them to move together.

FIGURE 3

Blowing between soda cans
resting on a slick magazine
causes them to "clang"
together because of the
Bernoulli effect.

Bernoulli's principle is working here because the faster-moving air blown between the paper strips has less pressure than the air on the other side of the paper. This higher pressure pushes the strips toward each other.

Now, place the two empty soda cans an inch apart upon the slick surface of a magazine. When you blow between the cans, they will move toward each other, producing a clanging sound. See **Figure 3**.

Air Pressure Demonstration V

Here's another sneaky, easy-to-perform demonstration of air pressure's causing an unexpected result.

What's Needed
    Scissors
    Piece of paper

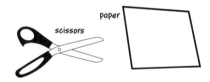

What to Do
Cut the piece of paper into a 5 by 3-inch shape. Fold the paper in half lengthwise, as shown in **Figure 1**.

Next, unfold the paper and place it on a flat surface so that it has a slight rise near its center crease. See **Figure 2**.

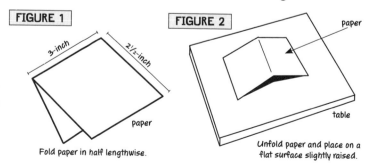

FIGURE 1

3-inch

2½-inch

paper

Fold paper in half lengthwise.

FIGURE 2

paper

table

Unfold paper and place on a
flat surface slightly raised.

Then, as shown in **Figure 3**, bring your face close to the surface of the table and blow underneath the paper.

You would expect the paper to rise but it actually flattens downward. The higher air pressure on top of the paper, compared to the fast-moving air beneath it, pushes the paper flat on the table, as shown in **Figure 4**.

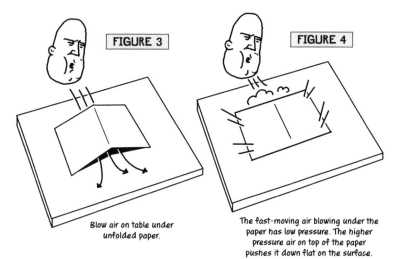

Blow air on table under
unfolded paper.

The fast-moving air blowing under the
paper has low pressure. The higher
pressure air on top of the paper
pushes it down flat on the surface.

Air Pressure Demonstration VI

You can use Bernoulli's principle to perform a neat magic trick by making a ball rise from a cup and jump into another one without touching it.

Ping-Pong ball

What's Needed
  Ping-Pong ball
  Two small cups

small cups

What to Do

This project requires small cups that are slightly smaller in diameter than the Ping-Pong ball. Since the Ping-Pong ball can barely fit in the cup, rapidly moving air above the ball will not affect the air pressure beneath it.

Put the ball into one of the cups and place it about 3 inches away from the second cup, as shown in **Figure 1**. Blow as hard as you can above the first cup and the ball should start to rise. See **Figure 2**. The force of your breath will push the raised Ping-Pong ball over to the empty cup, where it will drop inside, as shown in **Figure 3**. With a little practice, you can make this sneaky trick work every time.

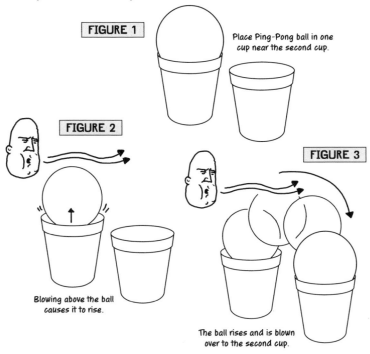

FIGURE 1

Place Ping-Pong ball in one cup near the second cup.

FIGURE 2

Blowing above the ball causes it to rise.

FIGURE 3

The ball rises and is blown over to the second cup.

Sneaky Flying Disk

You've seen how Bernoulli's principle works. Now it's time to put it to use and make a sneaky flyer, similar to flying disk toys, using paper and tape.

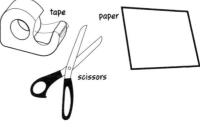

What's Needed
>   Scissors
>   Paper, 8$\frac{1}{2}$ x 11 inches
>   Transparent tape

What to Do

Cut eight 2-inch square pieces of paper as shown in **Figure 1**. Fold the top right corner of one square down to the lower left corner. See **Figure 2**. Then, fold the top left corner down to the bottom, as shown in **Figure 3**.

Repeat these two folds with the remaining seven squares. See **Figure 4**.

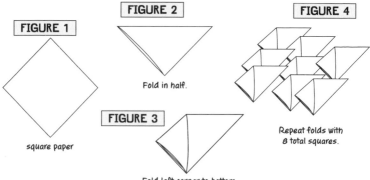

FIGURE 2

Fold in half.

FIGURE 1

square paper

FIGURE 3

Fold left corner to bottom.

FIGURE 4

Repeat folds with 8 total squares.

Insert one paper figure into the left pocket of another, as shown in **Figure 5**. Repeat inserting the figures into one another until they form an eight-sided doughnut shape; see **Figure 6**. Apply tape as needed to keep the origami flyer together and turn over, as shown in **Figure 7**.

Next, bend up the outer edge of the sneaky flyer to form a lip, as shown in **Figure 8**. This outer lip will cause the air to take a longer path over it, producing a Bernoulli effect.

Turn the device so the lip is bent downward. Throw the Sneaky Flying Disk with a quick snap of your wrist and it should stay aloft for a great distance.

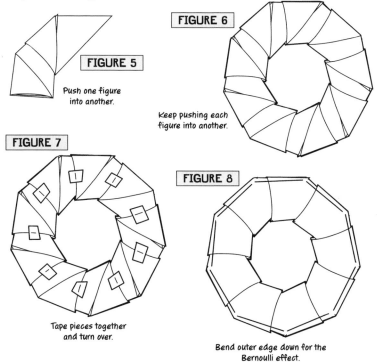

FIGURE 5

Push one figure into another.

FIGURE 6

Keep pushing each figure into another.

FIGURE 7

Tape pieces together and turn over.

FIGURE 8

Bend outer edge down for the Bernoulli effect.

Sneaky Boomerang

Want a sneaky way to play catch alone? You just need a piece of cardboard and foam rubber to make a working boomerang that will actually fly up to 30 feet away and return.

What's Needed

Scissors
Cardboard from a food box
Foam rubber, from an old pillow
Transparent tape

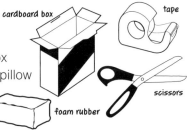

What to Do

Cut the cardboard into the boomerang shape shown in **Figure 1**. Each wing of the boomerang should be 9 inches long by 2 inches wide.

Then, cut two foam pieces into 6 by 2-inch oval shapes with one side rising into a curve. The rising shape should resemble the side view of an airplane wing. See **Figure 2**. Place the oval foam pieces on the leading edges of the boomerang and secure them with tape.

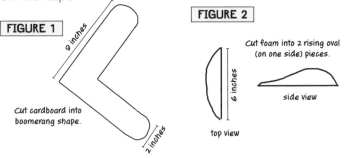

FIGURE 1

9 inches

2 inches

Cut cardboard into boomerang shape.

FIGURE 2

Cut foam into 2 rising oval (on one side) pieces.

6 inches

top view

side view

Note: Look carefully at the placement of the ovals on the boomerang wings in **Figure 3** before taping them. The foam creates a curved shape on the boomerang wing, which will cause air to move faster across its top than across the bottom surface. This will produce lift for the boomerang.

Hold the boomerang as if you were going to throw a baseball and throw it straight overhead (not to the side). See **Figure 4**. The Sneaky Boomerang should fly straight and return to the left. Experiment with different angles of throw to obtain a desired return pattern.

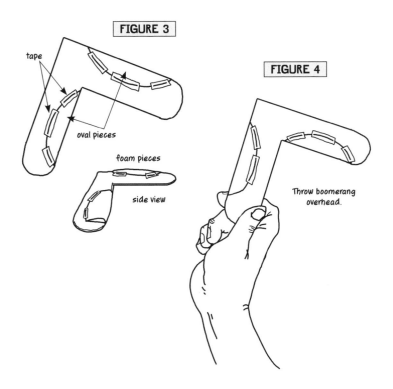

Sneaky Mini-Boomerang

You can use postcards, business cards, or cardboard food boxes to make a miniature, palm-size boomerang that actually flies and returns to you, for indoor fun.

What's Needed

Scissors
Cardboard from food
    boxes or postcards

What to Do

Cut out the boomerang shapes shown in **Figure 1**. The boomerang wings can be any length between 2 to 4 inches. For optimal flight height and return performance, cut each wing of the boomerang 2½ inches long and ½ inch wide.

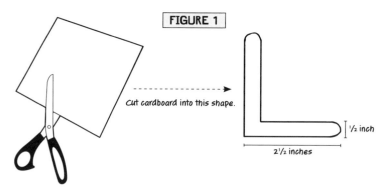

Set the Sneaky Mini-Boomerang on the palm of your raised hand with one wing hanging off. Tilt your hand slightly upward. With your other hand's thumb and middle finger $1/2$ inch away, snap the outer boomerang wing. You'll discover (after a few attempts) that it will fly forward and return to you. See **Figure 2**.

Note: You must snap your finger with a strong snapping action to make the boomerang fly away and return properly, as shown in **Figure 3**.

Experiment with different hand positions and angles to control the boomerang's flight pattern.

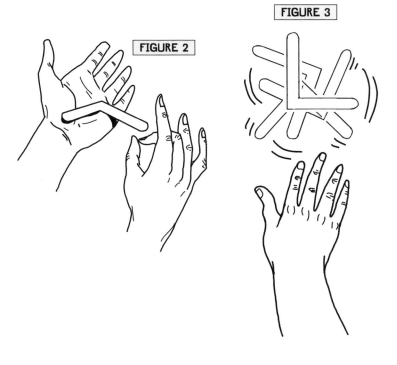

FIGURE 3

FIGURE 2

Sneaky Gliders

You don't have to spend money on a balsa wood kit to make a simple working glider. A working glider, made from discarded cardboard or Styrofoam material, can produce plenty of sneaky flyers for safe fun.

What's Needed

Scissors
Flat corrugated cardboard or Styrofoam
Transparent tape

tape

corrugated cardboard

scissors

What to Do

The sneaky glider body, or fuselage, can be cut out from the pattern shown in **Figure 1**. The plane will require at least one wing near the center for stability. A smaller wing near the rear rudder can also be added. Simply insert the wing(s) into the body slits and use tape to secure them properly as shown in **Figure 2**.

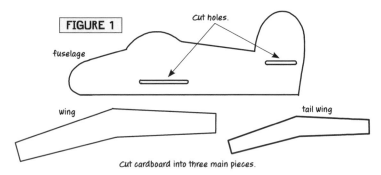

FIGURE 1

Cut holes.

fuselage

wing

tail wing

Cut cardboard into three main pieces.

Launch the Sneaky Glider with a snap of the wrist near your ear and it should fly up to 30 feet away. See **Figure 3**. Test the glider wing(s) shapes to achieve various flight paths as desired.

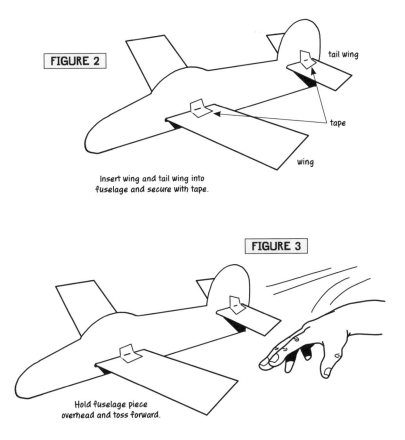

FIGURE 2

tail wing

tape

wing

Insert wing and tail wing into fuselage and secure with tape.

FIGURE 3

Hold fuselage piece overhead and toss forward.

Sneaky Hoop Paper Flyer

Paper airplane designs are not hard to find. But if you want to stand out from the crowd, make this unique sneaky flyer using just a straw and paper.

What's Needed
Scissors
Sheet of paper
Tape
Straight drinking straw

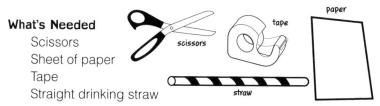

What to Do

First, cut two paper strips ½ inch wide by 4 inches long and then tape each strip into a loop, as shown in **Figure 1**. Next, tape a loop to each end of the straw. See **Figure 2**.

Now launch the sneaky straw flyer with your hand as if you were throwing a dart. It should fly up to 40 feet away.

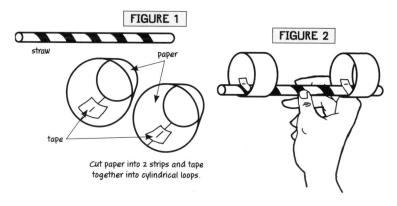

FIGURE 1

Cut paper into 2 strips and tape together into cylindrical loops.

FIGURE 2

Sneaky Soaring Cylinder

Paper airplanes don't have to have a standard-looking shape to glide long distances. Believe it or not, you can fold an ordinary piece of paper into the shape of a cup and amaze your friends with a Sneaky Soaring Cylinder.

What's Needed

paper

Sheet of paper

What to Do

First, fold the left side of the paper 2 inches to the right, as shown in **Figure 1**. Next, fold the paper from the left side one more inch, and crease it firmly. See **Figure 2**.

Roll the paper into a cylinder, then slide one end of the paper into the other end's folded-over area, as shown in **Figure 3**. Push the left side of the paper into the right side until about two inches' worth is securely in place. Then, roll over and firmly crease the edge of the folded paper into a lip to secure it. See **Figures 4** and **5**.

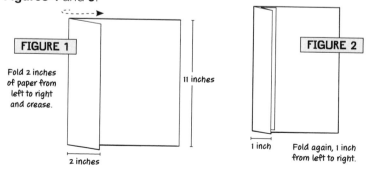

FIGURE 1

Fold 2 inches of paper from left to right and crease.

11 inches

2 inches

FIGURE 2

1 inch

Fold again, 1 inch from left to right.

Next, bend over the top layer of paper into a fin shape, shown in **Figure 6**, so it stands vertically. This will act as a wind stabilizer to keep the cylinder in the air.

Last, toss the cylinder like a football, but don't add a spinning motion. See **Figure 7**. The Sneaky Soaring Cylinder should fly up to 40 feet away. Experiment with the shape of the stabilizer fin to achieve the desired various flight paths.

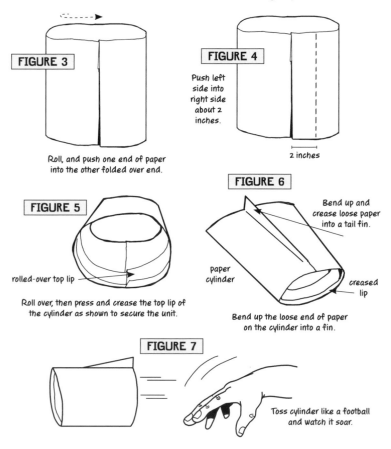

FIGURE 3

Roll, and push one end of paper into the other folded over end.

FIGURE 4

Push left side into right side about 2 inches.

2 inches

FIGURE 5

rolled-over top lip

Roll over, then press and crease the top lip of the cylinder as shown to secure the unit.

FIGURE 6

Bend up and crease loose paper into a tail fin.

paper cylinder

creased lip

Bend up the loose end of paper on the cylinder into a fin.

FIGURE 7

Toss cylinder like a football and watch it soar.

Sneaky Intercom

Like motors and generators, speakers are made with magnets
and coils of wires. By connecting two of them together with
connecting wire, you can create a sneaky intercom that requires
no external power source. This project also demonstrates the
versatility of coils of wire and magnets.

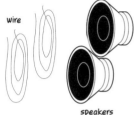

wire

speakers

What's Needed

    2 speakers (not mounted in a case)
    Fifty feet (or more) of wire,
        cut into two wires

What to Do

As illustrated in **Figure 1**, connect both wires to each speaker
and wrap them tightly around the lug connections. If you
carefully press the cone of one speaker, the other should move.

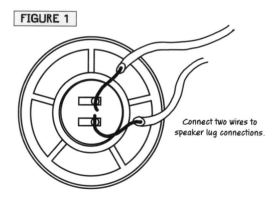

FIGURE 1

Connect two wires to
speaker lug connections.

Pressing the speaker cone, with the speaker coil, or voice coil, of wire attached to it generates an electrical current as it moves near the speaker's internal magnet. This current travels through the wire and into the other speaker's coil, creating an electromagnetic field. This causes its voice coil to repel against the magnet and move rapidly, producing sound.

The field is repelled by the speaker's magnet and moves slightly. Now, with the speakers separated, talk loudly in one speaker and have a friend listen to the other, as shown in **Figure 2**.

Your voice will be heard. Congratulations, you've just completed a no-electrical-power-supplied Sneaky Intercom.

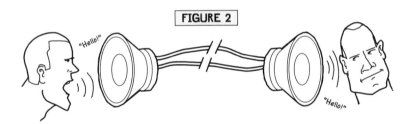

FIGURE 2

Sneaky Pencil Microphone

A typical pencil contains graphite (not actual lead) that can be used as a resistor. A resistor impedes the flow of electrical current and, if its value is varied, can carry sound in an electrical circuit.

A bare pencil lead placed on two others can act as a microphone.

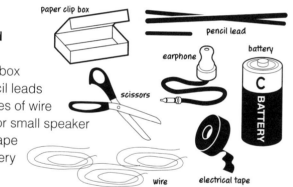

paper clip box

pencil lead

earphone

battery

scissors

C BATTERY

wire

electrical tape

What's Needed

Scissors
Paper clip box
Three pencil leads
Three pieces of wire
Earphone or small speaker
Electrical tape
C-size battery

What to Do

Cut four holes in the box and slide two pencil leads into the holes, as shown in **Figure 1**. Next, lay the third lead rod, broken to be half the length of the others, on the other two, as shown in **Figure 2**.

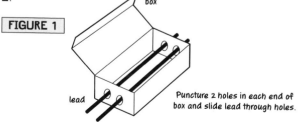

FIGURE 1

box

lead

Puncture 2 holes in each end of box and slide lead through holes.

Connect two of the wires to the earphone/speaker. Of those two, connect one to a pencil lead sticking out of the box and the other to the battery terminal, using tape to secure it. Then tape the third wire from the battery and connect it to the other pencil lead. See **Figure 3**.

Now bring your mouth close to the small rod of lead and speak loudly. The sound will be heard from the speaker. Your voice moves the pencil lead on the other two pieces and changes its resistance level, which modulates the current flow. The earphone reproduces this as sound waves.

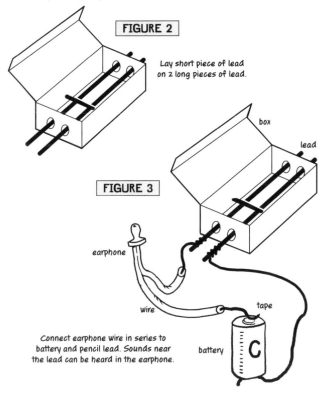

FIGURE 2

Lay short piece of lead on 2 long pieces of lead.

box

lead

FIGURE 3

earphone

wire

tape

battery

Connect earphone wire in series to battery and pencil lead. Sounds near the lead can be heard in the earphone.

Sneaky Tornado in a Bottle

You can produce a simulation of a tornado, using two-liter bottles and a few other common household items.

What's Needed

electrical tape

two-liter bottles

Two empty two-liter bottles,
    washed and dried
Scissors
Stiff, flat plastic from product
    packaging, or a 1-inch washer
Electrical tape

scissors

flat plastic

What to Do

Fill one bottle with water nearly all of the way to the top. See **Figure 1**.

Cut a 1-inch circle from the piece of stiff plastic, then cut a small hole in the center, ³⁄₈ inch in diameter, as shown in **Figure 2**, or use a 1-inch washer.

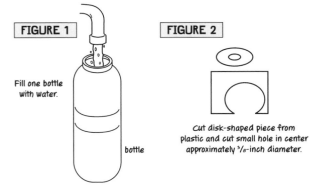

FIGURE 1

Fill one bottle
with water.

bottle

FIGURE 2

Cut disk-shaped piece from
plastic and cut small hole in center
approximately ³⁄₈-inch diameter.

Place the disk on top of the bottle filled with water, as shown in **Figure 3**, and place the other bottle on top of it (mouth to mouth), as shown in **Figure 4**. Wrap electrical tape tightly around the two bottle threads, as shown in **Figure 5**.

Turn the bottles upside down. As the water flows from the top to the bottom, air from the lower bottle will flow into the top, forming a swirling tornado-like vortex. See **Figure 6**. If this does not happen immediately or if the water just slowly drips down, shake the bottles to start the water flowing.

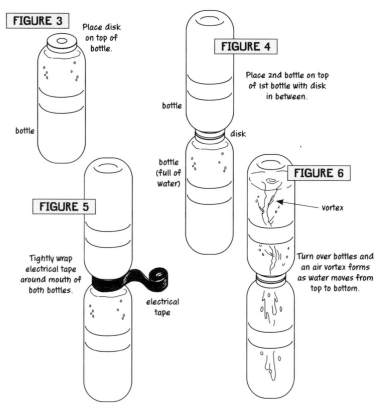

FIGURE 3
Place disk on top of bottle.
bottle

FIGURE 4
Place 2nd bottle on top of 1st bottle with disk in between.
bottle
disk
bottle (full of water)

FIGURE 5
Tightly wrap electrical tape around mouth of both bottles.
electrical tape

FIGURE 6
vortex
Turn over bottles and an air vortex forms as water moves from top to bottom.

PART II

Sneaky Gadgets

If you're curious about the sneaky adaptation possibilities of household devices, you're in the right place. People frequently throw away damaged gadgets and toys without realizing they can serve additional purposes.

This part of *Sneakiest Uses for Everyday Things* presents sneaky adaptation methods to make paper into animated origami designs, sugar into glass, a cup into a calculator, a quiz tester, motors, and robots, including a version that's six feet tall.

All the items have tested safe and can be made in no time. If you enjoy the idea of high-tech resourcefulness, the following projects will undoubtedly provide plenty of resourceful ideas.

You, too, can do more with less!

Sneaky Animated Origami

Paper folding is fun but you can enhance your enjoyment by making the following sneaky origami designs that include motion action using everyday things.

Sneaky Head-Bobbing Bird

What's Needed
  Scissors
  Paper
  Pencil

pencil

scissors

paper

What to Do
Cut the paper into a square and fold/unfold both the diagonals, as shown in **Figure 1**. Fold over the top left and right corners to the center. See **Figure 2**.

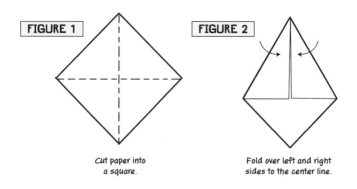

FIGURE 1

Cut paper into
a square.

FIGURE 2

Fold over left and right
sides to the center line.

Then, fold over the lower left and right corners toward the center as shown in **Figure 3**. Fold up the bottom point to the center line to form a tail and fold the top corner toward the back of the figure to make the head, as shown in **Figures 4** and **5**.

Next, fold the figure in half vertically along the center toward the tail. This will bend the tail and head outward as shown in **Figure 6**. Draw eyes and a beak on the figure as desired.

Last, with the sneaky bird standing upright, push down on the center of the tail. The head should move downward. See **Figure 7**.

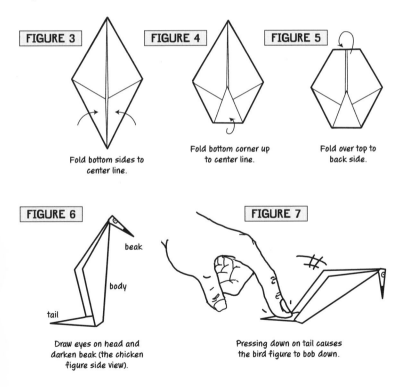

FIGURE 3

Fold bottom sides to center line.

FIGURE 4

Fold bottom corner up to center line.

FIGURE 5

Fold over top to back side.

FIGURE 6

beak

body

tail

Draw eyes on head and darken beak (the chicken figure side view).

FIGURE 7

Pressing down on tail causes the bird figure to bob down.

Sneaky Mouth Flapper

What's Needed

Scissors
Paper
Pencil

pencil   scissors   paper

What to Do

Cut the paper into a square, as shown in **Figure 1**. Next, fold and unfold the square on both the diagonals. Fold over the lower left and right corners to the center. See **Figure 2**.

Then, fold over the upper left and right corners toward the center, as shown in **Figure 3**. Fold up the bottom half of the figure along the center crease. See **Figure 4**. Fold down the top front corner to the bottom of the figure, as shown in **Figure 5**.

Fold the top back tip down and to the left along the fold line shown in **Figure 5**. Then, fold the bottom front tip up and to the left along its indicated diagonal fold line, until it resembles the shape in **Figure 6**. Unfold the left-pointing tips back to their positions shown in **Figure 5**. See **Figure 7**.

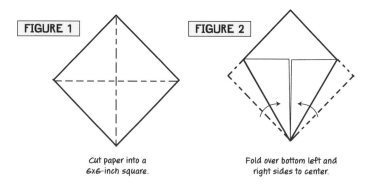

FIGURE 1	FIGURE 2

Cut paper into a
6x6-inch square.

Fold over bottom left and
right sides to center.

Next, fold the top corner down and to the right in the opposite direction of how you folded it to make **Figure 6**. Similarly, fold the bottom corner up but to the right, until the shape appears like the one in **Figure 8**.

Fold the bottom right corner to the center—it will fold the figure in half. See **Figure 9**. While you are folding it, shape the top right-pointing corners into a mouth shape by pushing the beak with your hand. See **Figure 10**. If necessary, fold and unfold the figure until this section resembles a mouth.

Last, draw eyes on both sides of the top portion of the figure. Now you can pull on the two bottom corners and the mouth will flap open and closed, as shown in **Figure 11**. If not, unfold the beak and refold it while adjusting it with your hand until the mouth moves properly.

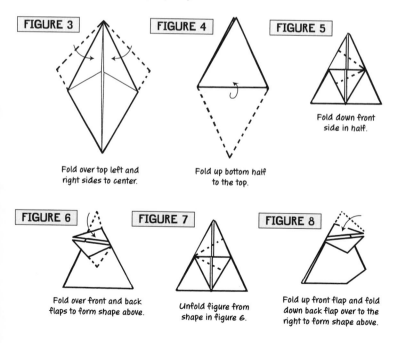

FIGURE 3
Fold over top left and right sides to center.

FIGURE 4
Fold up bottom half to the top.

FIGURE 5
Fold down front side in half.

FIGURE 6
Fold over front and back flaps to form shape above.

FIGURE 7
Unfold figure from shape in figure 6.

FIGURE 8
Fold up front flap and fold down back flap over to the right to form shape above.

FIGURE 9	FIGURE 10	FIGURE 11

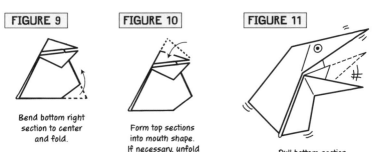

Bend bottom right
section to center
and fold.

Form top sections
into mouth shape.
If necessary, unfold
and fold bottom section.

Pull bottom section
apart and the mouth
will open and close.

Sneaky Origami Animator

You can add motion to your origami designs, and other craft
creations, by making a Sneaky Origami Animator with everyday
objects.

What's Needed

Two large paper clips
Electrical tape
Five by three-inch piece of cardboard
Needle-nose pliers

What to Do

This project illustrates how to make a cam-crank toy to add
locomotion to your still figure designs. You can produce variations
on this design by using larger pieces of cardboard and stiff wire,
but it's recommended to make a simple version first. Later, you
can alter the size of the parts to produce your desired results.

First, bend one paper clip into the shape shown in **Figure 1**.
It will act as a mount for your origami figure.

Next, bend the second paper clip into the shape shown in **Figure 2**. It will act as a cranking cam that will move the first paper clip up and down. Wrap electrical tape around both paper clips.

Poke holes in the cardboard at 1-inch, 2$\frac{1}{2}$-inch, and 4-inch intervals, as shown in **Figure 3**. Then, stand the card along its long side and fold it into a **U** shape.

Push the first paper clip into the center hole. Use pliers to bend the top of the clip into a **C** shape so it will not fall through the hole. See **Figures 4** and **5**.

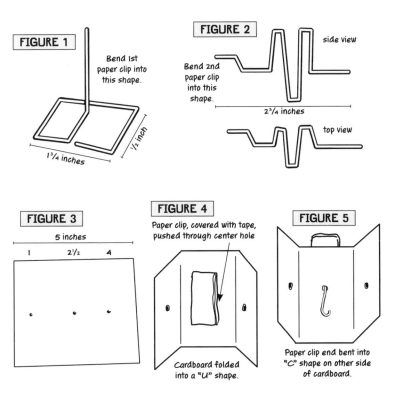

FIGURE 1

Bend 1st paper clip into this shape.

1$\frac{3}{4}$ inches

$\frac{1}{2}$ inch

FIGURE 2

Bend 2nd paper clip into this shape.

side view

2$\frac{3}{4}$ inches

top view

FIGURE 3

5 inches

1   2$\frac{1}{2}$ 4

FIGURE 4

Paper clip, covered with tape, pushed through center hole

Cardboard folded into a "U" shape.

FIGURE 5

Paper clip end bent into "C" shape on other side of cardboard.

Next, push the second paper clip into the side holes of the cardboard so it rests underneath the first paper clip, as shown in **Figure 6**. Apply tape to the bottom of the cardboard to keep its shape.

Last, turn the paper clip crank on the side of the Sneaky Origami Animator and the top paper clip will move up and down. See **Figure 7**. Since the first paper clip has an irregular shape, it acts as a cam mechanism and causes erratic movement on the other paper clip resting on it.

You can attach small paper figures to the top paper clip with tape. Experiment with an assortment of shapes for your paper clip cam (e.g., oval or triangular shapes) to produce a variety of motion effects. See the moving-arm figure in **Figure 8**.

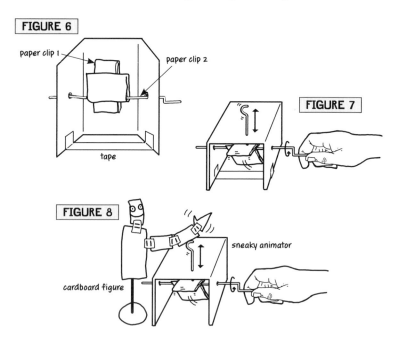

FIGURE 6

paper clip 1

paper clip 2

tape

FIGURE 7

FIGURE 8

sneaky animator

cardboard figure

Sneaky Solonoid

When electricity flows through a wire, it produces a magnetic field around it. If a magnet is brought near the wire, it will cause the wire to move toward it (or away, depending on its position). This project shows how to use this principle to create a Sneaky Solonoid—a mechanical switch activated by a magnetic coil, commonly used to open and close an electric circuit, a lock, or a valve.

What's Needed

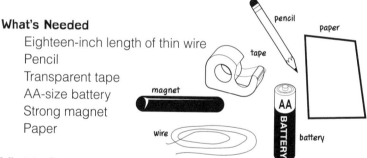

Eighteen-inch length of thin wire
Pencil
Transparent tape
AA-size battery
Strong magnet
Paper

What to Do

Strip the ends from the wire and wrap it ten turns around a pencil, using the center of the wire length to begin wrapping so that both ends are free. See **Figure 1**. Apply a small piece of tape to the wire coil to retain its shape, as shown in **Figure 2**.

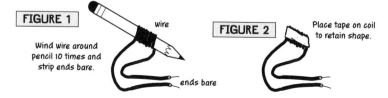

FIGURE 1

Wind wire around pencil 10 times and strip ends bare.

wire

ends bare

FIGURE 2

Place tape on coil to retain shape.

Tape one end of the wire to the AA battery's positive terminal and the other end to the side of the battery near the negative terminal. See **Figure 3**.

Place a magnet on the table and position the coil directly over it. When you press the wire on the battery's negative terminal, the wire coil will jump. If it moves toward the magnet, turn the magnet over. See **Figure 4**.

You've made a simple solonoid. Solonoids are used in many devices, such as an electric door lock, to allow a pushbutton to control motion or allow entry through the door. They are also used in radio control models to control the wings' ailerons and rudders for flight control.

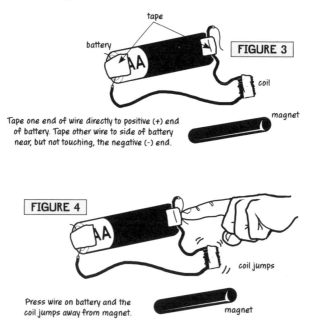

tape

battery

FIGURE 3

coil

Tape one end of wire directly to positive (+) end of battery. Tape other wire to side of battery near, but not touching, the negative (-) end.

magnet

FIGURE 4

coil jumps

Press wire on battery and the coil jumps away from magnet.

magnet

Going Further

You can make the Sneaky Solonoid animate a small origami figure by taping it to the wire coil. See **Figure 5**.

To make a simple origami beetle, follow the directions below:

Start with a 2-inch square piece of thin paper, as shown in **Figure 6A**. Fold down the top corner to the bottom corner. See **Figure 6B**. Fold over the left and right corners close, but not all the way, to the center, as shown in **Figure 6C**. **Figure 6D** shows how to fold down the top and side corners to give the origami beetle a buglike appearance. Simply tape the beetle to the wire coil and have fun making it hop and dance.

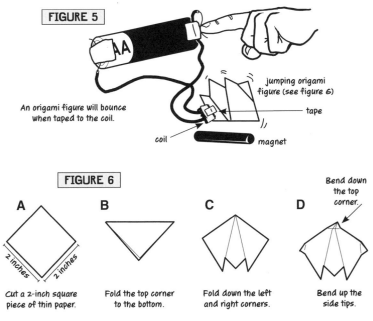

FIGURE 5

jumping origami figure (see figure 6)

An origami figure will bounce when taped to the coil.

tape

coil

magnet

FIGURE 6

Bend down the top corner.

A

2 inches
2 inches

Cut a 2-inch square piece of thin paper.

B

Fold the top corner to the bottom.

C

Fold down the left and right corners.

D

Bend up the side tips.

The origami "beetle" is complete.

Sneaky Motor

When electrical current passes through a wire it produces a magnetic field that will attract some metals and other magnets. You can make a simple electromagnet with a battery, wire, and a nail or bolt.

When you press the wire ends against the battery, the current flow induces a magnetic field in the coil of wire. The nail amplifies the effect and you can attract small metallic objects or a magnet. Magnets have a north and south pole, and so does your electromagnet. If you turn the magnet over, it will be either attracted to or repelled by the nail.

Using this knowledge, you can create a Sneaky Motor using the same parts in a different way.

What's Needed

Transparent tape
Three D-size batteries, one of
    which is to be used as a mold
Cardboard
Two paper clips
Ten feet of insulated 14-gauge magnet wire
Strong disk-shaped or square magnet
Pliers

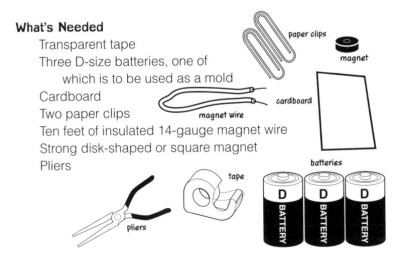

paper clips

magnet

cardboard

magnet wire

batteries

tape

pliers

What to Do

For this Sneaky Motor, you must use magnet wire found at electronic parts or hardware stores. Although it appears to be regular copper wire, it has copper-colored insulation that can be scraped off.

Tape two D-size batteries next to each other on to the cardboard as shown in **Figure 1**. Bend the two paper clips, as shown in **Figure 2**, and tape them to the ends of the batteries, perpendicular to the terminal ends so that they extend out in front of the batteries.

Next, wrap the wire around one D-size battery twelve times and wrap the ends to form a loop (making sure to leave a wire end free on each side of the coil), as shown in **Figures 3** and **4**. Then, very carefully use the rough inner surface of the pliers to scrape just one side of each end of the wires as shown in **Figure 5**. Do not scrape off the entire insulation, just one side (180 degrees).

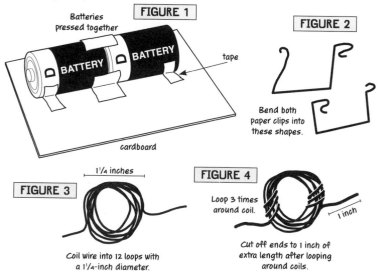

FIGURE 1

Batteries pressed together

tape

BATTERY BATTERY

cardboard

FIGURE 2

Bend both paper clips into these shapes.

FIGURE 3

1¼ inches

Coil wire into 12 loops with a 1¼-inch diameter.

FIGURE 4

Loop 3 times around coil.

1 inch

Cut off ends to 1 inch of extra length after looping around coils.

Then, place the wire coil on the paper clip hooks and position the magnet below the wire coil. Finally, spin the coil, which should continue spinning on its own. If it does not, turn the coil around or reposition the magnet until it spins freely. See **Figure 6**.

When the coil is at rest, the insulation on the ends prevents battery power from flowing through it. When you spin the coil, the bare wire touches the paper clips and the battery current flows through the wire coil, inducing a magnetic field in it. This field repels the magnet and the coil turns. When the insulated side of the coil touches the paper clips, the current stops but the momentum keeps it going until the bare wire makes contact again.

You may wonder why you bare only one side of the coil ends. If the coil wire ends were completely bare, the coil would start to spin but then immediately stop because the coil's other side, or magnetic pole, would then attract the magnet. In addition, this constant current flow would cause the battery to heat and to rapidly lose power.

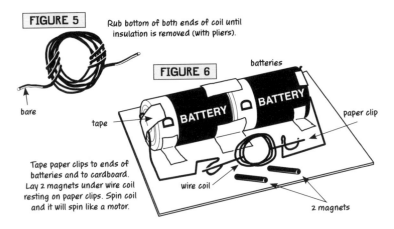

FIGURE 5

Rub bottom of both ends of coil until insulation is removed (with pliers).

bare

FIGURE 6

batteries

tape

BATTERY

BATTERY

paper clip

Tape paper clips to ends of batteries and to cardboard. Lay 2 magnets under wire coil resting on paper clips. Spin coil and it will spin like a motor.

wire coil

2 magnets

Sneaky Motor II

You've seen how a magnet will attract or repel a wire that has electrical current flowing through it. This project shows how to use this principle to create a Sneaky Motor. Although most motors produce circular motion, a motor is actually any device that uses electricity to obtain repetitive movement.

What's Needed

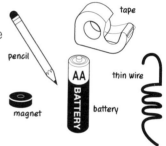

Eighteen-inch length of thin wire
Pencil
Transparent tape
Strong metallic disk magnet
AA-size battery

What to Do

This project uses the same design shown in the Sneaky Solonoid project, except the magnet is placed on the battery.

First, strip the ends from the wire, wrap it ten turns around a pencil leaving the wire ends free from the coil shape, and apply a small piece of tape to the wire coil to retain its shape, as shown in **Figure 1**.

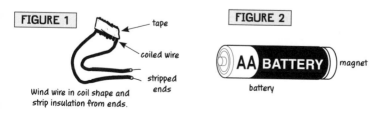

| FIGURE 1 | FIGURE 2 |

FIGURE 1
tape
coiled wire
stripped ends
Wind wire in coil shape and strip insulation from ends.

FIGURE 2
magnet
battery

Next, place the metallic disk magnet on the battery's negative terminal. See **Figure 2**. Then, tape one end of the wire coil to the battery's positive terminal. See **Figure 3**.

When you bend the wire coil so it rests on top of the magnet, it should start to move back and forth, as shown in **Figures 4** and **5**. (If it does not, turn over the magnet and test it again.)

How does it work? When the wire touches the magnet, electricity flows through it. It becomes magnetic and is repelled by the magnet. When it moves away from the magnet, it disconnects from the battery, loses it magnetic field, and falls back to its original position. It then reconnects to the battery through the metallic magnet, becomes magnetically charged again, and the cycle repeats.

For a more dramatic effect, bend the wire unto a **V** shape and tilt the battery downward. Ensure that the wire coil rests just above the magnet. When the wire is bent into a right angle, you will see the wire coil bounce up and down much farther. See **Figure 6**.

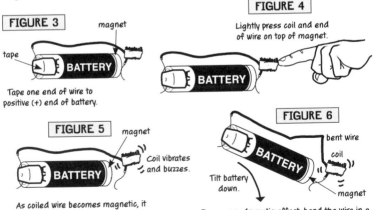

FIGURE 3

magnet

tape

BATTERY

Tape one end of wire to positive (+) end of battery.

FIGURE 4

Lightly press coil and end of wire on top of magnet.

BATTERY

FIGURE 5

magnet

BATTERY

Coil vibrates and buzzes.

As coiled wire becomes magnetic, it repels against magnet and disconnects, then pushes back to magnet. This cycle produces buzzing action.

FIGURE 6

bent wire

coil

BATTERY

Tilt battery down.

magnet

For a more dramatic effect, bend the wire in a "V" shpae and tilt the battery down. The coil will move a greater distance back and forth.

Sneaky Motor III

This project illustrates the versatility of the Sneaky Motor design but has a workaround in case you cannot locate a metallic disk magnet. A bonus application is included, using the motor to demonstrate how a radio control transmitter works.

What's Needed

Paper clip
Strong disk magnet
Pliers
Eighteen-inch length of thin wire
Pencil
Transparent tape
AA-size battery

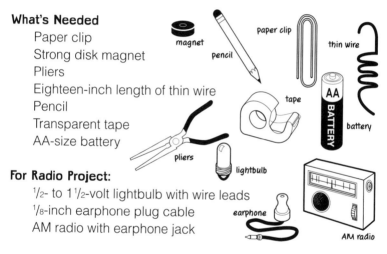

For Radio Project:

$1/2$- to $1 1/2$-volt lightbulb with wire leads
$1/8$-inch earphone plug cable
AM radio with earphone jack

What to Do

First, bend a paper clip into the shape shown in **Figure 1**. It should allow the magnet to slip in with a tight grip. See **Figure 2**.

FIGURE 1

Bend paper clip into a "C" shape.

FIGURE 2

Slide magnet between paper clip.

Note: If you cannot locate a small metallic disk magnet for
your Sneaky Motor, a plain magnet can be used. You must add
a small paper clip to act as a magnet holder. The paper clip also
conducts electricity from the battery to the wire coil in this design.

Then, set up the battery as follows:

First, strip the ends from the wire, wrap it around a pencil
ten times, and apply a small piece of tape to the wire coil to
retain its shape. Then, tape one end of the wire coil to the
battery's positive terminal, as shown in **Figure 3**.

When you bend the wire coil so it rests on top of the paper
clip above the magnet, it should start to move back and forth. If
it does not, turn over the magnet and test it again.

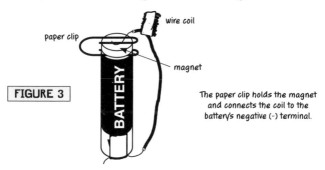

wire coil

paper clip

magnet

FIGURE 3

The paper clip holds the magnet
and connects the coil to the
battery's negative (-) terminal.

Bonus Sneaky Radio Control Demonstration

This project will take advantage of ordinary AM radio's sensitivity
to electromagnetic interference. If you activate the Sneaky Motor
near an AM radio that is tuned between stations with the volume
turned up, you will hear a loud buzzing sound. When you move the
motor away from the radio, the tone level decreases. See **Figure 4**.

The Sneaky Motor emits a magnetic field that is opening
and closing. This produces a low-frequency interference signal,
which the radio detects and amplifies. This signal can be used
to power a small light connected to the radio's earphone jack.

Obtain a small lightbulb with leads from a single-cell flashlight or from an electronics parts store. The lightbulb should be rated to work with only 1½ volts of power. Connect the light leads to the ⅛-inch earphone plug leads, as shown in **Figure 5**. If you tune the radio to an active station with the volume level high, the light should turn on when the earphone plug is plugged in.

For this project you must first tune the radio between stations, with the volume high. The light should not turn on. If it does, turn down the volume until it goes out. Then, bring the Sneaky Motor near the radio and activate it. This should produce enough interference that the light turns on. If not, adjust the volume level until it does. See **Figure 6**.

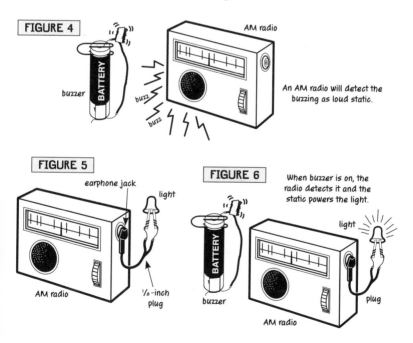

FIGURE 4

buzzer

BATTERY

buzz

buzz

AM radio

An AM radio will detect the buzzing as loud static.

FIGURE 5

earphone jack

light

AM radio

⅛-inch plug

FIGURE 6

When buzzer is on, the radio detects it and the static powers the light.

BATTERY

buzzer

light

plug

AM radio

Sneaky Motor IV

You can also make a motor using a battery, magnet, and piece of stiff copper wire to produce a spiraling circular motion around the battery.

What's Needed

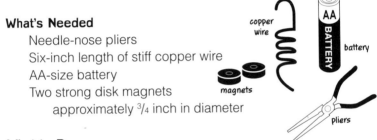

Needle-nose pliers
Six-inch length of stiff copper wire
AA-size battery
Two strong disk magnets
approximately ¾ inch in diameter

What to Do

This project uses the same design shown in the Sneaky Solonoid project, except that two magnets are placed on the battery's negative (−) terminal.

Note: In this design, the magnets must be larger in diameter than the battery.

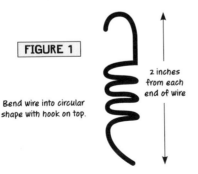

FIGURE 1

Bend wire into circular shape with hook on top.

2 inches from each end of wire

First, strip the insulation off the wire. Bend the top of the wire into a hook shape. Press the tip into a sharp point with the pliers. Wrap the wire in a spiral form that will fit around the body of the battery as shown in **Figure 1**. The wire should be just loose enough to not contact the battery case.

Next, place two disk magnets on the battery's negative terminal. See **Figure 2**. Adjust the shape of the wire so the top rests on the center positive (+) terminal and the bottom just touches the side of the magnet, as shown in **Figure 3**. The length from the tip of the top hook and the bottom of the wire should be 2 inches.

Once the wire makes contact with the top battery terminal, it will spin around. See **Figure 4**. If it does not, carefully bend and adjust the wire so that it is free to move and make contact properly.

You can also turn the magnets over to make the wire spin in the other direction.

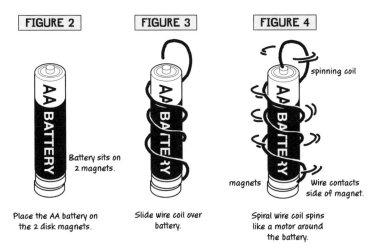

| FIGURE 2 | FIGURE 3 | FIGURE 4 |

spinning coil

Battery sits on 2 magnets.

magnets

Wire contacts side of magnet.

Place the AA battery on the 2 disk magnets.

Slide wire coil over battery.

Spiral wire coil spins like a motor around the battery.

How It Works

When the wire touches the battery's top positive terminal and the side of the magnet, electricity flows through it. The wire becomes magnetic and is repelled by the two disk magnets. When the wire moves away from the magnet, it disconnects from the battery and loses its magnetic field. It falls back to its original position and contacts the side of the magnet. Then, it connects to the battery via the magnet and becomes magnetically charged again, and the cycle repeats.

Since the wire coil is suspended by its sharp tip on top of the battery's positive terminal, when it repels from and returns to the magnet, it rotates slightly. The cycle occurs so quickly that it generates a circular motor motion.

Sneaky Motor V

Another motor can be put together using a battery and two disk magnets. This time, a small pointed screw and a piece of thin stranded wire are added to the mix.

What's Needed

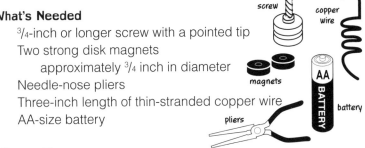

¾-inch or longer screw with a pointed tip
Two strong disk magnets
   approximately ¾ inch in diameter
Needle-nose pliers
Three-inch length of thin-stranded copper wire
AA-size battery

What to Do

Place the base of the screw on the two magnets, as shown in **Figure 1**. Then, point the tip of the screw at the positive (+) battery terminal until it sticks to it because of magnetic attraction. See **Figure 2**.

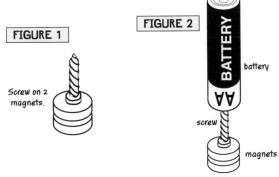

Then, strip the insulation off the stranded wire using the pliers. Next, hold the battery, hanging screw, and magnets with your thumb and middle finger. Hold one end of the wire to the battery's negative (–) terminal with your forefinger, as shown in **Figure 3**.

To start the Sneaky Motor turning, press the other end of the wire to the top edge of the topmost magnet, using your other hand. See **Figure 4**. The magnets and screw should start spinning and will continue even when you disconnect the wire. If you turn the magnets over, they will spin in the other direction.

How It Works

When the wire touches the battery's top negative terminal and the edge of the magnet, electricity flows through it. The wire becomes magnetic, causing the magnets to repel it. When this happens, the wire loses its magnetic field and the magnets fall back to their original position of resting on the wire. Then, the wire reconnects to the battery, through the magnets, and becomes magnetically charged again, thus repeating the cycle.

The cycle of movement makes the magnets rotate slightly, because they pivot on the battery terminal via the point of the screw.

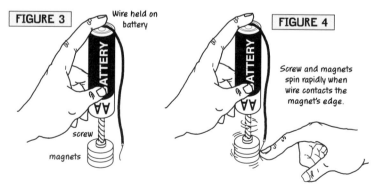

FIGURE 3 — Wire held on battery; screw; magnets

FIGURE 4 — Screw and magnets spin rapidly when wire contacts the magnet's edge.

Sneaky Sugar Glass

When you see a character in a TV show or movie crash through a window, it's not really glass they are breaking. Special effects men use a sheet of clear substance that's actually made of sugar!

You can make your own fake glass for models and hobby projects like they do in the movies. All you need are a few common kitchen items.

What's Needed

    Butter
    Nonstick pan or baking sheet
    One cup of sugar
    Nonstick frying pan
    One tablespoon of water

baking sheet

butter

frying pan

sugar

water

What to Do

First, spread a thin layer of butter on the surface of the baking sheet and let it cool for one hour in the refrigerator. Then, pour a cup of sugar into the frying pan, add the water, and place the pan on a stove-top burner. Turn the heat on low. See **Figures 1** and **2**.

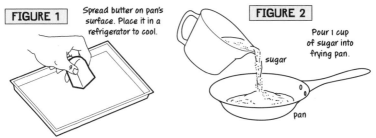

FIGURE 1 — Spread butter on pan's surface. Place it in a refrigerator to cool.

FIGURE 2 — Pour 1 cup of sugar into frying pan.

sugar

pan

Next, stir the sugar continually so it will not burn. It will liquefy when heated. See **Figures 3** and **4**. When the sugar is completely liquefied but before it starts to turn brown, remove the baking sheet from the refrigerator and pour the sugar onto it, as shown in **Figure 5**. (Be sure to turn off the heat, and to allow the pan to cool on an unheated burner before you wash it.)

Let the sugar cool and you will have a sheet of fake glass that you can use for hobby models and other projects. See **Figure 6**.

FIGURE 3

Add 1 tablespoon of water at low temperature.

FIGURE 4

Stir the sugar to prevent burning.

pan

FIGURE 5

Once the sugar liquefies but before it turns brown, pour it onto the cooled pan.

FIGURE 6

After the sugar cools and hardens, remove it carefully from the tray.

Sneaky Calculator

You can make a simple-to-make toy for young children just learning addition and subtraction. You just need a couple of discarded Styrofoam cups and a pen. Plus, you'll prevent the cups from needlessly filling up landfill space.

What's Needed

Two white, rimmed Styrofoam cups
Pen
Ruler

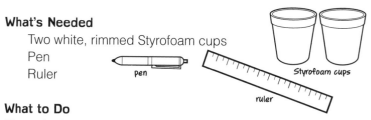

pen

ruler

Styrofoam cups

What to Do

First, obtain two cups that have a lip at the top. Place one cup into the other as shown in **Figure 1**.

Next, using the pen and ruler, draw a plus sign (+) on the lip of the top cup and the numbers 1 through 20 exactly ¼ inch apart. Similarly, draw a negative sign (–) on the rim of the bottom cup and the numbers 1 through 20 exactly ¼ inch apart. See **Figure 2**.

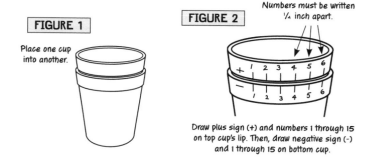

FIGURE 1

Place one cup into another.

FIGURE 2

Numbers must be written ¼ inch apart.

Draw plus sign (+) and numbers 1 through 15 on top cup's lip. Then, draw negative sign (-) and 1 through 15 on bottom cup.

How to Add Numbers

Following the arrows in the example shown in **Figure 3**, start with a number on the bottom cup, in this case the number 5. Turn the top cup so the plus sign (+) is above the number 5 on the bottom cup. Then, select a number on the top cup that you want to add to 5. In this instance, it is the number 3. Look at the number below 3, on the bottom cup, and the answer is 8.

You can repeat this process with any number adding up to 20. Select a number on the lower cup, align the plus sign above it, and then on the top cup select a number to add. You will see the sum immediately below the number you added.

How to Subtract Numbers

See the example problem in **Figure 4** and follow the arrows. Start with a number on the bottom cup, in this case the number 10. Turn the top cup so the number you wish to subtract is above the first number you selected on the bottom cup. In this instance it is the number 7. Then, look at the plus sign (+) on the top cup. Below the symbol, on the bottom cup, is the answer: the number 3.

You can repeat this process with any number up to 20. Select a number on the lower cup and turn the cup to align it with the number on the top cup that you wish to subtract. Look at the plus sign on the top cup and you'll see the answer below it on the lower cup.

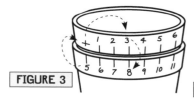

FIGURE 3

To add, start with bottom cup's number; match with (+) on top cup and number to add. The sum is below that number on the lower cup.
Example: 5 (+) 3 = 8

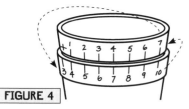

FIGURE 4

To subtract, select a number on the bottom cup, in this example 10. Align it with the number to subtract, which is 7. The answer is below the (+) sign: 3.

Sneaky School Quiz Tester 1

You can add a little fun to the chore of studying for a test by making a sneaky quiz tester. This 3-D model complements written material and adds a little fun in the process.

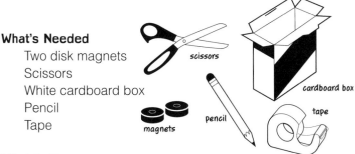

What's Needed
- Two disk magnets
- Scissors
- White cardboard box
- Pencil
- Tape

What to Do

First, test the two magnets to see which ends are north and which are south. When magnets stick together, the north end of one is attracted to the south end of the other. Indicate both magnets' north and south ends with a marker.

Next, cut the cardboard into the shape illustrated (an unfolded box) in **Figure 1**, being careful to follow the exact dimensions shown. Fold the segments into 1¼-inch square sections, as shown. Tape a magnet, north side up, to one of the square sections.

On the second cutout, tape another magnet in place with its south side up. See **Figure 2**.

Fold each cutout into a box shape, fitting the tabs into the slots. Write, with a pencil, a sample quiz question on the surface of one box, on the outside of the section that has the magnet taped to its inner side. See **Figure 3**. Write an assortment of answers on the second box, one answer per side, placing the correct answer on the section whose magnet is attached to its inner surface.

As shown in **Figure 4**, when the two boxes are brought together, they will attract each other only when the question and the correct answer are aligned.

You can erase and write additional quiz questions and answers on the front of the boxes as desired.

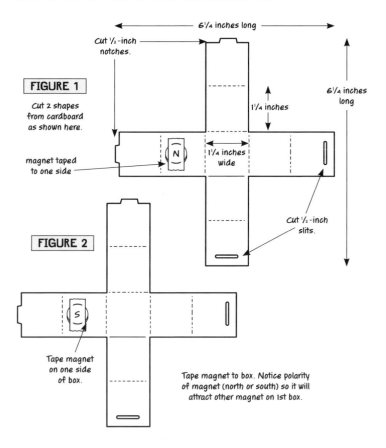

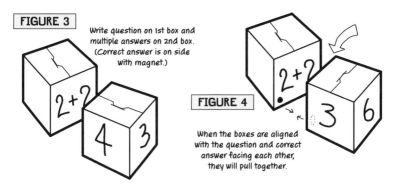

FIGURE 3

Write question on 1st box and multiple answers on 2nd box. (Correct answer is on side with magnet.)

$2+2$

4 3

FIGURE 4

When the boxes are aligned with the question and correct answer facing each other, they will pull together.

$2+2$

3 6

Sneaky School Quiz Tester II

Here's another Sneaky Quiz Tester you can build with everyday things. Its larger size allows for more questions and answers to be selected, as well as greater visibility, for a group of students.

What's Needed

Cardboard box
Scissors
Tape
Pliers
$1\frac{1}{2}$-volt lightbulb
Ten paper clips
Five feet of insulated wire
AA-size battery
Paper
Pencil

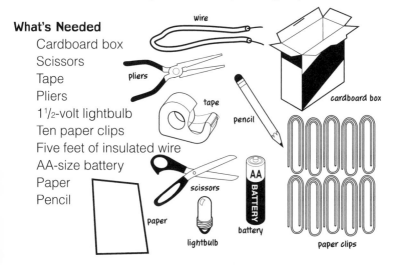

What to Do

You can use a cardboard box from a food product for this project. An empty cereal box is perfect. Simply unfold it, cut off the top flap and back, and turn it inside out. Tape the corners together, as shown in **Figure 1**, so it stands upright.

Next, using the scissors, carefully puncture five small holes on each side of the box and two at the top. Also cut a small hole at the top of the box for the bulb, as shown in **Figure 2**. Then, push the bulb through the top hole. Also, unbend ten paper clips so you can push them through the back of the box. See **Figure 3**.

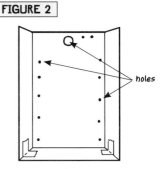

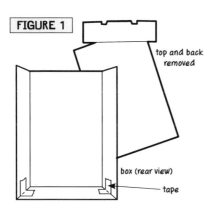

top and back removed

box (rear view)

tape

Dismantle box, turn inside out, and remove
top flaps and back side. Tape bottom
together so it stands upright.

holes

Cut holes into box front—small ones 5
on each side and 2 at the top, plus one
in the center for the lightbulb.

FIGURE 3

Push bulb and paper
clips into holes from
front of box.

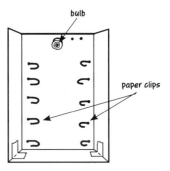

bulb

paper clips

Cut a 3-inch length of wire and two 10-inch lengths. Strip the insulation off the ends of the wires.

Tape the AA battery to the top of the box and secure the 3-inch length of wire from the battery around the side of the lightbulb's base. Tape one of the 10-inch wires to the bottom of the bulb and push its other end through one of the two small holes at the top. Tape the other 10-inch wire to the remaining battery terminal and push its other end through the other small hole at the top. See **Figure 4**. When the two wires touch, the lightbulb should turn on. If it doesn't, check the connections to all of the parts and test it again.

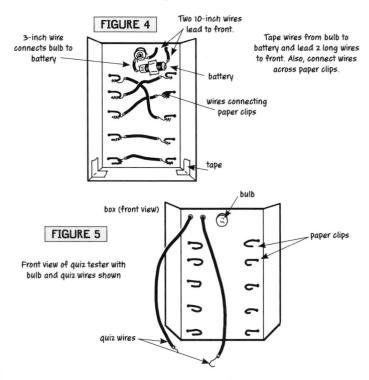

FIGURE 4

Two 10-inch wires lead to front.

3-inch wire connects bulb to battery

Tape wires from bulb to battery and lead 2 long wires to front. Also, connect wires across paper clips.

battery

wires connecting paper clips

tape

bulb

box (front view)

FIGURE 5

Front view of quiz tester with bulb and quiz wires shown

paper clips

quiz wires

Cut five 7-inch lengths from the remaining wire and strip the insulation from their ends. Wrap the wires around the paper clips on the box, running them side to side in various patterns (straight and crisscross), as shown in **Figure 4**. When the two 10-inch quiz wires make contact with the proper paper clips in the front of the Quiz Tester (in the example shown in **Figure 6**, 1 + 4 = 5), it will make a complete circuit and turn on the light. When you look from the front of the Quiz Tester box, the bulb and 10-inch wires should be protruding from the back to the front. The 10-inch wires will be used to connect to a paper clip to each side of the box and light the bulb, indicating a correct answer. See **Figure 5**.

Cut a piece of paper so it will fit between the columns of paper clips on the front of the box. Write some math questions on the left side and some answers on the right with a pencil. Be sure to use the correct pattern of wire connections on the back as a guide. See **Figure 4** as an example. When the two 10-inch-long quiz wires touch the top left-side paper clip and the second to top paper clip on the right side, respectively, the light will turn on to indicate the correct answer, as shown in **Figure 6**.

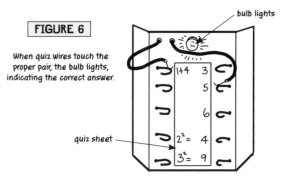

| FIGURE 6 |

When quiz wires touch the proper pair, the bulb lights, indicating the correct answer.

bulb lights

quiz sheet

1+4 3
5
6
2^2 = 4
3^2 = 9

Sneaky Robot

Robots are fascinating because of their utility and resemblance to humans. But you don't have to buy an expensive and complicated kit when you can make a Sneaky Robot from everyday things.

In the projects that follow, you'll learn how to use discarded toy cars, cardboard, and other items to make a modular "trashformer" that's easy to construct and disassemble. If desired, you can go all the way and make your own giant 6-foot sneakbot out of parts found around the house.

Chassis and Body

What's Needed

> Motorized toy car, wire- or radio-controlled
> Plastic ice trays or small
>   parts box
> Pringles containers (chip cans)
> Two wire garment hangers
> Double-stick Velcro pads
> Transparent tape
> Scissors
> Pliers
> *Optional:*
> Tablecloth
> Plastic dining tray

pliers
tape
tablecloth
scissors
Velcro
hangers
ice trays or small parts box
toy car
dining tray
chip cans

What to Do

The simplest robot can be constructed using an inexpensive radio-controlled car as its base. The car should include a full-function remote control. Small, cheap radio-control cars that are always in motion and only go in reverse when you press the remote's single button are not recommended for this robot project. A medium-to-large car model with a full-function remote control should be used to provide ample torque. (Of course, if you do not want mobility for your robot, then the car is unnecessary.) The robot's body is mounted on the car's chassis with Velcro pads, allowing for easy construction and disassembly.

Sneaky Robots can be assembled using just two basic parts: plastic ice trays and Pringles chip cans. Ice trays provide an excellent modular, low-cost horizontal base that can support the upper parts. They allow you to easily increase the height of the robot by placing one section on top of another.

Pringles containers, which hereon we'll refer to as chip cans, are great for adding vertical height to the robot's body. Like ice trays, they, too, are modular and, with their plastic cap, allow for easy construction and disassembly.

Double-stick Velcro pads, tape, and wire hangers are used for connecting the parts and to keep the body rigid. See how to fit the materials together in **Figures 1** through **4**.

Besides being a fun toy, a Sneaky Robot can be used as a mobile TV dinner tray, as shown in **Figure 5**.

When making a tall Sneaky Robot, it's important to stabilize the lowest ice tray to the car with strong rubber bands and to use three chip cans, in a tripod arrangement, to prevent the robot from tipping over. See **Figure 6**.

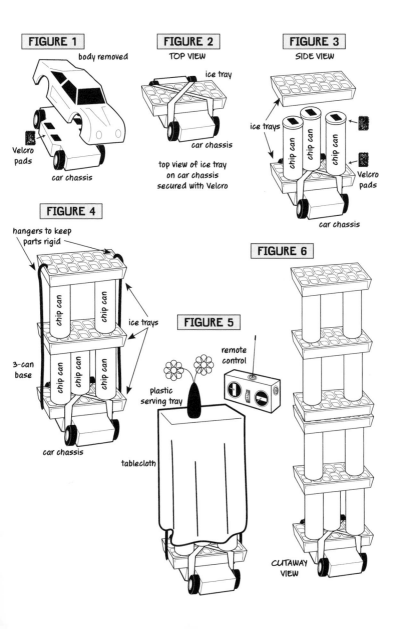

FIGURE 1
body removed

Velcro pads

car chassis

FIGURE 2
TOP VIEW

ice tray

car chassis

top view of ice tray
on car chassis
secured with Velcro

FIGURE 3
SIDE VIEW

ice trays

chip can chip can chip can

Velcro pads

car chassis

FIGURE 4

hangers to keep
parts rigid

chip can chip can

ice trays

3-can base

chip can chip can

car chassis

FIGURE 5

plastic serving tray

remote control

tablecloth

FIGURE 6

chip can

CUTAWAY VIEW

Body Decoration and Accessories

After designing and assembling the basic robot chassis and frame, you'll want to decorate it so that it resembles a cybernetic being. You probably already have plenty of materials in the house that can decorate your robot. Additional inexpensive materials and useful accessories can be obtained from discarded toys and local thrift stores.

Note: The suggested parts list below will depend on the extent of your robot design.

What's Needed (Suggested)
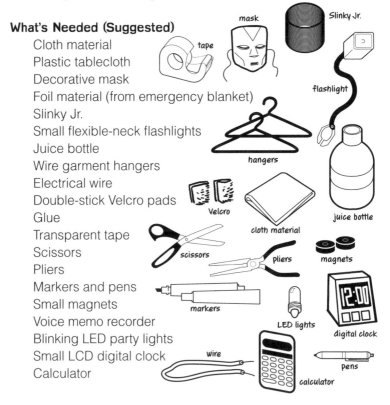

- Cloth material
- Plastic tablecloth
- Decorative mask
- Foil material (from emergency blanket)
- Slinky Jr.
- Small flexible-neck flashlights
- Juice bottle
- Wire garment hangers
- Electrical wire
- Double-stick Velcro pads
- Glue
- Transparent tape
- Scissors
- Pliers
- Markers and pens
- Small magnets
- Voice memo recorder
- Blinking LED party lights
- Small LCD digital clock
- Calculator

Walkie-talkies
Toy metal detector
Personal battery-powered fan
CDs
Antennas
Umbrella
Pie pans
Circuit board from toy
TV dinner tray
Mini radio
Vacuum cleaner hose
Plastic cups
Plastic tray

What to Do

Figure 1 illustrates several robot head designs. Or, you can substitute an available decorative mask at the top of the robot.

The robot's arms can be constructed using wire hangers covered with cloth material, plastic vacuum cleaner hoses, or Slinky Jr. coils. Attach strong magnets or clamps so the robot can transport objects. See **Figure 2**.

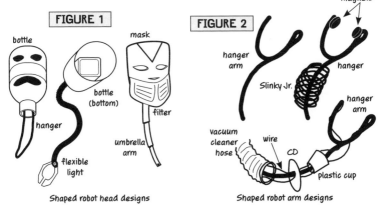

Shaped robot head designs

Shaped robot arm designs

You can buy inexpensive decorative accessories at dollar stores, and mount such devices as LED lights, an LCD clock, or a calculator keypad in or on the robot body, as desired. If your robot design uses a soft body covering, such as foil material, mount the accessory parts with double-stick Velcro strips directly on one of the upper trays. You can cut holes in the body covering and apply tape around the decorative objects as needed. See **Figure 3**.

Why not use the mobility of your Sneaky Robot to do some surveillance or search for hidden treasures? You can easily attach a couple of accessories you probably already have for added fun.

A walkie-talkie, compact radio, or a small toy metal detector can be useful additions, as shown in **Figure 4**. The robot's walkie-talkie can be used to transmit your voice from a remote location. Or, if you'd rather listen in, place the button in its TRANSMIT mode (if the button will not stay in the TRANSMIT mode, you can secure it with tape). In this way, you can send the robot to a remote location and monitor the environment from afar.

Similarly, you can attach a compact metal detector, the type with a removable handle, to the lower part of the robot chassis with Velcro strips, to enable you to walk along without holding the handle, as shown in **Figure 5**.

Going Further

Your Sneaky Robot has virtually limitless accessory and utility options. For added convenience, you may want to remount the robot's main ON/OFF switch to a more accessible location.

Consider adding sound-effect devices from toys, plus radio control receivers, obtained from micro radio-control cars, to control these optional devices.

If you build more than one robot, you can stage friendly battles by outfitting them with foam or plastic toy bats and

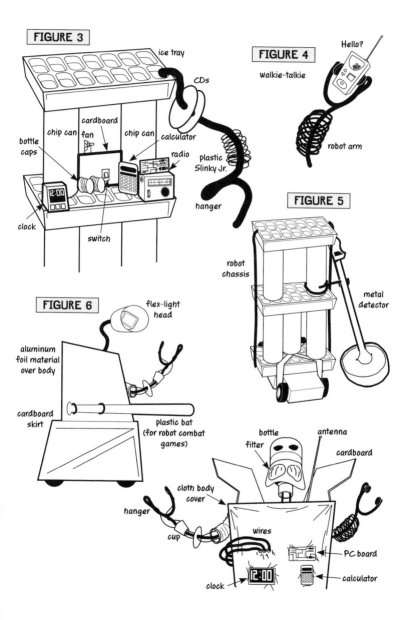

FIGURE 3

ice tray
CDs
cardboard fan
chip can
chip can
calculator
bottle caps
radio
plastic Slinky Jr.
clock
switch
hanger

FIGURE 4

Hello?
walkie-talkie
robot arm

FIGURE 5

robot chassis
metal detector

FIGURE 6

flex-light head
aluminum foil material over body
cardboard skirt
plastic bat (for robot combat games)

bottle filter
antenna
cardboard
cloth body cover
hanger
cup
wires
PC board
clock
calculator

light sabers, as shown in **Figure 6**. Be sure to use radio-controlled cars with different transmission frequencies to avoid interference.

For versatility, design a robot chestplate that can be easily attached and removed with Velcro strips. You can easily alter the robot's style to fit your tastes or a special event (such as Halloween, a birthday, or a competition). Simply cut a piece of cardboard slightly smaller than the upper body area on the robot and, using Velcro strips (or glue), apply spare electronic parts from old computers and toys such as wire cables, printed circuit boards, LEDs, voice memo recorders, digital clocks, and calculators to the cardboard for a high-tech look. See **Figure 7**. When you've completed the chestplate, attach Velcro to the back and simply press it onto the Velcro strips on the front of the robot, as shown in **Figure 8**.

Sneaky Robot arms can be made with stiff wire or a clothes hanger. Bend the hanger until it resembles the shape shown in **Figure 9**. One side will clip onto the ice tray and the other end forms a claw shape. Decorate the robot arm with found items like old CDs or a Slinky Jr. toy, and secure the parts with tape. See **Figure 10**. Last, bend the end of the hanger until it clips securely to the edge of the ice tray and secure it firmly with tape. If desired, small magnets can be attached to the end of the robot arms so it can hang on to lightweight metallic objects. See **Figure 11**.

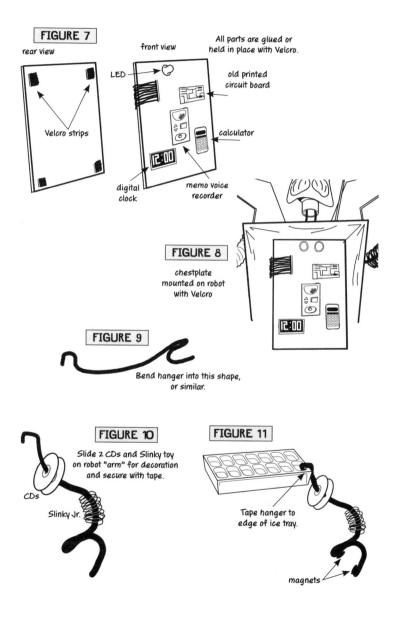

FIGURE 7

rear view

front view

All parts are glued or
held in place with Velcro.

LED

old printed
circuit board

calculator

Velcro strips

digital
clock

memo voice
recorder

FIGURE 8

chestplate
mounted on robot
with Velcro

FIGURE 9

Bend hanger into this shape,
or similar.

FIGURE 10

Slide 2 CDs and Slinky toy
on robot "arm" for decoration
and secure with tape.

CDs

Slinky Jr.

FIGURE 11

Tape hanger to
edge of ice tray.

magnets

Sneaky 6-Foot Sneakbot

To really make a big impression you can create your own giant
sneakbot easily enough by adding another level or two of chip
cans and ice trays.

What's Needed

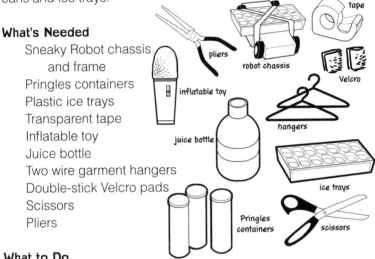

- Sneaky Robot chassis
  and frame
- Pringles containers
- Plastic ice trays
- Transparent tape
- Inflatable toy
- Juice bottle
- Two wire garment hangers
- Double-stick Velcro pads
- Scissors
- Pliers

What to Do

First, assemble the chassis and body from the Sneaky Robot
project.

Then, assemble an additional level or two of chip can and
ice tray segments, as shown in the previous robot project, and
place the bottommost ice tray of that portion atop the ice tray
that completes the lower level of the robot, as shown in **Figure
1**. Secure the ice trays with tape.

To increase the robot's height without adding additional
ice tray/chip can segments, you can attach an inflatable toy,
with mask, to act as the head. Your lower body decorations,

accessories, and arms can be mounted to the upper sections,
as shown in **Figure 2**.

Note: If necessary, use a three-can tripod arrangement and
add weight to the lowest segments, to lower the center of gravity
and prevent the robot from tipping over when it accelerates.
Also, add more wire hangers to the side of the ice trays as
needed, to keep the upper segments rigid.

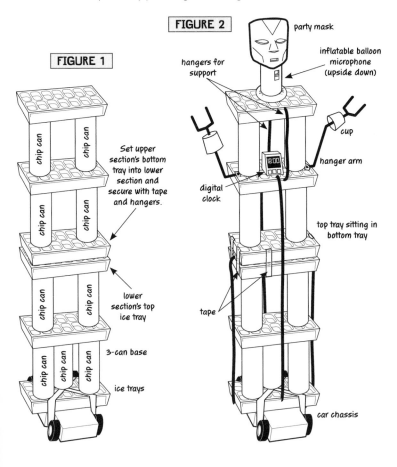

FIGURE 1

chip can

Set upper
section's bottom
tray into lower
section and
secure with tape
and hangers.

lower
section's top
ice tray

3-can base

ice trays

FIGURE 2

party mask

hangers for
support

inflatable balloon
microphone
(upside down)

cup

hanger arm

digital
clock

top tray sitting in
bottom tray

tape

car chassis

PART III

Sneaky Energy Projects and Simulations

Energy affects everybody. We depend on it for transportation, industry, and to power our homes. Yet the average person doesn't fully comprehend the ever-increasing ways that energy is obtained, produced, and distributed. This part of *Sneakiest Uses for Everyday Things* includes background details, experiments, and simulations to help you understand your options for choosing cleaner, renewable energy.

Do you know how oil is refined and how biofuels can substitute for gasoline and diesel fuel? If you're curious about how a hybrid car can utilize normally wasted energy during braking or whether hydrogen fuel cells will soon power vehicles, or want details about atomic energy, then this part of the book is for you. Here, you'll learn the basic techniques used to obtain energy from coal, oil, gas, the sun, wind, and water and from the atom. The nuclear power simulation project, made with cardboard and paper clips, can also be adapted to demonstrate other energy-related projects.

Whether you want to know energy theory or want a practical guide to making unique energy-related science simulations, the following projects will expand your knowledge of energy in a fun and interesting way, to help you make more informed choices that protect our planet.

Energy Fundamentals

Energy is what makes things change or move. It is found in many forms, including heat, chemical, light, electrical, and mechanical energy.

Kinetic energy is the energy in moving things. Energy that can be stored for later use is called *potential energy*. Gases, solids, and chemicals can all store potential energy that may be released later in a variety of ways.

For instance, when certain substances, such as coal, are burned, the process releases energy in the form of heat. In a coal-fired electrical power plant, the heat that the released energy produces is used to boil water into steam, which in turn propels turbine blades to power an electrical generator. See **Figure 1**.

Food, oil, and batteries have potential energy stored within their chemicals. Springs and rubber bands do, as well. They can be wound up to store *strain energy* for later use.

Energy can be converted from one form or another for practical use. Common energy conversions take place all the time, all around you. For example:

- The sun provides energy for plants to make food. This food is stored as *chemical energy*. When animals eat plants, they convert the chemical energy into motion and heat.
- Chemical energy is stored in consumer batteries, where it is converted into electricity. The electricity is changed into heat, light, motion, or sound, depending on whether the batteries are in a flashlight, toy, radio, or other device.

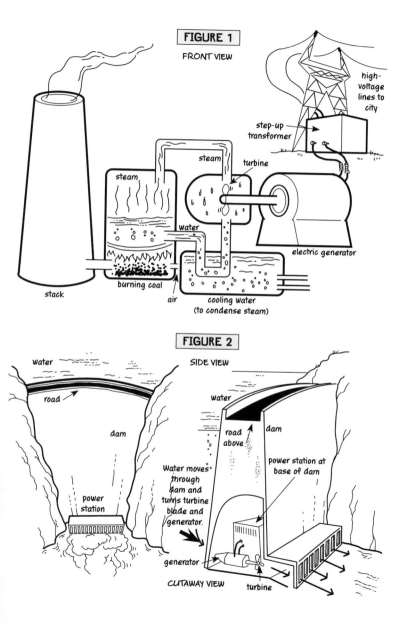

FIGURE 1

FRONT VIEW

high-voltage lines to city

step-up transformer

steam

turbine

steam

steam

water

electric generator

burning coal

air

cooling water (to condense steam)

stack

FIGURE 2

SIDE VIEW

water

road

dam

power station

water

road above

dam

power station at base of dam

Water moves through dam and turns turbine blade and generator.

generator

CUTAWAY VIEW

turbine

- Hydroelectric power plants use water at a high elevation to fall on turbine blades, which turn electrical generators. As shown in **Figure 2**, water, blocked by a dam, flows through a penstock channel where it eventually reaches a turbine. The rushing water spins the turbine blades and provides mechanical energy to an electrical generator.
- Wood, oil, and coal store energy from the sun as chemical energy. In the case of gas, oil, and coal, they are burned to release chemical energy in the form of heat. Geothermal power plants use underground pockets of steam to power turbines.

Electrical power stations have large water, gas, or steam turbines that turn electrical generators. An electrical generator diagram is shown in **Figure 3**. To reduce energy loss while traveling over long-distance power lines, step-up transformers increase the voltage level from about 15,000 to 20,000 volts, to several hundred thousand volts. Electric power substations, located near cities, use distribution transformers to step down the voltage to about 7,200 volts. Line transformers, near homes and businesses, step down the voltage level to 240 volts.

Wires leading from line transformers can be tapped to produce 120 volts, for most needs, or 240 volts for heavy-duty appliances such as washers and dryers. See **Figure 4**.

The next project illustrates an easy-to-make multistage example of energy storage and conversion.

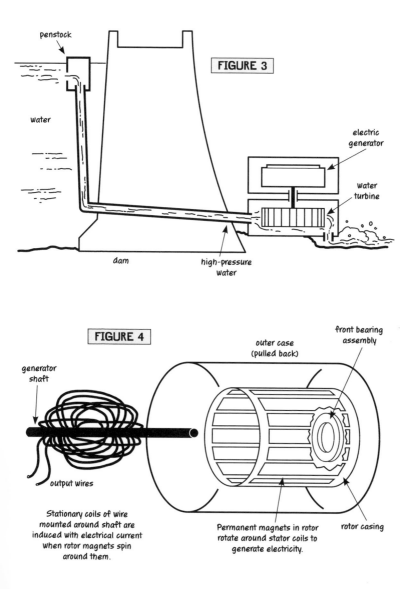

penstock

FIGURE 3

water

electric generator

water turbine

dam

high-pressure water

FIGURE 4

front bearing assembly

outer case (pulled back)

generator shaft

output wires

Stationary coils of wire mounted around shaft are induced with electrical current when rotor magnets spin around them.

Permanent magnets in rotor rotate around stator coils to generate electricity.

rotor casing

FIGURE 5

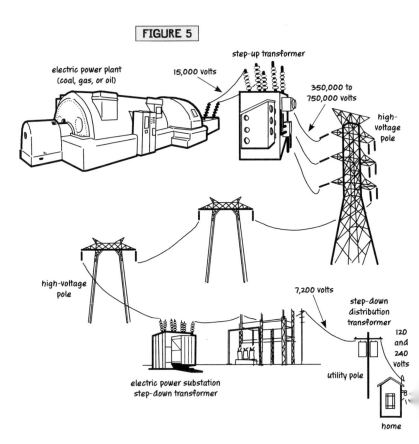

Energy Conversion and Storage Demonstration

If you tire of constantly manually rewinding the rubber band–powered planes or other toy models, you can use everyday things to make an automatic rewinder. This project demonstrates how one form of energy can be converted and stored in another form.

The chemical energy in a battery is converted into electrical energy that is converted, by a toy car's motor, into mechanical energy. This mechanical energy is then used to wind a rubber band taut and is stored as potential energy.

What's Needed

Large paper clip
Toy car
Rubber band–operated plane

paper clip

toy car

airplane

What to Do

This project requires a medium-size toy car, not the small ones found in dollar stores. Smaller model motors do not generate enough power to wind a rubber band tightly.

First, bend the large paper clip into the **V** shape shown in **Figure 1**. Most toy cars have holes in the wheels that make it easy to push the paper clip through, as shown in **Figure 2**. Once it's in position, spread the ends of the paper clip apart slightly to secure it in place. See **Figure 3**.

FIGURE 1

Bend paper clip into "V" shape.

Then, place the paper clip ends on each side of the model plane's propeller and turn on the car. The car motor will spin the propeller and the motor will spin the blades, to wind the rubber band as shown in **Figure 4**.

When disconnected from the paper clips, the rubber band releases its stored energy. See **Figure 5**.

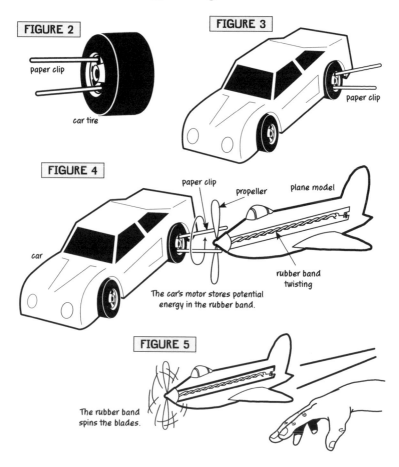

FIGURE 2

paper clip

car tire

FIGURE 3

paper clip

FIGURE 4

paper clip   propeller   plane model

car

rubber band twisting

The car's motor stores potential energy in the rubber band.

FIGURE 5

The rubber band spins the blades.

Solar Power Demonstrations

In the following projects we will take advantage of the sun's radiation by using its heat, as well as utilizing solar cells to generate electricity.

Sneaky Solar Cooker

What's Needed
Aluminum foil
Transparent tape
Bowl
Large paper clip
Potato
Rock

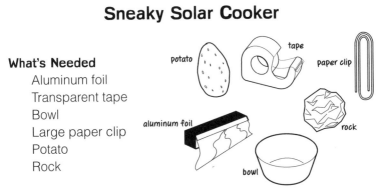

What to Do
Wrap the aluminum foil into a cone shape and tape it to the inside of the bowl as shown in **Figure 1**.

Bend the paper clip into a **C** shape, as shown in **Figure 2**. Tear away a small piece of foil in the center of the bowl and tape the paper clip to the bowl.

To test your solar cooker, stick a small potato on the end of the paper clip, as shown in **Figure 3**. Place the bowl in direct sunlight for one to two hours and move it occasionally to keep it in line with the sun until the potato is cooked, as shown in **Figure 4**. You now have a free Sneaky Solar Cooker.

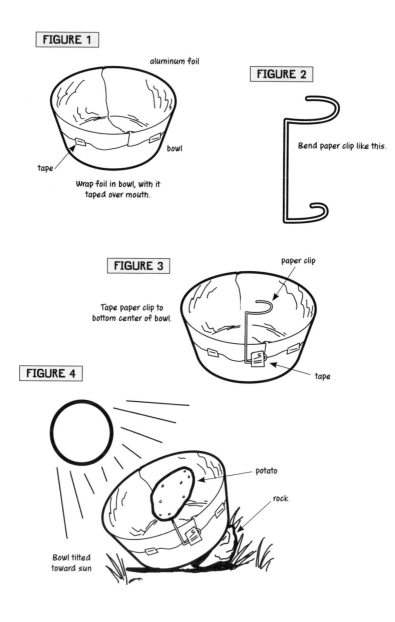

FIGURE 1

aluminum foil

bowl

tape

Wrap foil in bowl, with it taped over mouth.

FIGURE 2

Bend paper clip like this.

FIGURE 3

Tape paper clip to bottom center of bowl.

paper clip

tape

FIGURE 4

potato

rock

Bowl tilted toward sun

Solar Power Generator

Solar cells convert light from the sun into electricity. A photovoltaic (PV) cell is a semiconductor that needs a little energy to allow electron flow between its N- and P-type layers. Solar cells have a protective cover, an antireflective coating, and electrical contacts that collect photons, particles of solar energy, and transfer them into electric current. See **Figure 1**.

Solar cells can be removed from small toys and calculators or purchased separately from electronic parts supply houses and hobby stores.

You can demonstrate how solar power can be used to power devices by connecting a solar cell to a miniature radio-controlled car.

What's Needed

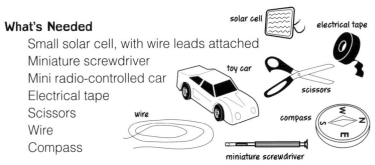

Small solar cell, with wire leads attached
Miniature screwdriver
Mini radio-controlled car
Electrical tape
Scissors
Wire
Compass

What to Do

First, obtain a small solar cell with wire leads already attached (so you do not have to solder).

Next, carefully remove the body from the mini radio-controlled car. Most models allow you to pry off the body from the chassis with a miniature flat-bladed screwdriver. The motor can usually be lifted out of the chassis once the motor cover (if found) is pried open as shown in **Figure 2**.

FIGURE 1

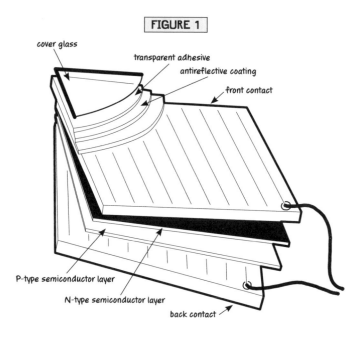

Connect the solar cell wires to the terminals of the motor with tape, as shown in **Figure 3**. If you only see one terminal or wire, the motor casing is its negative (–) terminal. Place the solar cell and motor under a bright light or in the sun and it should start to spin.

The car should move on its own when exposed to sunlight and, possibly, a bright room lamp. See **Figure 4**.

Wire that is connected to the solar cell can move a compass needle when it's wrapped around a compass. See **Figure 5**.

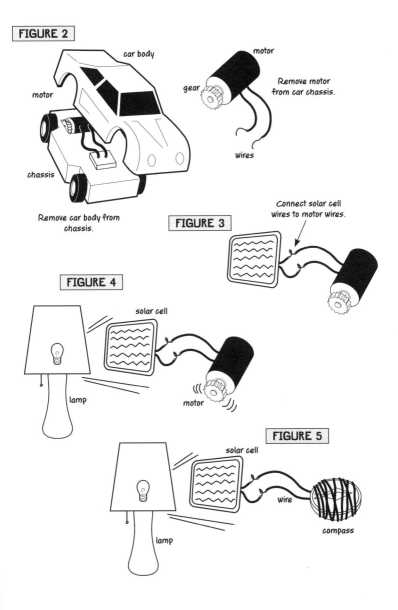

FIGURE 2

car body

motor

motor

gear

Remove motor from car chassis.

wires

chassis

Remove car body from chassis.

FIGURE 3

Connect solar cell wires to motor wires.

FIGURE 4

solar cell

lamp

motor

FIGURE 5

solar cell

wire

compass

lamp

Sneaky Oil Refinery Demonstration

Over 60 percent of the world's energy is derived from oil and natural gas. Much as time and pressure can turn coal into diamonds, organic remains from plants and animals were converted to oil deposits by millions of years of heat and pressure.

Basically, when oil is discovered, it is brought to the surface, gas and water are removed, and what remains is then pumped through pipelines to a refinery. An oil rig at sea and an oil refinery are shown in **Figures 1** and **2**. This project will illustrate how an oil refinery converts crude oil into useful products, including gasoline.

In a refinery, crude oil is pumped into a large furnace and boiled into a gas. It is then pumped into a distillation tower to condense back into different liquid substances at various temperatures. You've witnessed evidence of condensation on a cold glass of liquid, or on grass in the early morning in the form of dew droplets. The water in the air turns into a liquid when it comes in contact with a cooler surface.

A refinery's distillation tower uses the same principle to gather different types of oil products as the heated oil condenses. **Figure 3** shows the distillation tower, which has multiple levels of saucer-shaped cool surfaces against which the oil will form condensation (liquid). This condensation drips into trays and flows to gathering tanks. The higher tanks gather oil that is cooler than what is produced in the lower ones. By this process, the key ingredients for various petroleum products, including bitumen, diesel, gasoline, kerosene, and plastics, are obtained.

You can demonstrate how a refinery works, using common items found in every kitchen.

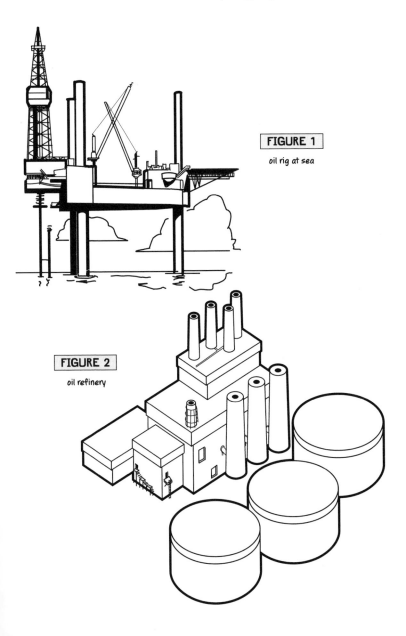

FIGURE 1

oil rig at sea

FIGURE 2

oil refinery

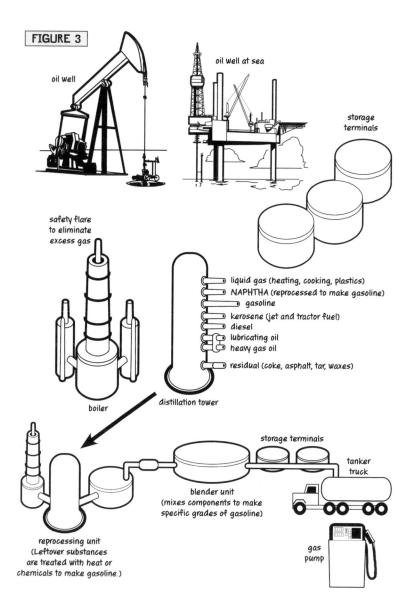

FIGURE 3

oil well

oil well at sea

storage terminals

safety flare to eliminate excess gas

liquid gas (heating, cooking, plastics)
NAPHTHA (reprocessed to make gasoline)
gasoline
kerosene (jet and tractor fuel)
diesel
lubricating oil
heavy gas oil
residual (coke, asphalt, tar, waxes)

boiler

distillation tower

storage terminals

tanker truck

blender unit
(mixes components to make
specific grades of gasoline)

reprocessing unit
(Leftover substances
are treated with heat or
chemicals to make gasoline.)

gas pump

What's Needed

Teakettle filled with water
Bowl
Metal pan
Ice cubes
Oven mitt

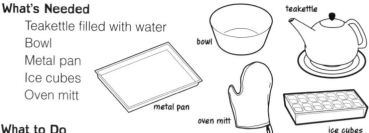

What to Do

Bring water to a boil in the teakettle. Place a bowl near the stove a few inches away from the kettle, as shown in **Figure 1**.

Next, fill the metal pan with ice cubes. See **Figure 2**. With an oven mitt, hold the pan over the bowl, near the kettle's spout, as shown in **Figure 3**.

When the steam gathers on the pan's bottom surface, which is cooled by the ice cubes, it condenses (turns into a liquid), and drips into the bowl.

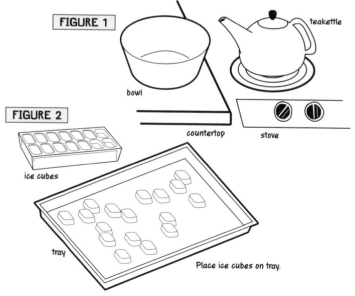

Place ice cubes on tray.

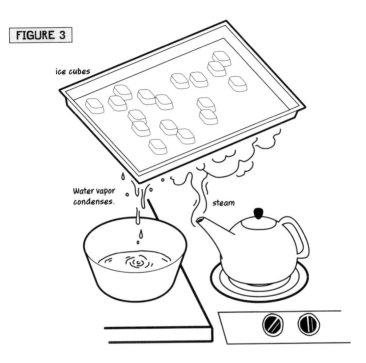

FIGURE 3

ice cubes

Water vapor condenses.

steam

Biofuels

Biofuels are liquid fuels derived from crops. They include methanol (wood alcohol), ethanol (grain alcohol), and biodiesel.

Biodiesel

Rudolf Diesel made diesel engines in 1895 that could run on peanut oil. Diesel engines differ from gasoline engines because of their higher compression ratio.

Currently, in the United States, diesel cars account for less than 4 percent of the market while in Europe over 50 percent of passenger vehicles are diesel powered. A diesel engine produces higher torque at lower RPMs (rotations per minute) and gets better gas mileage, compared with its gasoline counterpart.

Standard gasoline engines use a spark plug to ignite the air-fuel mixture as shown in **Figure 1**.

In a diesel engine, the pistons compress the air-fuel mixture in the cylinder so much that the extreme heat ignites it without requiring a spark plug. See **Figure 2**.

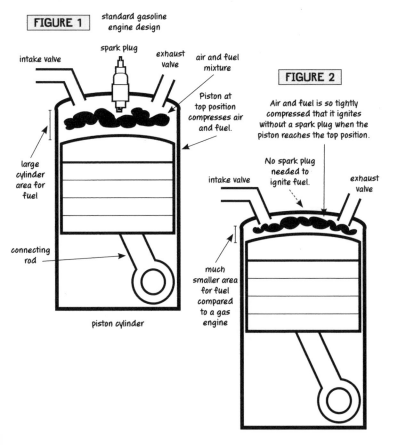

FIGURE 1 standard gasoline engine design

spark plug

intake valve

exhaust valve

air and fuel mixture

Piston at top position compresses air and fuel.

large cylinder area for fuel

connecting rod

piston cylinder

FIGURE 2

Air and fuel is so tightly compressed that it ignites without a spark plug when the piston reaches the top position.

No spark plug needed to ignite fuel.

intake valve

exhaust valve

much smaller area for fuel compared to a gas engine

All diesel engines can use biodiesel fuel if it is heated and filtered properly. Biodiesel can be made, via a chemical process, from recycled cooking oil, animal fats, soy, corn, sunflower seeds, canola, peanuts, mustard seeds, or cottonseeds. Solar energy, combined with water and carbon dioxide, provides the stored energy captured by feedstock.

Even ordinary vegetable oil or filtered cooking oil from restaurants can power biodiesel-ready vehicles.

Since the crops use carbon dioxide from the atmosphere in their energy absorption process, they are virtually a carbon-neutral source of fuel. When the vehicle's exhaust emits carbon dioxide, it's absorbed by crops and the biodiesel carbon cycle continues, as shown in **Figure 3**.

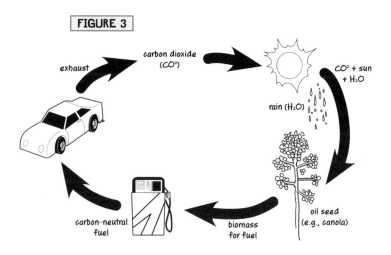

FIGURE 3

exhaust — carbon dioxide (CO_2) — CO_2 + sun + H_2O — rain (H_2O) — oil seed (e.g., canola) — biomass for fuel — carbon-neutral fuel

BIODIESEL CARBON CYCLE

Sneaky Ethanol Demonstration

Ethanol has been used to power vehicles since the early twentieth century—Henry Ford had ethanol-fueled Model T vehicles. Ethanol (specifically, E85—a mixture of 85 percent ethanol and 15 percent gasoline) vehicles have been available for consumers since 1992.

Ethanol can also be produced from biomass feedstocks, including corn stalks, grasses, paper, wood wastes (e.g., wood chips and sawdust), and green wastes (e.g., vegetable and fruit wastes, leaves, and grass clippings).

Figure 1 illustrates the basic ethanol production process. Corn is crushed and mixed with water. It is heated and mixed with enzymes to convert its starch into sugar. Then, it is fermented with yeast to make alcohol. To boost the alcohol content, the mixture is boiled and then dehydrated.

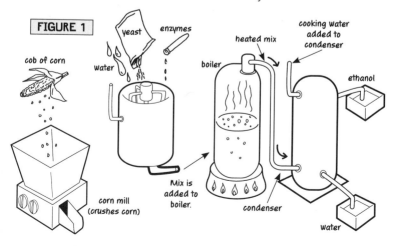

Ethanol emits cleaner emissions (carbon dioxide or CO_2, carbon monoxide, and particulate emissions) compared with gasoline and diesel fuel.

This project will enable you to demonstrate how sugar breaks down into ethyl alcohol, ethanol, and carbon dioxide.

What's Needed

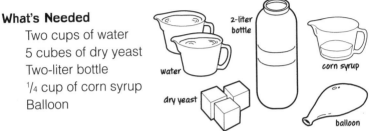

Two cups of water
5 cubes of dry yeast
Two-liter bottle
$1/4$ cup of corn syrup
Balloon

What to Do

First, pour the 2 cups of water and 5 cubes of yeast into the bottle and mix them by shaking the bottle for one minute. See **Figure 2**.

Then, pour the $1/4$ cup of corn syrup in the bottle and shake it for a minute. Wrap the lip of the balloon over the mouth of the bottle, as shown in **Figure 3**. Let the bottle sit, and monitor the liquid and the balloon every two hours.

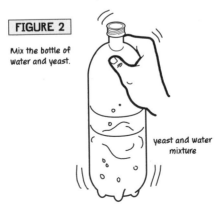

FIGURE 2

Mix the bottle of water and yeast.

yeast and water mixture

You will first see some bubbles appear on the surface of the mixture, and eventually the balloon will inflate. Fermentation is taking place. This is the process by which the yeast breaks down the sugar in the corn syrup into ethyl alcohol (ethanol) and carbon dioxide (which rises and inflates the balloon). See **Figure 4**.

You can also perform this demonstration by substituting a cola drink or table sugar for the corn syrup. Try testing all three mixtures with three separate bottles and note the amount of time for bubbles to form and the rate of inflation of the balloon.

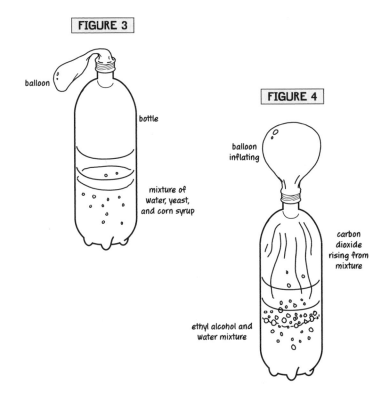

FIGURE 3

balloon

bottle

mixture of water, yeast, and corn syrup

FIGURE 4

balloon inflating

carbon dioxide rising from mixture

ethyl alcohol and water mixture

Sneaky Electrical Generator

New energy sources are being found and refined every day, and you can demonstrate how industry, smaller businesses, and individuals take advantage of various forms of alternate energy sources. This project illustrates three methods that harness the power of wind, water, and steam to produce electricity.

When a wire moves near a magnet, an electrical current is induced. Using this knowledge, you can create a Sneaky Electrical Generator with a toy motor.

What's Needed

Three large paper clips
Electrical tape
Toy car motor
Pliers
Voltmeter
Wire (optional)

What to Do

First, bend the three paper clips into the shapes shown in **Figure 1**. Paper clip 1 will act as a hand crank. The other two paper clips will act as propeller blades.

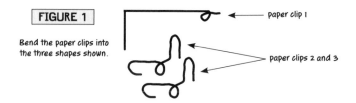

FIGURE 1

Bend the paper clips into the three shapes shown.

paper clip 1

paper clips 2 and 3

Next, wrap electrical tape around the shaft of the toy car motor. See **Figure 2**.

If the motor does not have wires on its two terminals, tape two 4-inch lengths of wire to them with tape.

Then, attach the first paper clip to the motor shaft and press it tight with pliers. Place the voltmeter on its lowest direct current (DC) setting and wrap the motor wires around its probes. Cranking the motor should cause the voltmeter to indicate a current has been generated, as shown in **Figure 3**.

Next, remove the first paper clip and press the other two paper clips onto the motor shaft as shown in **Figure 4**. Reshape the first paper clip to resemble the other two and press it onto the motor shaft also. See **Figure 5**.

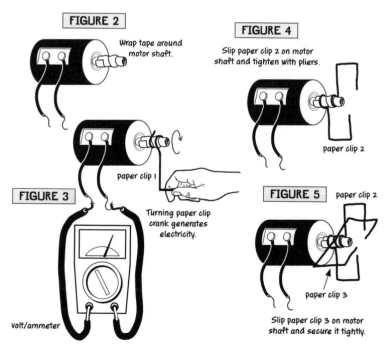

FIGURE 2

Wrap tape around motor shaft.

FIGURE 4

Slip paper clip 2 on motor shaft and tighten with pliers.

paper clip 2

paper clip 1

FIGURE 3

Turning paper clip crank generates electricity.

FIGURE 5

paper clip 2

paper clip 3

Slip paper clip 3 on motor shaft and secure it tightly.

volt/ammeter

Apply tape to all three paper clips to form propeller blades, as shown in **Figure 6**.

If you blow on the propeller or use a small hair dryer on it, the blades will turn and you will be harnessing wind power to generate electricity.

You can carefully hold the motor blades near a teakettle spout to harness steam power or place the propeller under a faucet's stream of running water to harness hydro power as shown in **Figure 7**.

Note: If you have a personal battery-powered fan, you can connect it to the voltmeter and spin its blades with your fingers to attain the same effect. See **Figure 8**.

Figure 9 illustrates the internal parts of a wind turbine. Multiple wind turbines, called a wind farm, are shown in **Figure 10**.

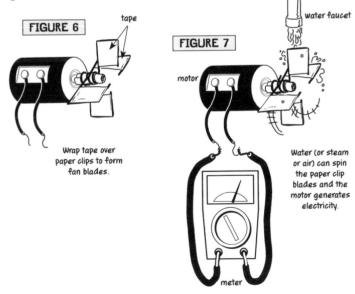

FIGURE 6

tape

Wrap tape over paper clips to form fan blades.

FIGURE 7

water faucet

motor

Water (or steam or air) can spin the paper clip blades and the motor generates electricity.

meter

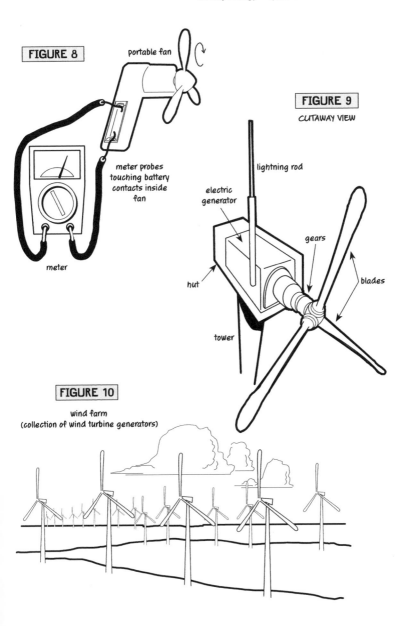

FIGURE 8

portable fan

meter probes
touching battery
contacts inside
fan

meter

FIGURE 9

CUTAWAY VIEW

lightning rod

electric
generator

gears

hut

blades

tower

FIGURE 10

wind farm
(collection of wind turbine generators)

Sneaky Hybrid Car Demonstration

Hybrid cars utilize two different methods of power—usually a gas combustion engine and an electrical motor—to power the vehicle. Depending on the design, a hybrid car can use one type of power for initial movement at low speeds and then another form of propulsion at higher speed, to optimize gas savings. Some hybrid models use both types of power simultaneously to complement each other.

For instance, a Toyota Prius hybrid initially uses an electric motor for low speeds, usually under 10 miles per hour, and switches to its gasoline engine for high-speed operation.

During braking, standard vehicles use mechanical pressure against brake drums or disks to slow the vehicle. Energy is lost as heat during this process. The Prius has another power-saving technology: a second, smaller motor/generator uses energy normally lost to heat during braking, to recharge its battery or act as a motor itself to add power to the engine's output. See **Figure 1**.

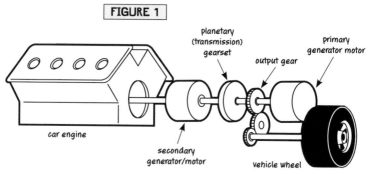

FIGURE 1

planetary (transmission) gearset

primary generator motor

output gear

car engine

secondary generator/motor

vehicle wheel

This project will show how to make a hybrid car that stores energy for use when the primary source is not active.

What's Needed

Rubber band
Two paper clips
Wire or thread spool
Transparent tape
1 large paper clip
Toy wire- or radio-controlled car

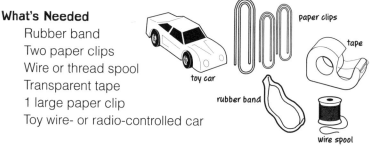

paper clips

tape

toy car

rubber band

wire spool

What to Do

First, thread the rubber band into the opening of a regular paper clip and back through the hole on the other end of the rubber band. Pull tightly until a knot is formed, as shown in **Figure 2**. Push the rubber band through the spool and use tape to secure the paper clip to the outside. See **Figure 3**.

Bend another regular paper clip into a **V** shape, as shown in **Figure 4**. Slip the loose end of the rubber band onto the middle of the **V**-shaped paper clip. See **Figure 5**.

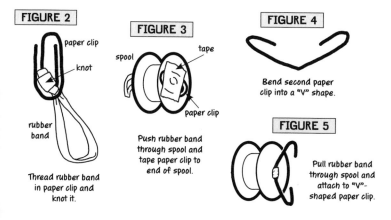

FIGURE 2

paper clip

knot

rubber band

Thread rubber band in paper clip and knot it.

FIGURE 3

spool

tape

paper clip

Push rubber band through spool and tape paper clip to end of spool.

FIGURE 4

Bend second paper clip into a "V" shape.

FIGURE 5

Pull rubber band through spool and attach to "V"-shaped paper clip.

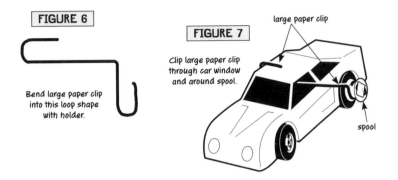

FIGURE 6

Bend large paper clip into this loop shape with holder.

large paper clip

FIGURE 7

Clip large paper clip through car window and around spool.

spool

Next, bend the large paper clip so that one side has a round hook to hold the spool (see **Figure 6**) and the other end will fit through the toy car window. **Figure 7** shows how to mount the spool onto the large paper clip and secure it to the car.

Next, bend the large paper clip so the spool will touch the floor surface and spin when the car moves on the floor. Using the remote control, run the toy car in circles on the floor at least five times around the room. Carefully lift the car while holding the spool. Pull the spool off the large paper clip and set it on the floor. It will spin on its own because the rubber band was wound by the toy car's movement.

Sneaky Hydrogen Power Demonstration

Hydrogen is an energy carrier, not an energy source. In the future, hydrogen fuel cells will be virtually emission-free forms of energy storage devices.

Fuel cells use a chemical reaction to produce electricity by combining hydrogen and oxygen. A diagram of a polymer electrolyte membrane (PEM) fuel cell is shown in **Figure 1**. Hydrogen enters the fuel cell's anode, where its electrons and protons are separated. The protons pass through the PEM while the electrons are forced to take an external route, which makes electricity. Oxygen is fed into the cathode side and combines with the protons and electrons to form water. The cycle repeats and produces an electrical current. See **Figure 2**. This process is called *electrolysis.*

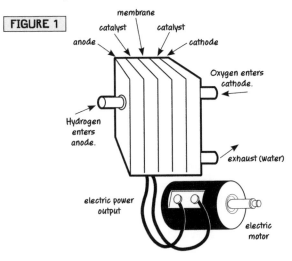

FIGURE 1

membrane
catalyst   catalyst
anode   cathode

Oxygen enters
cathode.

Hydrogen
enters
anode.

exhaust (water)

electric power
output

electric
motor

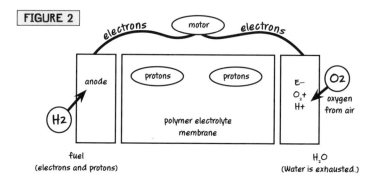

FIGURE 2

electrons — motor — electrons

anode

protons   protons

H_2

polymer electrolyte membrane

E−
O_2+
H+

O_2

oxygen from air

fuel
(electrons and protons)

H_2O
(Water is exhausted.)

You can demonstrate this process by separating water (H_2O, composed of hydrogen and oxygen) into its two elements with electricity.

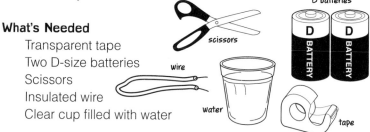

scissors

wire

water

D batteries

D BATTERY   D BATTERY

tape

What's Needed

Transparent tape
Two D-size batteries
Scissors
Insulated wire
Clear cup filled with water

What to Do

Tape the two D-size batteries together with one positive end connected to the negative end of the other. See **Figure 3**.

Cut two pieces of insulated wire and strip the insulation from both ends of them. Tape the wires to the ends of the battery terminals, as shown in **Figure 4**.

Next, place both of the free wire ends in the cup of water. See **Figure 5**. You should soon see bubbles appear on the ends of the wire lead. One of them will have about twice as many bubbles. This is hydrogen gas separating from the oxygen, as shown in **Figure 6**.

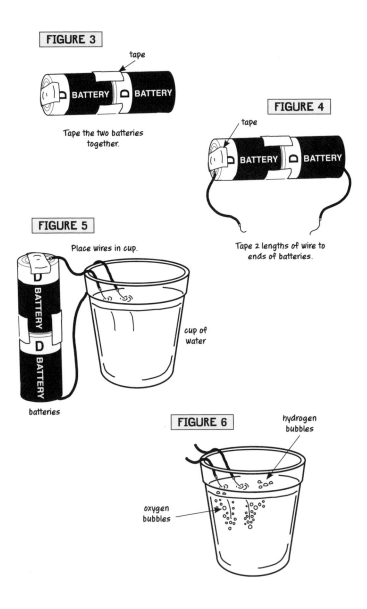

FIGURE 3

tape

Tape the two batteries together.

FIGURE 4

tape

Tape 2 lengths of wire to ends of batteries.

FIGURE 5

Place wires in cup.

cup of water

batteries

FIGURE 6

hydrogen bubbles

oxygen bubbles

Sneaky Atomic Fundamentals Simulation

Nuclear Power

Radioactive material, like uranium, must be located, mined, and enriched before it can be put to use in nuclear power plants. The following projects provide experiments and simulations for unique science projects.

Nuclear Fission Simulation

Elements are the basic building blocks of matter in the universe and are made from just one type of atom.

Atoms are the building blocks of an element. A group of atoms bound together is called a *molecule.* Compounds are two or more different type of atoms bound together. For instance, water (H_2O) consists of two hydrogen atoms and one oxygen atom.

Although atoms are the smallest bit of a pure substance, atoms are made up of still smaller particles. They include *neutrons* and *protons* in its center (or nucleus) with *electrons* circling around them. See **Figure 1**.

Note: An element's *atomic number* is the number of protons in the nucleus.

FIGURE 1

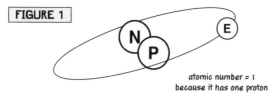

atomic number = 1
because it has one proton

Atoms of the same substance that have a different number of neutrons are called *isotopes.* For example, most hydrogen atoms have just one electron and one proton in their nucleus. A rare form of hydrogen that instead has one proton and one neutron in its nucleus is called *deuterium.* Another hydrogen isotope, which has one proton and two neutrons, is called *tritium.* See **Figure 2**.

Nuclear fission is the process of releasing nuclear energy by splitting the nucleus of uranium or plutonium atoms. Most uranium is the type called U-238 because it has 92 protons and 146 neutrons in its nucleus, for a total of 238 nuclear particles. It is radioactive but, when bombarded by neutrons, it absorbs them and the nucleus does not split. This type does not produce a fission chain reaction on its own.

An isotope of uranium that has three fewer neutrons (143) in its nucleus is called U-235. It is very rare and volatile. U-235 atoms will easily produce a fission chain reaction because there are already stray neutrons in the air. When a stray neutron flies into the nucleus of a U-235 atom and splits it, two neutrons fly out. These two neutrons split more atoms, releasing four more neutrons, and so on, starting a chain reaction that produces tremendous heat energy. See **Figure 3**.

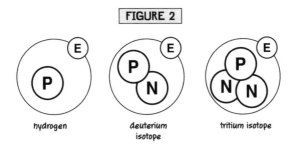

| FIGURE 2 |

hydrogen

deuterium
isotope

tritium isotope

Hydrogen atoms and their isotopes

fission reaction   **FIGURE 3**   Heat is emitted.

Stray neutron
collides with U-235
atom and splits
it, causing more
neutrons to emit
that split more
atoms.

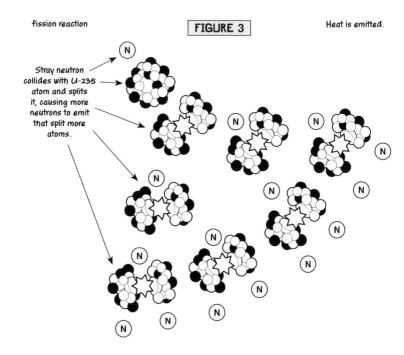

You can make a simple simulation of nuclear fission, using 3 by 5-inch cards. Draw illustrations of a single neutron, then an atom splitting and emitting more neutrons and more atoms splitting on the next cards, as shown in **Figure 4**.

When you push over the first card, which represents a stray neutron, it causes the other cards to fall. This chain reaction represents the splitting uranium 235 atoms, whose ejected neutrons split more atoms. See **Figure 5**.

Uranium enrichment is the process of separating U-235 isotopes from the more prevalent U-238. Two methods are widely used to enrich uranium: gas diffusion and centrifuge diffusion.

FIGURE 4

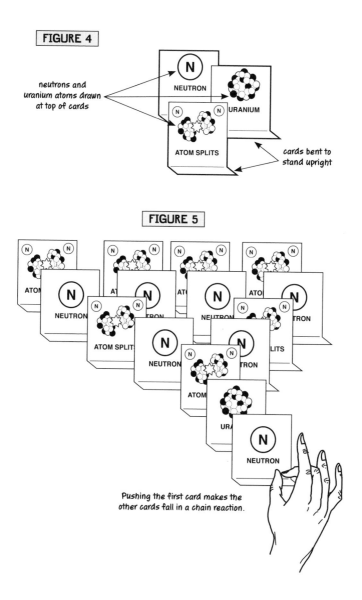

neutrons and uranium atoms drawn at top of cards

NEUTRON

URANIUM

ATOM SPLITS

cards bent to stand upright

FIGURE 5

NEUTRON

ATOM SPLITS

Pushing the first card makes the other cards fall in a chain reaction.

Gas diffusion consists of using a filter, like a kitchen strainer, to block larger particles from going through.

Centrifuge diffusion spins a substance to separate the heavier material, the way a clothes washer extracts water from garments during its spin cycle.

Gas Diffusion Enrichment Simulation

The gas diffusion method mixes uranium with fluoride to create uranium fluoride gas. This gas is pumped into filters that block the heavier uranium 238, with its three extra neutrons, but allow the lighter U-235 atoms through.

You can demonstrate this isotope-filtering process, using common household items.

What's Needed
Scissors
Waxed paper
Bowl
Tape
Needle
Large spoon
Salt
Flour

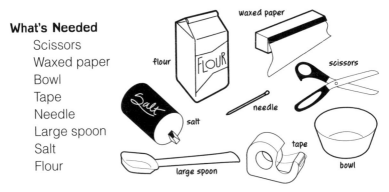

What to Do
First, cut a piece of waxed paper that will cover the top of the bowl and affix it with tape so that it stays in place, as shown in **Figure 1**. Carefully using the needle, puncture about thirty holes in the waxed paper. See **Figure 2**.

Then, use the spoon to pour equal parts of salt and flour on the waxed paper, as shown in **Figure 3**. (The salt will represent a U-238 atom; and the flour, a U-235 atom.)

Rub the mixture around on the surface with the bottom of the spoon. See **Figure 4**. Remove the rubber band and waxed paper, and check the bowl. It should have more flour, which is finer and lighter than the salt, as shown in **Figure 5**. The waxed paper and holes acted as a filter for the larger salt granules, which is similar to the gas diffusion method used for uranium.

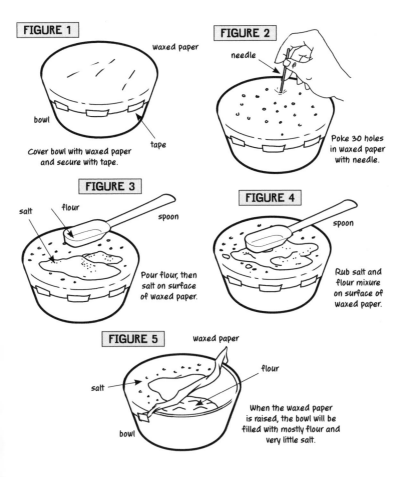

FIGURE 1

waxed paper

bowl

tape

Cover bowl with waxed paper and secure with tape.

FIGURE 2

needle

Poke 30 holes in waxed paper with needle.

FIGURE 3

salt   flour   spoon

Pour flour, then salt on surface of waxed paper.

FIGURE 4

spoon

Rub salt and flour mixure on surface of waxed paper.

FIGURE 5   waxed paper

flour

salt

bowl

When the waxed paper is raised, the bowl will be filled with mostly flour and very little salt.

Centrifuge Enrichment Simulation

A centrifuge is a cylindrical device that spins. When substances are placed in it, centrifugal force causes the heavier materials to separate and move toward the outer surface.

You can make a sneaky centrifuge to demonstrate this technique.

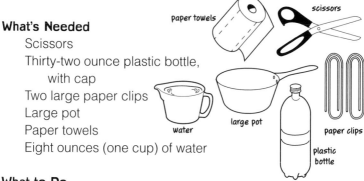

What's Needed
Scissors
Thirty-two ounce plastic bottle,
    with cap
Two large paper clips
Large pot
Paper towels
Eight ounces (one cup) of water

What to Do
First, carefully cut off the top third of the small bottle and use the points of the scissors to puncture small holes all around its body, as shown in **Figure 1**.

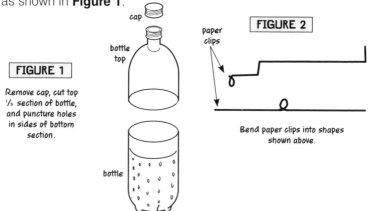

cap

bottle top

| FIGURE 1 |

Remove cap, cut top
⅓ section of bottle,
and puncture holes
in sides of bottom
section.

bottle

paper clips

| FIGURE 2 |

Bend paper clips into shapes
shown above.

Bend the two paper clips into the shapes shown in **Figure 2**.

Next, connect the first paper clip with the center loop into the top holes on the side of the bottle. Then, attach the second paper clip into the first one's center loop hole. See **Figure 3**. They will act as a handle and stirring lever for the bottle.

Place the bottle cap into the bottom of the pot and then place the bottle on top of it. Place paper towels inside the bottle and pour 8 ounces of water onto the paper towels. See **Figure 4**.

Now turn the paper clip handle rapidly to spin the bottle. Keep the bottle spinning for about five minutes. Afterward, examine the paper towels to see how much they've dried and check the pot for water droplets. See **Figure 5**.

You'll discover that the centrifugal force removed water from the towels through the holes in the bottle and into the pot.

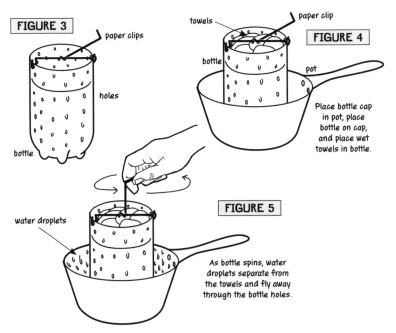

FIGURE 3

paper clips

holes

bottle

towels

paper clip

FIGURE 4

bottle

pot

Place bottle cap in pot, place bottle on cap, and place wet towels in bottle.

water droplets

FIGURE 5

As bottle spins, water droplets separate from the towels and fly away through the bottle holes.

Nuclear Energy Simulation

This project will illustrate the multiple stages of nuclear energy production and power distribution, using everyday items. It's a perfect simulation for a school science project. First, let's review how nuclear energy is produced and converted into a form that can be used by consumers.

Similar to other power plants, nuclear power plants produce heat energy to boil water into steam that runs a turbine, which in turn powers an electrical generator. The main difference is that the heat is generated from a nuclear reaction (fission) in a lead-lined reactor, rather than without fission from burning coal.

Radioactive material, such as uranium, is mined and enriched, as discussed in Nuclear Fission Simulation. Once the U-235 materials are collected, they are stored as pellets inside aluminum rods. When placed near other rods, stray neutrons will start a nuclear fusion chain reaction, producing tremendous heat energy. To control the nuclear fission process, control rods are placed near them.

Control rods have pellets of cadmium or boron inside them, which absorb neutrons to halt the fission reaction. The control rods are placed between the U-235 rods in a matrix pattern (U-235 rod, control rod, U-235 rod, and so on), as shown in **Figure 1**.

When the control rods are lifted up and away from the U-235 rods, the fission reaction accelerates and heat is given off. The heat is used to turn water into steam, which turns an electrical turbine generator.

This project will show the four stages of a nuclear reactor in action, using household items.

FIGURE 1

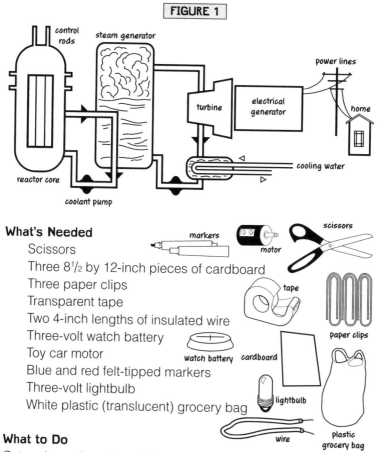

What's Needed

Scissors
Three 8½ by 12-inch pieces of cardboard
Three paper clips
Transparent tape
Two 4-inch lengths of insulated wire
Three-volt watch battery
Toy car motor
Blue and red felt-tipped markers
Three-volt lightbulb
White plastic (translucent) grocery bag

What to Do

Cut a piece of cardboard into the shape and dimensions shown in **Figure 2**. Be sure to cut the slits in the corners.

Bend two paper clips into an **S** shape and tape them to the center of the board. See **Figure 3**.

Strip the insulation from the ends of the two wires and tape one on each side of the watch battery, as shown in **Figure 4**.

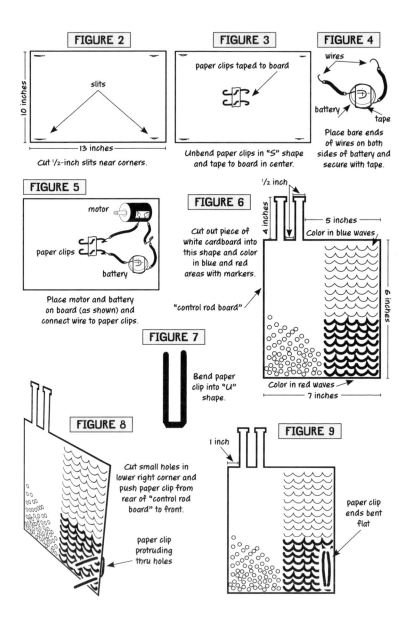

FIGURE 2

10 inches

13 inches

slits

Cut ½-inch slits near corners.

FIGURE 3

paper clips taped to board

Unbend paper clips in "S" shape and tape to board in center.

FIGURE 4

wires

battery

tape

Place bare ends of wires on both sides of battery and secure with tape.

FIGURE 5

motor

paper clips

battery

Place motor and battery on board (as shown) and connect wire to paper clips.

FIGURE 6

½ inch

4 inches

5 inches

Color in blue waves

6 inches

Cut out piece of white cardboard into this shape and color in blue and red areas with markers.

"control rod board"

Color in red waves

7 inches

FIGURE 7

Bend paper clip into "U" shape.

FIGURE 8

Cut small holes in lower right corner and push paper clip from rear of "control rod board" to front.

paper clip protruding thru holes

FIGURE 9

1 inch

paper clip ends bent flat

Next, position the battery and motor on the cardboard. Connect the wires in series from the paper clips to the motor to the battery, as shown in **Figure 5**.

Cut out the second piece of cardboard in the shape and dimensions shown in **Figure 6**. Notice the control rod "handles" at the top. Draw the neutron chain reaction onto the cardboard to represent the U-235 atom fission process of electrons bombarding other atoms, splitting them, and continuing the chain reaction: on the right side of the cardboard, draw blue water waves on the top half and red water waves on the bottom. The red shows the steamy, hot water from the heating process.

Next, bend a paper clip into a **U** shape. See **Figure 7**. Cut small holes in the control rod board's right corner area (the same corner as your red water waves). Push the paper clip through the holes from the back and bend the ends flat. See **Figures 8** and **9**.

When the control rod board is positioned properly on the main board, the "red water wave" paper clip will contact the other two paper clips and complete the electrical circuit, activating the motor. See **Figure 10**.

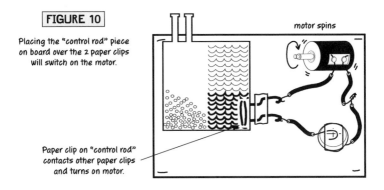

FIGURE 10

Placing the "control rod" piece on board over the 2 paper clips will switch on the motor.

motor spins

Paper clip on "control rod" contacts other paper clips and turns on motor.

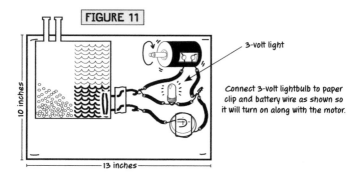

FIGURE 11

10 inches

13 inches

3-volt light

Connect 3-volt lightbulb to paper clip and battery wire as shown so it will turn on along with the motor.

Next, connect the light's wires across the motor's wires so it will turn on with the motor. See **Figure 11**.

Cut two strips of spare cardboard and tape them to the sides of the control rod board, to ensure that it slides in a straight path. See **Figure 12**.

Next, cut a piece of cardboard into the dimensions and shape shown in **Figure 13**. Notice the tabs on each corner. They will later fit into the main board's corner slots. Also cut out sections for the reactor core, steam generator, electrical generator (motor), and house window. Turn the cover board over, and cut out and tape white translucent plastic over the cutout sections.

Last, insert the cover board's tabs into the main board's slots and test to see if all three boards fit properly. Test the movement of the control rod board to ensure that it will activate the motor and light. See **Figure 14**.

When all of the sections fit and work properly, sliding the control rod up will show the reactor core's nuclear fission chain reaction, which generates steam and turns the turbine. This activates the electrical generator and distributes power to light the house. See **Figure 15**.

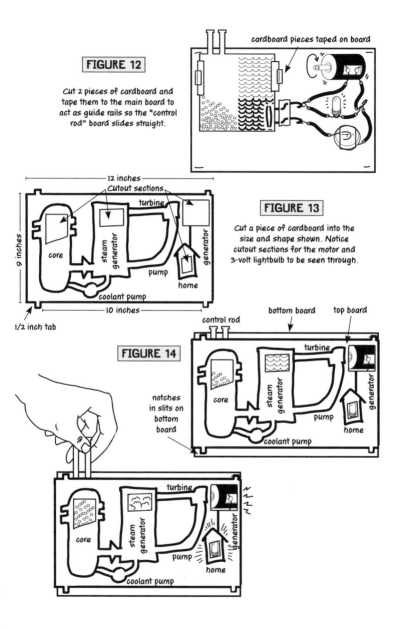

FIGURE 12

Cut 2 pieces of cardboard and tape them to the main board to act as guide rails so the "control rod" board slides straight.

cardboard pieces taped on board

12 inches

Cutout sections

turbine

9 inches

core

steam generator

generator

pump

home

coolant pump

10 inches

1/2 inch tab

FIGURE 13

Cut a piece of cardboard into the size and shape shown. Notice cutout sections for the motor and 3-volt lightbulb to be seen through.

bottom board   top board

control rod

turbine

FIGURE 14

notches in slits on bottom board

core

steam generator

generator

pump

home

coolant pump

turbine

core

steam generator

generator

pump

home

coolant pump

PART IV
Bonus Sections

Sneaky Uses for Everyday Things and
Sneakier Uses for Everyday Things **Project Updates**

If you weren't aware by now, this book is the third in the
Sneaky Uses series. As time goes on, you discover better
ways of doing things. That's what this bonus section is about.
It provides updates to projects and techniques found in
Sneaky Uses for Everyday Things and *Sneakier Uses for
Everyday Things*.

Sneaky project updates from *Sneaky Uses for Everyday
Things* include little-known sources for superstrong magnets
found in everyday things, an improved magnetically sensitive
switch, a direction-finding update, and a Sneaky Magnifier.

Updates to projects found in *Sneakier Uses for Everyday
Things* include a simple-to-make static electricity tester, more
Hide and Sneak techniques for passwords and personal
identification numbers, and several Gadget Jacket updates
and options.

Sneaky Direction Finding

In the *Sneaky Uses for Everyday Things* project Road Scholar: Down-to-Earth Direction Finding, readers learned that even without a compass, there are numerous ways to find directions in desolate areas. Here's another sneaky one:

What's Needed
Stick or branch about 3 feet long
Rock or leaf

What to Do
On a sunny day, you can find out which direction is north, south, east, or west by using shadows. Stand a stick upright in the ground, as shown in **Figure 1**. Notice the shadow it casts and, using a rock or leaf, mark the shadow's edge.

Wait about fifteen minutes and notice the new shadow that appears. Mark its tip, too. See **Figure 2**. Draw an imaginary line between the two marks. This is the east–west line (west is the first tip, and the second marker represents east). You can draw an imaginary or real line across the east–west line to determine the north and south directions. See **Figure 3**.

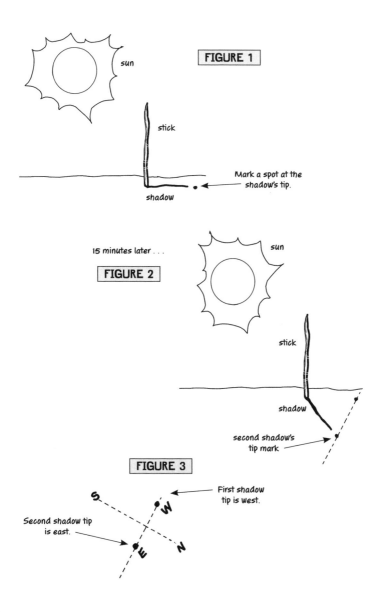

FIGURE 1

sun

stick

shadow

Mark a spot at the shadow's tip.

15 minutes later . . .

FIGURE 2

sun

stick

shadow

second shadow's tip mark

FIGURE 3

First shadow tip is west.

Second shadow tip is east.

Sneaky Magnifier

In the *Sneaky Uses for Everyday Things* project Make a Sneaky Magnifier, readers learned techniques to see tiny objects by using household objects. Here's a bonus Sneaky Magnifier you can make with paper:

What's Needed
    Needle or paper clip
    Paper or cardboard

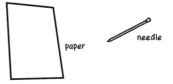

What to Do
If you're having trouble focusing on a small object or fine point, this Sneaky Magnifier will come in handy. Simply use a needle or paper clip to poke a small hole in a piece of paper (preferably a dark color), as shown in **Figure 1**.

    Place the paper over the object, and you will see that the image is now enlarged. See **Figure 2**.

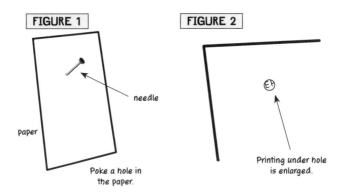

Sneaky Magnet Sources

In *Sneaky Uses for Everyday Things* project Make a Power Ring, readers learned how to attach a magnet to a ring, to control devices. Here's are additional sneaky sources for superstrong, miniature magnets:

Superstrong magnets can be found in the most unlikely everyday items. For instance, miniature radio-controlled (RC) toy cars, the type that can fit in the palm of your hand, use a very strong, tiny magnet for steering. If you obtain a broken, discarded RC car, pry the body off its frame and remove the tiny magnet located between the front wheels. See **Figure 1**.

Some hearing-aid battery packages include a tiny, strong magnet to prevent the batteries from falling when the device is removed from its packaging. You can easily extract the magnet and use it for your own projects. See **Figure 2**.

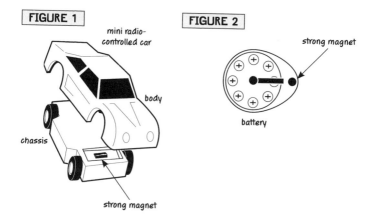

FIGURE 1

mini radio-controlled car

body

chassis

strong magnet

FIGURE 2

strong magnet

battery

Some toy dart kits use a metal board and powerful magnets on the tip of each of the darts. See **Figure 3**.

If you have a broken shaker-style flashlight, the type that uses no batteries, you can unscrew its case to access its superstrong magnet, as shown in **Figure 4**.

Sneaky Use for Magnets

You can test monetary currency for validity by folding a bill in half, as shown in **Figure 5**, and aiming the magnet near its edge. Real currency, unlike a counterfeit, has iron particles in the ink and will move toward a strong magnet.

Strong magnets can activate such devices as bulbs and buzzers, as shown in the next Sneaky Switch project.

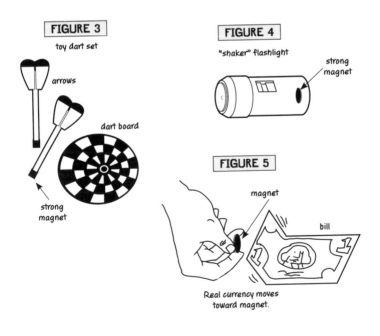

FIGURE 3

toy dart set

arrows

dart board

strong magnet

FIGURE 4

"shaker" flashlight

strong magnet

FIGURE 5

magnet

bill

Real currency moves toward magnet.

Sneaky Switch

In the *Sneaky Uses for Everyday Things* project Make Power Ring-Activated Gadgets, readers learned how to produce a switch that turns on when a magnet is in close proximity. Here's another way to design it for improved visual clarity (for science projects), using everyday things:

What's Needed

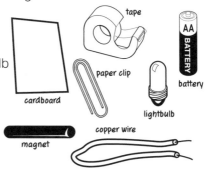

- AA-size battery
- Small 1½-volt lightbulb
- Transparent tape
- Cardboard
- Paper clip
- Stiff copper wire
- Strong magnet

What to Do

In this project, the parts are mounted with tape to a piece of cardboard (a postcard will work fine) so the operation of the Sneaky Switch can be seen by others or recorded on a digital camera.

First, place the battery and bulb end to end and tape them to the cardboard, as shown in **Figure 1**.

Next, bend the paper clip in the shape shown in **Figure 2**, so it wraps around the battery's positive (+) terminal.

Then, wrap the stiff copper wire around the bulb's base and bend it so it hovers over the paper clip, as shown in **Figure 3**. Place a piece of tape on the end of the paper clip to secure it to the board.

Last, ensure that the paper clip is bent upward slightly and is very close but not touching the copper wire above it. It should be able to move freely. Bring the strong magnet close to the top of the copper wire. The paper clip should move upward toward the magnet, contacting the copper wire and lighting the bulb as shown in **Figure 4**.

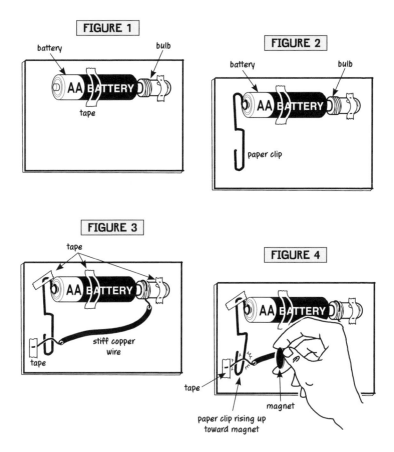

Gadget Jacket

Sneaky Sleeve Pocket

In *Sneakier Uses for Everyday Things,* readers learned how to make Sneaky Pockets, including a quick-release sleeve pocket, using fabric, elastic, and Velcro material. This updated project illustrates a simpler way to make a quick-release Sneaky Sleeve Pocket to access such devices as a pen, camera, flashlight, or calculator.

What's Needed

Scissors
Cloth
Needle
Thread
Double-stick Velcro strips
Jacket

What to Do

First, cut the cloth in the dimensions shown in **Figure 1**. Fold the material in half and use the needle and thread to sew it along the top and left side. See **Figure 2**.

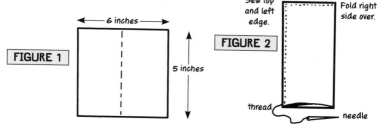

Apply two Velcro strips to the inside area of the lower sleeve of the jacket as shown in **Figure 3**. Next, turn the pocket inside out so the edges are smooth. Cut one side of the pocket so two small strips of fabric form latches, and apply small Velcro strips to them. Also apply Velcro strips on the back of the pocket. See **Figure 4**. **Figure 5** shows how the pocket appears when the latches are closed.

Place the pocket in the sleeve and press firmly so the Velcro secures it, as shown in **Figure 6**. When the pocket is attached inside the sleeve by the Velcro strips latched together, you can use your little finger to pry open the pocket latch. Your desired device will slide into the palm of your hand. See **Figure 7**.

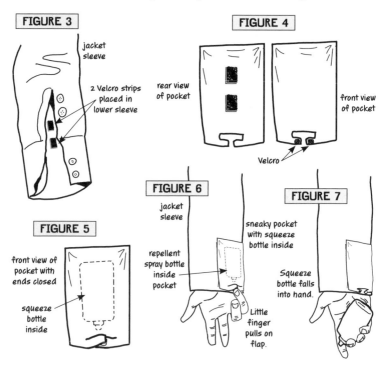

FIGURE 3

jacket
sleeve

2 Velcro strips
placed in
lower sleeve

FIGURE 4

rear view
of pocket

front view
of pocket

Velcro

FIGURE 5

front view of
pocket with
ends closed

squeeze
bottle
inside

FIGURE 6

jacket
sleeve

repellent
spray bottle
inside
pocket

Little
finger
pulls on
flap.

FIGURE 7

sneaky pocket
with squeeze
bottle inside

Squeeze
bottle falls
into hand.

Camera and Memory Drive

In *Sneakier Uses for Everyday Things,* Sneaky Collar, readers learned how to add devices to their gadget jacket's collar (with quick-release Velcro strips). Here are two additional applications:

What's Needed
Scissors
Double-stick Velcro strips
Mini digital camera
Jacket
USB flashdrive

What to Do
Miniature digital, keychain cameras are now commonplace, can fit in the palm of your hand, and are available for under ten dollars. Many of them even have a video-recording mode. Adding one to the Gadget Jacket allows you to be ready to capture once-in-a-lifetime events.

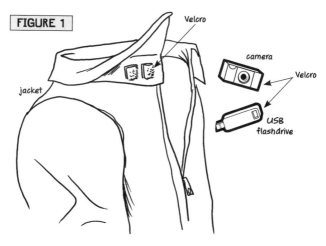

FIGURE 1

To mount the camera to the jacket, cut out small square pieces of Velcro. Apply them to the back of the camera and the matching Velcro pieces inside the collar area of the jacket. See **Figure 1**.

With many USB flashdrives now priced under five dollars, it makes sense to always have one with you. You can store text, graphics, music files, videos, and even entire Web sites on these miniature storage devices. Adding a flashdrive to your jacket will allow you to obtain and share files with others without having to log on to the Web. Plus, you'll have a convenient way to copy files from other computers whenever they are needed. With Velcro strips, the flashdrive always will be at hand.

Simply apply the appropriate Velcro strips to the flashdrive and under the collar area of the jacket, as shown in **Figure 2**, and you're ready to go.

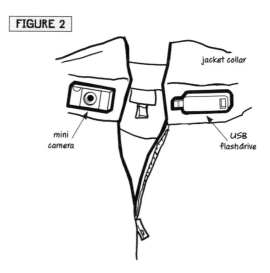

FIGURE 2

jacket collar

mini camera

USB flashdrive

Sneaky Static Electricity Tester

In *Sneakier Uses for Everyday Things,* readers learned how to
construct an Electroscope, a Static Electricity Tester. Here's a
simpler one you can make:

What's Needed

Large paper clip
Plastic cup or jar
Scissors
Aluminum foil
Comb or balloon

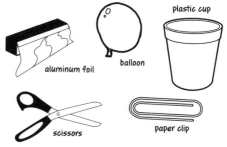

What to Do

To make a supersimple static electricity tester, bend the paper
clip into the **S** shape shown in **Figure 1**. Place the paper clip on
the edge of the cup. See **Figure 2**.

Next, cut two strips of aluminum foil, ½ inch by 2 inches,
and bend one end so they can be placed on the paper clips, as
shown in **Figure 3**.

FIGURE 1	FIGURE 2	FIGURE 3
Bend paper clip into this shape.	Place clip on lip of cup.	Place aluminum strips on paper clip.

Last, rub a comb or balloon on your hair or sweater and touch it to the top of the paper clip. You'll see the foil strips move. See **Figure 4**.

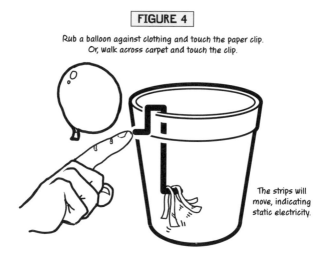

| FIGURE 4 |

Rub a balloon against clothing and touch the paper clip.
Or, walk across carpet and touch the clip.

The strips will move, indicating static electricity.

Hide and Sneak: Password and Personal Information Protection

You probably have a written record of your computer passwords and personal information numbers (PINs) that you need to keep hidden. Hiding your information is not hard but, to be on the safe side, you should assume that it could be found.

This project illustrates three sneaky methods of encoding your personal information so that in case it's found, it still can't be used by others.

Crease Message Encryption

What's Needed
Piece of paper
Pencil
Scissors

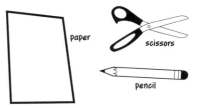

paper

scissors

pencil

What to Do
Fold a piece of paper in half and then fold it down to a square as shown in **Figure 1**. Next, unfold the paper, as shown in **Figure 2**, so you can see the center crease.

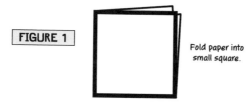

FIGURE 1

Fold paper into small square.

Then, write your password or message along the crease. See the example shown in **Figure 3**.

Last, write words on the paper that seem to describe an event or a message to disguise the secret cipher. See **Figure 4**. If the message is found, it will seem to be a simple message but you can follow the crease to discern the secret message.

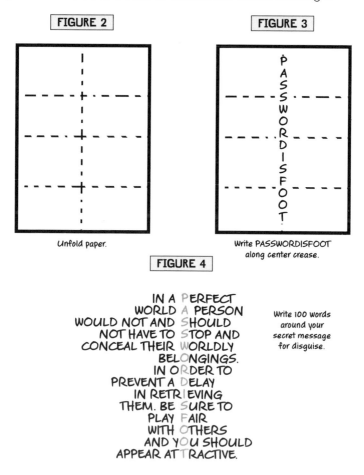

FIGURE 2

Unfold paper.

FIGURE 3

Write PASSWORDISFOOT along center crease.

FIGURE 4

IN A PERFECT
WORLD A PERSON
WOULD NOT AND SHOULD
NOT HAVE TO STOP AND
CONCEAL THEIR WORLDLY
BELONGINGS.
IN ORDER TO
PREVENT A DELAY
IN RETRIEVING
THEM. BE SURE TO
PLAY FAIR
WITH OTHERS
AND YOU SHOULD
APPEAR ATTRACTIVE.

Write 100 words
around your
secret message
for disguise.

Scroll Message Encryption

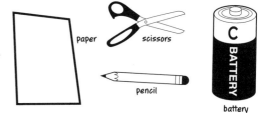

What's Needed
Scissors
Piece of paper
C-size battery
Pencil

paper

scissors

pencil

battery

What to Do
Cut a ½ by 11-inch strip of paper as shown in **Figure 1**. Tightly wrap the strip around a C-size battery and write your message across the strip from left to right. See **Figure 2**.

When you unwrap the strip, your original message is not intelligible. You can write more letters on the scroll to further disguise the message.

To recover your secret message, simply wrap your scroll around a C-size battery or similarly sized cylinder.

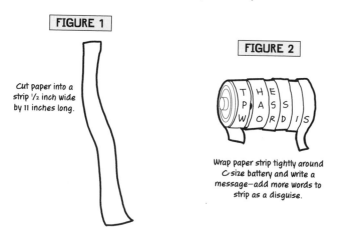

FIGURE 1

Cut paper into a strip ½ inch wide by 11 inches long.

FIGURE 2

Wrap paper strip tightly around C-size battery and write a message—add more words to strip as a disguise.

Label Code Encryption

To hide a record of one of your PIN codes, you can write a number code that refers to letters on a popular product label. If someone finds the code, it will not seem to have any meaning.

What's Needed
Product label
Pencil

pencil

label

What to Do
Be sure to select an easy-to-obtain, popular product that can be found in locations other than your home (in case you need to retrieve your PIN while traveling).

In the example shown in **Figure 1**, a mint package label is used for the code. On a piece of paper, write two letters to represent the product—TT for Tic Tac, in this example.

The numbers that follow represent the letters on a phrase you select from the product label, in order of appearance. The code TT 3, 2, 10, 14, 16, 24 represent the message: Tic Tac SECRET.

You can produce similar codes using other product labels, including the larger label on the back of the product.

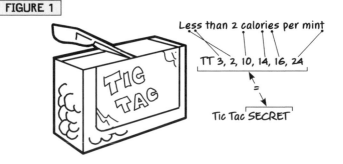

FIGURE 1

Less than 2 calories per mint

TT 3, 2, 10, 14, 16, 24

=

Tic Tac SECRET

Sneaky Uses for a Magnet

Magnets are one of the most versatile items for use with resourceful projects. They are used in telephones, computers, doorbells, electronic door locks, maglev (magnetic-levitation) trains, tape recorders, car crushers, scrap metal sorters, speakers, electric motors, generators, and more.

Here are more sneaky applications for magnets:

Parts Locater: An old antenna glued to a magnet makes a great parts locator. See **Figure 1**.

Tape Eraser: A magnet, when stroked near recording tape, will erase its contents. See **Figure 2**.

Cereal Iron Separator: Iron-fortified particles can be separated from cereal by placing magnets at the bottom of a bowl. See **Figure 3**.

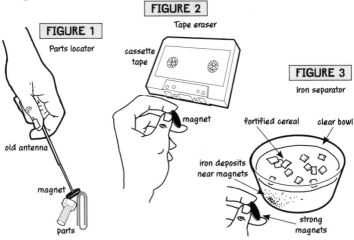

FIGURE 2
Tape eraser

FIGURE 1
Parts locator

cassette tape

magnet

old antenna

magnet

parts

FIGURE 3
Iron separator

fortified cereal   clear bowl

iron deposits near magnets

strong magnets

Levitator: Bend a large paper clip into a stand for a disk magnet, and a smaller paper clip, connected by a thread, will magically hover just below the magnet at the top. Turn the stand sideways or upside down, and spin the little paper clip for more fun. See **Figure 4**.

Magnet Maker: Stroke a thin piece of steel, iron, or tin at least twenty times in the same direction and you'll make it magnetic. See **Figure 5**.

Compass Maker: Stroke a needle at least twenty times in the same direction and, when it hangs or floats, it'll point north and south. See **Figures 6** and **7**.

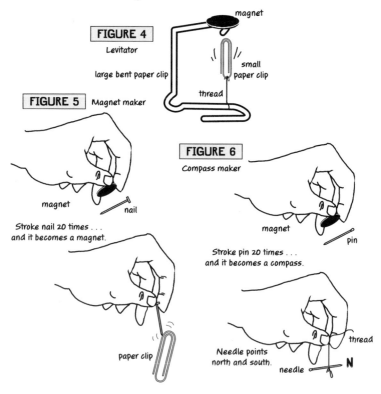

magnet

FIGURE 4

Levitator

large bent paper clip

small paper clip

thread

FIGURE 5 | Magnet maker

FIGURE 6

Compass maker

magnet

nail

Stroke nail 20 times . . .
and it becomes a magnet.

magnet

pin

Stroke pin 20 times . . .
and it becomes a compass.

paper clip

thread

Needle points
north and south.

needle

N

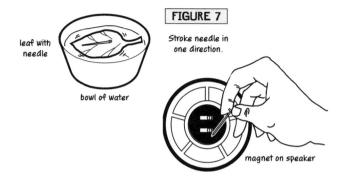

You will find more sneaky magnet projects throughout this book. See the following projects for details:

Buzzer

Motor

Magnetic Switch

Electrical Generator

Tape Design Wiggler

Quiz Tester

Science and Technology Resources

If you find that you like science and want to go still further in your quest for knowledge, this section provides a multitude of science education resources. It contains links to city, state, and national science fairs; science camps and schools; science organizations; and educational scholarships.

You'll also find special inventor resources and contests, grants and awards, free government programs, educator lesson plans, and additional links to free science project Web sites.

Check out some of the resource sites listed to see what free projects and fantastic career opportunities await you.

Science Freebies, Grants, and Scholarships
Community of Science www.cos.com
Education Freebies www.thehomeschoolmom.com/
    teacherslounge/freebies.php
Science Magazine www.sciencemag.org
Science Master www.sciencemaster.com
Science Teacher Freebies www.teacherhelp.org/freebies.htm
Siemens Foundation www.siemens-foundation.org
U.S. Government Science Grants www.science.doe.gov/grants

Inventors and Inventing
About Inventors http://inventors.about.com/od/campinventio1/
    index_r.ht

AMA Science www.sciencetoymaker.org

American Solar Energy Society www.ases.org

Association of Science: Technology Centers www.astc.org

Biodiesel Board http://biodiesel.org

By Kids for Kids www.bkfk.com

The Discovery Channel: Young Scientist Challenge www.
    discovery.com/dcysc

Electric Auto Association http://eaaev.org

Energy Information Administration www.eia.doe.gov

Energy Star www.energystar.gov

Exploratorium www.exploratorium.edu

Funology www.funology.com

Intel Science Talent Search www.sciserv.org

Inventors Digest http://inventorsdigest.com

Inventors HQ www.inventorshq.com/just %20for %20kids.htm

Inventor Resources http://invention.lifetips.com/cat/61342/kid-
    inventors-internet-resources/index.html

National Ethanol Vehicle Coalition http://e85fuel.com/index.php

National Geographic Kids www.nationalgeographic.com/ngkids/
    index.html

Nuclear Energy Institute www.nei.org

Plug in America http://pluginamerica.com

Science Toymaker www.funology.com

Smart Homeowner www.smart-homeowner.com

United Inventors Association www.uiausa.com

Wind Works www.wind-works.org/index.html

Women in Technology www.witi.com/index-c.shtml

Yahooligans http://yahooligans.yahoo.com/Science_and_Nature/
    Machines/Inventions/Inventors

Science Fairs

Children's Museum List www.childrensmuseums.org/visit/
reciprocal.htm
More Science Centers www.astc.org/sciencecenters/find_
scicenter.htm
Science Centers Worldwide http://physics.usc.edu/ScienceFairs
and www.cs.cmu.edu/~mwm/sci.html
Science Camps www.campresource.com
Science Camps for Girls www.sallyridecamps.com and www.
sme.org
Science Catalogs www.amasci.com/suppliers.html
U.S. Government Science Resources http://sciencedems.house.
gov/resources/science_education.htm

Energy-Saving Information

http://auto.howstuffworks.com/alternative-fuel-channel.htm
www.consumerenergycenter.org/errebate
www.ecohome.org
Energy Efficiency and Renewable Energy www.eere.energy.gov
and www1.eere.energy.gov/consumer/tips/
www.energystar.gov/
www.epa.gov/epahome/athome.htm
www.findsolar.com
www.homepower.com
http://savepower.lbl.gov
http://science.howstuffworks.com/fuel-cell.htm
http://science.howstuffworks.com/nuclear-power.htm
www.solarcooking.org
www.windenergy.com
www.windturbine.net

Web Sites of Interest

Have fun devising and making your own sneaky jacket adaptations and be sure to check for additional ideas (and post your own) at www.sneakyuses.com.

Science Sites

amasci.com
build-it-yourself.com
discovercircuits.com
exploratorium.edu
howtoons.net
kidsinvent.org
sciencetoymaker.org
sneakyuses.com
theteachersguide.com/QuickScienceActivities.html
us.brainium.com
uspto.gov/go/kids
wildplanet.com

Frugal and Thrift Sites

choose2reuse.org
freegiftclub.net
frugalcorner.com
frugalitynetwork.com
getfrugal.com
make-stuff.com
ready-made.com
Recycle.net
thefrugalshopper.com
thriftydeluxe.com
wackyuses.com
watchthepennies.com

Gadgets Sites

advanced-intelligence.com
berberblades.com
casio.com
colibri.com
dailygadget.com
equalizers1.com
girltech.com
gizmodo.com
ijustgottahavethat.com
inventorsdigest.com
johnson-smith.com
leatherman.com
netgadget.net
nutsandvolts.com
popgadget.net
robotstore.com
scientificsonline.com
smartplanet.net
spy-gear.net
spyderco.com
spymall.com
swissarmy.com
swisstechtools.com
the-gadgeteer.com/cgi-bin/redirect.cgi/gadget
thinkgeek.com
topeak.com
undercovergirl.com

Survival Sites

americansurvivalist.com
backwoodshome.com

backwoodsmanmag.com

basegear.com

beprepared.com

campmor.com

emergencypreparednessgear.com

equipped.com

fieldandstream.com

hikercentral.com/survival

homepower.com

productsforanywhere.com

ruhooked.com

secretsofsurvival.com

self-reliance.net

simply-survival.com

Survival.com

survival-center.com

Survivaliq.com

survivalplus.com

Survivalx.com

wildernesssurvival.com

wilderness-survival.net

windpower.org

Home Security Sites

mcgruff.org

ncpc.org

safesolutionsystems.com

X10.com

youdoitsecurity.com

Science and Technology Sites

about.com

boydhouse.com/crystalradio
craftsitedirectory.com
discover.com
hallscience.com
homeautomationmag.com
howstuffworks.com
johnson-smith.com
midnightscience.com
radioshack.com
scienceproject.com
scientificsonline.com
scitoys.com
thinkgeek.com
wildplanet.com

Other Web Sites of Interest

almanac.com
beprepared.com
casio.com
doityourself.com
equalizers1.com
movie-mistakes.com
nitpickers.com
popsci.com
popularmechanics.com
rube-goldberg.com
smarthome.com
tbotech.comrotorsportz.com
thefunplace.com
tipking.com
toollogic.com

Recommended Books

David Borgenicht and Joe Borgenicht, *The Action Hero's Handbook* (Quirk Books)

Robert Young Decton, *Come Back Alive* (Doubleday)

Dept. of the Air Force, *U.S. Air Force Search & Rescue Handbook* (The Lyons Press)

Dept. of the Army, *U.S. Army Survival Handbook* (The Lyons Press)

Simon Field, *Gonzo Gizmos* Simon (Chicago Review Press)

Ira Flatow, *They All Laughed . . . From Light Bulbs to Lasers: The Fascinating Stories Behind the Great Inventions That Have Changed Our Lives* (Perennial)

Joey Green, *Clean It! Fix It! Eat It!: Easy Ways to Solve Everyday Problems with Brand-Name Products You've Already Got Around the House* (Prentice Hall)

————. *Clean Your Clothes with Cheez Wiz: And Hundreds of Offbeat Uses for Dozens More Brand-Name Products* (Prentice Hall)

————. *Joey Green's Encyclopedia of Offbeat Uses for Brand-Name Products* (Prentice Hall)

Lois H. Gresh and Robert Weinberg, *The Science of Superheroes* (John Wiley & Sons)

William Gurstelle, *Backyard Ballistics* (Chicago Review Press)

Garth Hattingh, *The Outdoor Survival Handbook* (New Holland Publishers)

Vicky Lansky, *Another Use for 101 Common Household Items* (Book Peddlers)

————. *Baking Soda: Over 500 Fabulous, Fun, and Frugal Uses* (Book Peddlers)

————. *Don't Throw That Out: A Pennywise Parent's Guide* (Book Peddlers)

———. *Transparent Tape: Over 350 Super, Simple, and Surprising Uses* (Book Peddlers)

Hugh McManners, *The Complete Wilderness Training Book* (Dorling Kindersley)

Forrest M. Mims III, *Circuits and Projects* (Radio Shack)

———. *Science and Communications Circuits and Projects* (Radio Shack)

Steven W. Moje, *Paper Clip Science* (Sterling Publishing Co., Inc.)

Bob Newman, *Wilderness Wayfinding: How to Survive in the Wilderness as You Travel* (Paladin Press)

Tim Nyberg and Jim Berg, *The Duct Tape Book* (Workman Publishing Company, 1994)

———. *Duct Tape Book Too: Real Stories* (Workman Publishing Company)

———. *The Ultimate Duct Tape Book* (Workman Publishing Company)

Larry Dean Olsen, *Outdoor Survival Skills* (Chicago Review Press)

Joshua Piven and David Borgenicht, *The Worst-Case Scenario Survival* (Chronicle Books)

———. *The Worst-Case Scenario Travel* (Chronicle Books)

Royston M. Roberts, *Serendipity* (John Wiley & Sons)

Jim Wilkinson and Neil A. Downie, *Vacuum Bazookas, Electric Rainbow Jelly, and 27 Other Saturday Science Projects* (Princeton University Press)

John Wiseman, *The SAS Survival Handbook* (Harvill Books)

Magazines
Backpacker
Craft
E Magazine
Make
Mother Earth News
Nuts and Volts
Outdoor Life
Outside
Poptronics
Popular Mechanics
Popular Science
ReadyMade

Sneaky Notes